THE HALLOWING OF TIME

A DAILY PRAYER RESOURCE

THE HALLOWING OF TIME

A DAILY PRAYER RESOURCE

VOLUME II

LENT

HOLY WEEK

EASTER

BY CAROL WILKINSON

Hodder & Stoughton
LONDON SYDNEY AUCKLAND

The Hallowing of Time: Volume II
A Daily Prayer Resource
Copyright © 1998 Carol Wilkinson

First published in Great Britain in 1998 by Hodder & Stoughton

10 9 8 7 6 5 4 3 2 1

British Library Cataloguing in Publication Data
A record for this book is available from the British Library

ISBN 0 340 71411 5

Printed and bound in Great Britain by Clays Ltd., St. Ives plc.

Hodder & Stoughton Ltd
A division of Hodder Headline PLC
338 Euston Road
London NW1 3BH

CONTENTS

'Lent is a time for self-indulgence – and rightly so.' These were the words of a sermon I heard at College. They contrast considerably with the gloomy atmosphere of the season when I was a boy. We were expected to give up nice food and consume bleaker spiritual fare. No wonder that the whole pattern needed to be re-thought.

And re-thought it certainly has been. We have recovered a sense of the ancient past. For example, the *Prayer Book* Collects for Eastertide date back many centuries, and they were written to pray for new Christians baptised at Easter, and for the whole people of God renewing their Easter faith. There is one which prays, 'that they may eschew those things that are contrary to their profession, and to follow all such things as are agreeable to the same.' But there are yet profounder truths to ponder, for Easter – not Christmas – is the *primal* festival of the Christian year. The life of faith can be said to begin again at the start of Lent in a way even more poignant than the great themes of judgment and kingship with which Advent is inaugurated. The 'Easter Cycle', as it is often called, consists of the Easter festival itself, and has its own time of preparation beforehand and extended celebration after. There is always more to ponder, more to celebrate, more to discern of God's truth, as Carol Wilkinson's second volume in this series shows.

This is why *The Hallowing of Time* is such a useful resource for prayer. It is rooted in the liturgical tradition but not limited by it. Bible readings find their place alongside devotional prayers, which are themselves interpreted by short readings from Christian writers across the centuries. Light and shade, so central to the Easter gospel, provide a balance of mood and texture throughout.

The outcome is a balanced diet which may not quite (perhaps) result in self-indulgence. But it will certainly go a long way towards ensuring genuine spiritual nourishment. I commend this book warmly.

+ KENNETH PORTSMOUTH
Feast of St Andrew the Apostle 1998

ACKNOWLEDGMENTS

I am grateful to the many publishers and authors who have given their permissions to include their work. Every effort has been made to determine the ownership of all the texts and to make proper arrangements for their use. I apologise for any errors or omissions that may remain, and would ask those concerned to contact the publishers, who will ensure that full acknowledgment is made in the future.

Acknowledgements for sources are contained within the *Resources* section and in the endnotes of *Morning & Evening Prayer* and the *Penitential Rite*.

I would like to thank my redoubtable team of "test-pilots" for all their hard work, advice, and inspiration; and my family and friends for their unfailing support of this project and their encouragement.

My thanks to Emma Sealey and Judith Longman of Hodder & Stoughton for their editorial assistance.

How To Use This Book

This book may be used in a variety of ways. It is primarily intended for the use of those who wish to have some order in their devotional lives, but lack the time to celebrate the daily offices.

A form of worship is provided for each day, centred upon a weekly seasonal theme. A three year cycle of readings is provided. Readings are taken from Scripture on week-days, and from other Christian sources on Saturday and Sunday (whatever our occupation, the week-end marks a change in the pace of life). Thus, the only variable for the day is the reading.

For those who wish to use the daily material in a more formal "office type" style of worship, three forms of Morning and Evening Prayer are provided into which the order for the day can be incorporated easily. These forms are also suitable for worship with small groups.

Forms of penance, intercessions, and meditations, are provided at the end of each week, to be used as the reader wishes.

This book may also be used as a seasonal resource.

The celebration of the Paschal Mystery is the centre of the Christian year, and the Christian life, therefore, at the request of my "test pilots", considerable weight has been given to the seasonal themes. It is a difficult time of the liturgical year for lay people. So many demands are made of us in our daily lives, and yet we want to enter into the time of reflection and repentance, to walk with Jesus to Jerusalem, to rejoice in the resurrection, and to feel empowered by the Holy Spirit. I hope that this volume will help us do that.

Carol Wilkinson

THE LITURGICAL YEAR: *LENT–HOLY WEEK–EASTER*

Lent: There is some disagreement about when the beginning of Lent occurs, some would say Ash Wednesday, others the first Sunday in Lent. However, for the purposes of this book Lent begins on Ash Wednesday, which will occur on the following dates:

1998	25 Feb	2002	13 Feb	2006	1 Mar
1999	17 Feb	2003	5 Mar	2007	21 Feb
2000	8 Mar	2004	25 Feb	2008	6 Feb
2001	28 Feb	2005	9 Feb	2009	25 Feb

Easter: Easter Sunday will occur on the following dates:

1998	12 Apr	2002	31 Mar	2006	16 Apr
1999	4 Apr	2003	20 Apr	2007	8 Apr
2000	23 Apr	2004	11 Apr	2008	23 Mar
2001	15 Apr	2005	27 Mar	2009	12 Apr

Ascension Day: will occur on the following dates:

1998	21 May	2002	9 May	2006	25 May
1999	13 May	2003	29 May	2007	17 May
2000	1 Jun	2004	20 May	2008	1 May
2001	24 May	2005	5 May	2009	21 May

Pentecost: will occur on the following dates:

1998	31 May	2002	19 May	2006	4 Jun
1999	23 May	2003	8 Jun	2007	27 May
2000	11 Jun	2004	30 May	2008	11 May
2001	3 Jun	2005	15 May	2009	31 May

The Three-Year Cycle of Readings: The yearly readings do not belong to any particular calendar year. However, if the reader wishes, Year 1 may being in 1998, Year 2 – 1999, Year 3 – 2000, etc.

THE ORIGINS OF THE SEASONS

The celebration of Lent, Holy Week and Easter is the focal point of the Christian year, indeed the centre of the Christian Mystery has always been the death and resurrection of Jesus Christ. However, the manner of the keeping of the fast and the feast has developed over a considerable period of time.

In the observation of Lent we see three strands of tradition. The first of these is that of a fast in preparation for Easter. But it was not until the early part of the fourth century, after the Council of Nicaea (A.D. 325), that Athanasius tells us of a fast of forty days. Lent was also the time when those who were to be baptised at Easter entered into a final period of preparation. The candidates would be examined as to their fitness for baptism, and if approved, they would receive teaching, and periodic exorcisms. The third strand lies in the restoration of penitents to full communion with the Church. At the beginning of the fourth century Bishop Peter of Alexandria issued a series of canons giving instructions for the restoration of those who had capitulated under duress during times of persecution. The canons stipulated probation for a period of three years before the penitent could undertake a final preparatory fast.

We must note that the association of the Lenten fast with the time Jesus spent in the wilderness is a later development. In addition to these traditions we have a period of contemplation on the passion of Christ.

The early Christians would not recognise the way we keep Holy Week. For the first three centuries Christians observed the death and resurrection of Jesus in a single all-night service, rather than in a series of pre-planned liturgies. Thus the Jewish Passover was replaced by the Christian Passover. Baptism was later incorporated into this single service, forming a highly impressive liturgy of vigil, baptism and eucharist. It is not until the fourth century that we begin to see the kind of liturgical developments which we associate with the celebration of Holy Week. Egeria, a nun of the fourth century, has left us a graphic account of the Holy Week services she experienced in Jerusalem during her pilgrimage to the Holy Land. She records a procession of the people and clergy on Palm Sunday, and a variety of devotions some of which began before sunrise:

The following day, Sunday, marks the beginning of Holy Week, which they call here the Great Week. On this Sunday morning, at the

1

completion of those rites which are customarily celebrated at the Anastasis or the Cross from the first cockcrow until dawn, everyone assembles for the liturgy, according to custom in the major church called the Martyrium...

When the dismissal has been given... everyone retires to his home to eat hastily, so that at the beginning of the seventh hour everyone will be ready to assemble at the church on the Eleona, by which I mean the Mount of Olives, where the grotto in which the Lord taught is located [1]

In the early church Easter was a unified period of fifty days of rejoicing culminating in a feast of the Holy Spirit. It was not until the fourth century that we begin to see the separation of the celebrations of Easter and Ascension, and Pentecost treated as a separate feast of the Holy Spirit.

Over the centuries traditions have been lost and made. During the Reformation some abandoned the liturgical year completely, others adapted and changed their manner of observation. The 'Three Hours Devotion', which gained popularity in the Church of England, had its origins in seventeenth century Peru under the influence of the Jesuits.

Today, many Christian denominations look back to the practices of the early church. They have tried to re-establish a more primitive and symbolic celebration of the Paschal Mystery. For example, we have seen the re-introduction of the footwashing at the Maundy Thursday eucharist, the keeping of the Easter vigil, and the celebration of baptism during the Easter liturgy. But, despite these efforts we cannot ignore the fact that for the most part our rehearsal of God's mighty acts of salvation is lamentable.

Lent, Holy Week and the Great Fifty Days of Easter are an integrated whole, a celebration of the Paschal Mystery by preparation, remembrance and rejoicing. The heart of the Christian year deserves our fullest attention.

---

[1] *Egeria: Diary of a Pilgrimage*, trans and annotated by G. E. Gingras, Newman/Paulist Press, New York, 1970.

LENT

LENT

The path through Lent is paved with good advice. The stones cry out to us, 'do something positive', and 'not *that* way, but *this* way'. The words echo down the busy streets of our lives. We can become all ways distracted and find ourselves feeling inadequate and disappointed.

But how rarely do we hear of the 'joy' of Lent, and of the privileges that the season offers. Here we are given the opportunity to reflect upon the spiritual life, to joyfully embrace this time of self-denial and repentance, to heed the call to 'a devout and holy life', as we contemplate the Way of the Cross.

Come, then, let us celebrate the Great and Holy Season of Lent. Let us rejoice in the knowledge that we can repent of our sins, and be forgiven, that redemption is not just a pretty theory, but a living – and dying – reality.

> 'When you fast, do not look sombre as the hypocrites do ... I tell you the truth, they have received their reward in full. But when you fast, put oil on your head and wash your face, so that it will not be obvious to others that you are fasting, but only to your Father, who is unseen; and your Father, who sees what is done in secret, will reward you.' (Matthew 6:16-18)

ASH WEDNESDAY

Although I do not hope to turn again
Although I do not hope
Although I do not hope to turn

This is the time of tension between dying and birth
The place of solitude where three dreams cross
Between three rocks
But when voices shaken from the yew-tree drift away
Let the other yew be shaken and reply.

Blessed sister, holy mother, spirit of the fountain, spirit of
the garden,
Suffer us not to mock ourselves with falsehood
Teach us to care and not to care
Teach us to sit still
Even among these rocks,
Our peace is his will
And even among these rocks
Sister, mother
And spirit of the river, spirit of the sea,
Suffer me not to be separated

And let my cry come unto Thee.

T. S. Eliot
From 'Ash Wednesday 1930'[1]

---

[1] T. S. Eliot, *Collected Poems 1909 – 1962,* Faber & Faber, London, 1963,
pp. 104-5

ASH
WEDNESDAY

ASH WEDNESDAY

Let us enter the season of Lent in the spirit of joy,
giving ourselves to spiritual strife,
cleansing our soul and body, controlling our passions,
as we limit our food, living on the virtues of the Spirit;
let us persevere in our longing for Him
so as to be worthy to behold the most solemn Passion of Christ
and the most holy Passover,
rejoicing the while with spiritual joy.

Psalm 90:1-12

1. Lord, you have been our refuge
from one generation to the other.

2. Before the mountains were brought forth,
or the land and the earth were born,
from age to age you are God.

3. You turn us back to dust and say,
'Go back, O child of earth.'

4. For a thousand years in your sight
are like yesterday when it is past
and like a watch in the night.

5. You sweep us away like a dream;
we fade away suddenly like the grass.

6. In the morning it is green and flourishes;
in the evening it is dried up and withered.

7. For we consume away in your displeasure;
we are afraid because of your wrathful indignation.

8. Our iniquities you have set before you,
and our secret sins in the light of your countenance.

9. When you are angry, all our days are gone;
we bring our years to an end like a sigh.

10. The span of our life is seventy years,
perhaps in strength even eighty;
yet the sum of them is but labour and sorrow,
for they pass away quickly and are gone.

11. Who regards the power of your wrath?
Who rightly fears your indignation?
12. So teach us to number our days
that we may apply our hearts to wisdom.

**Lord, you have been our refuge
from one generation to the other**

Joel 2:12-17

"Even now," declares the LORD, "return to me with all your heart,
with fasting and weeping and mourning." Rend your heart and not
your garments. Return to the LORD your God, for he is gracious and
compassionate, slow to anger and abounding in love, and he relents
from sending calamity. Who knows? He may turn and have pity and
leave behind a blessing—grain offerings and drink offerings for the
LORD your God. Blow the trumpet in Zion, declare a holy fast, call a
sacred assembly. Gather the people, consecrate the assembly; bring
together the elders, gather the children, those nursing at the breast.
Let the bridegroom leave his room and the bride her chamber. Let
the priests, who minister before the LORD, weep between the temple
porch and the altar. Let them say, "Spare your people, O LORD. Do
not make your inheritance an object of scorn, a byword among the
nations. Why should they say among the peoples, 'Where is their
God?'"

Silence

Meditation

*Most holy and merciful Father,
we confess to you, to one another,
and to the whole communion of saints
in heaven and on earth,
that we have sinned by our own fault
in thought, word, and deed;
by what we have done,
and by what we have left undone.*

We have not loved you with our whole heart, and mind, and strength,
We have not loved our neighbours as ourselves. We have not
forgiven others, as we have been forgiven.
Have mercy on us, Lord.

We have been deaf to your call to serve as Christ served us.
We have not been true to the mind of Christ.
We have grieved your Holy Spirit.
Have mercy on us, Lord.

We confess to you, Lord, all our past unfaithfulness;
the pride, hypocrisy, and impatience of our lives,
We confess to you, Lord.

Our self-indulgent appetites and ways,
and our exploitation of other people,
We confess to you, Lord.

Our anger at our own frustration, and our envy of
those more fortunate than ourselves,
We confess to you, Lord.

Our intemperate love of worldly goods and comforts,
and our dishonesty in daily life and work,
We confess to you, Lord.

Our negligence in prayer and worship, and our failure
to commend the faith that is in us.
We confess to you, Lord.

Accept our repentance, Lord, for the wrongs we have done:
for our blindness to human need and suffering,
and our indifference to injustice and cruelty,
Accept our repentance, Lord.

For all false judgements,
for uncharitable thoughts toward our neighbours, and for
our prejudice and contempt toward those who differ from us,
Accept our repentance, Lord.

For our waste and pollution of your creation,
and our lack of concern for those who come after us,
Accept our repentance, Lord.

Restore us, good Lord, and let your anger depart from us;
Hear us Lord, for your mercy is great.

Dust and ashes touch our face,
mark our failure and our falling.
Holy Spirit, come,
walk with us tomorrow,
take us as disciples,
washed and wakened by your calling.
Take us by the hands and lead us,
lead us through the desert sands,
bring us living water,
Holy Spirit, come.

THURSDAY

All life is but one day, so it is said,
To those who labour with love.
There are forty days in the Fast:
Let us keep them all with joy.

Psalm 102:1-12

1. Lord, hear my prayer and let my cry come before you;
hide not your face from me in the day of my trouble.
2. Incline your ear to me;
when I call, make haste to answer me,

3. For my days drift away like smoke,
   and my bones are hot as burning coals.
4. My heart is smitten like grass and withered,
   so that I forget to eat my bread.
5. Because of the voice of my groaning
   I am but skin and bones.
6. I have become like a vulture in the wilderness,
   like an owl among the ruins.
7. I lie awake and groan;
   I am like a sparrow, lonely on a house-top.
8. My enemies revile me all day long,
   and those who scoff at me have taken an oath against me.
9. For I have eaten ashes for bread
   and mingled my drink with weeping.
10. Because of your indignation and wrath
    you have lifted me up and thrown me away.
11. My days pass away like a shadow,
    and I wither like the grass.
12. But you, O Lord, endure for ever,
    and your name from age to age.

You, O Lord, endure for ever

James 1:19-27

My dear brothers and sisters, take note of this: Everyone should be quick to listen, slow to speak and slow to become angry, for human anger does not bring about the righteous life that God desires. Therefore, get rid of all moral filth and the evil that is so prevalent and humbly accept the word planted in you, which can save you. Do not merely listen to the word, and so deceive yourselves. Do what it says. Those who listen to the word but do not do what it says are like people who look at their faces in a mirror and, after looking at themselves, go away and immediately forget what they look like. But those who look intently into the perfect law that gives freedom, and continue to do this, not forgetting what they have heard, but doing it—they will be blessed in what they do. Those who consider themselves religious and yet do not keep a tight rein on their tongues deceive themselves, and their religion is worthless. Religion that God our Father accepts as pure and faultless is this: to look after orphans and widows in their distress and to keep oneself from being polluted by the world.

Silence

Meditation

Lord God,
you call us to repentance and self-denial.
While we can choose our penances, so many of
our brothers and sisters have not the basic needs of life.
Teach us humility in our works of penance, so that
our fast may be a victory over egotism and indulgence,
through Jesus, the Christ, our Lord. Amen.

FRIDAY

Come, O ye people, and today let us
accept the grace of the Fast as a gift from God
and as a time for repentance,
in which we may find mercy with the Saviour.
The time for combat is at hand and has begun already;
let all of us set forth eagerly upon the course of the fast,
offering our virtues as gifts to the Lord.

Song: Isaiah 1:11-17

13. "The multitude of your sacrifices -
what are they to me?" says the Lord.
"I have more than enough of burnt offerings,
of rams and the fat of fattened animals;
I have no pleasure in the blood of lambs and goats.

14. When you come to appear before me,
who has asked this of you, this trampling of my courts?
15. Stop bringing me meaningless offerings!
Your incense is detestable to me.
New Moons, Sabbaths and convocations-
I cannot bear your evil assemblies.
16. Your New Moon festivals and your appointed feasts
my soul hates.
They have become a burden unto me;
I am weary of bearing them.
17. When you spread out your hands in prayer,
I will hide my eyes from you;
even if you offer many prayers, I will not listen.
Your hands are full of blood;
18. wash and make yourselves clean.
Take your evil deeds out of my sight!
Stop doing wrong,
19. learn to do right!
Seek Justice, encourage the oppressed.
Defend the cause of the fatherless,
plead the case of the widow.

Stop doing wrong, learn to do right!

Matthew 16:24-end

Then Jesus said to his disciples, "If anyone would come after me, he must deny himself and take up his cross and follow me. For whoever wants to save his life will lose it, but whoever loses his life for me will find it. What good will it be for a man if he gains the whole world, yet forfeits his soul? Or what can a man give in exchange for his soul? For the Son of Man is going to come in his Father's glory with his angels, and then he will reward each person according to what he has done. I tell you the truth, some who are standing here will not taste death before they see the Son of Man coming in his kingdom."

Silence

Meditation

Jesus our only Saviour,
you renounced the way of ease
for the way of truth and life.
Draw us to seek God's kingdom
whatever the cost,
for the sake of the true treasure of heaven.
Amen.

SATURDAY

The springtime of the Fast has dawned,
the flower of repentance has begun to open.
O brothers and sisters,
let us cleanse ourselves from all impurity
And sing to the Giver of Light:
Glory be to You, who alone loves us all.

Song: Daniel 9:3-10

3. So I turned to the Lord God and pleaded with him in prayer and
petition, in fasting, and in sackcloth and ashes.
4. I prayed to the LORD my God and confessed:
"O Lord, the great and awesome God,
who keeps his covenant of love
with all who love him and obey his commands,
5. we have sinned and done wrong.
We have been wicked and have rebelled;
we have turned away from your commands and laws.
6. We have not listened to your servants the prophets,
who spoke in your name to our kings,
our princes and our ancestors,
and to all the people of the land.

7. Lord, you are righteous,
but this day we are covered with shame--
the people of Judah and Jerusalem and all Israel,
both near and far, in all the countries where you have scattered us
because of our unfaithfulness to you.
8. O LORD, we and our kings, our princes and our ancestors are
covered with shame because we have sinned against you.
9. The Lord our God is merciful and forgiving,
even though we have rebelled against him;
10. we have not obeyed the LORD our God
or kept the laws he gave us
through his servants the prophets."

Lord God, have mercy upon us

Mark Searle

The purpose of the first part of Lent is to bring us to compunction. "Compunction" is etymologically related to the verb "to puncture" and suggests the deflation of our inflated egos, a challenge to any self-deceit about the quality of our lives as disciples of Jesus. By hitting us again and again with demands which we not only fail to obey, but which we come to recognize as being quite beyond us, the gospel passages are meant to trouble us, to confront our illusions about ourselves. "Remember, you are dust ..." From this perspective, lenten penance may be more effective if we fail in our resolutions than if we succeed, for its purpose is not to confirm us in our sense of virtue but to bring home to us our radical need of salvation.

Silence

Meditation

Almighty and merciful God,
you hate nothing that you have made
and forgive the sins of all who are penitent;
create in us new and contrite hearts,
so that when we turn to you and confess our sins
we may receive your full and perfect forgiveness;
through Jesus Christ our Redeemer. Amen.

YEAR 2

WEEKDAY READINGS

ASH WEDNESDAY: Isaiah 58:1-9
THURSDAY: 1 Corinthians 9:19-27
FRIDAY: Matthew 6:16-24

SATURDAY

Thomas Merton

We must not imagine that the way of self-denial is always a way of tranquillity and uninterrupted peace. It does not resolve all doubts and deliver us from every care as if by magic. Self-denial attunes us to the Spirit of God and the Spirit may not always sing a tune that harmonizes with our nature. There may be terrible discords instead of tranquil harmonies. Self-denial brings order into our lives sometimes in the form of an apparent disorder, and we may sometimes have to find peace as best we can in the midst of confusion.

YEAR 3

WEEKDAY READINGS

ASH WEDNESDAY: Jonah 3
THURSDAY: 2 Timothy 2:1-7
FRIDAY: Mark 2:18-22

SATURDAY

Maximus the Confessor

Do not devote yourself entirely to disciplining your body. Arrange a programme that is within your capabilities and then concentrate on your spiritual work.

Those who do not know how to walk in the way of the Spirit are likely to fail to keep a watchful eye on the passions that rage within them, and let themselves be entirely taken up with the body. They then reach one of two opposite stages. Either they become gluttonous, profligate, miserable, choleric, full of rancour, and this quenches their spirit, or they overdo the mortification and lose their clarity of thought.

Not one of the things God has put at our disposal is forbidden in Scripture. The Bible limits itself to reproving excess and correcting what is unreasonable.

For example, there is no need to avoid eating, having children, possessing wealth and administering it with justice; only avoid gluttony, luxury, and so forth.

There is one further point. There is no need to avoid dwelling on these matters in your thoughts, they exist because we have thought of them in the first place, avoid only dwelling on them with immoderate eagerness.

A PRAYER OF PENITENCE

God of grace, I turn my face
To you, I cannot hide;
My nakedness, my shame, my guilt,
are all before Your eyes.

Strivings and all anguished dreams
In rags lie at my feet,
and only grace provides the way
For me to stand complete.

And your grace clothes me in righteousness,
And Your mercy covers me in love.
Your life adorns and beautifies,
I stand complete in You.

THE PRAYERS

Jesus invites us to a way of celebration,
meeting and feasting with the humble and poor.
Let us walk his way with joy.

Jesus beckons us to a way of risk,
letting go of our security.
Let us walk his way with joy.

Jesus challenges us to listen to the voices
of those who have nothing to lose.
Let us walk his way with joy.

Jesus points us to a way of self-giving,
where power and status are overturned.
Let us walk his way with joy.

Jesus calls us to follow the way of the cross,
where despair is transformed by the promise of new life.
Let us walk his way with joy.

MEDITATIONS

ASH WEDNESDAY: By the sweat of your brow you will eat your food until you return to the ground, since from it you were taken; for dust you are and to dust you will return. (Genesis 3:19)

THURSDAY: Many acts of self-denial are heroic only in imagination, justified by some inaccessible ideal more dreamt than lived. (A Monk)

FRIDAY: When the stomach is full it is easy to talk of fasting. (St. Jerome)

SATURDAY: Do not limit the benefit of fasting merely to abstinence from food, for a true fast means refraining from evil. Loose every unjust bond, put away your resentment against you neighbour, forgive him his offences. Do not let your fasting lead to wrangling and strife. You do not eat meat, but you devour your brother; you abstain from wine, but not from insults. So all the labour of your fast is useless. (St. Ambrose)

Madeleine L'Engle

Second Lazarus

O come, dear Lord, unbind, like Lazarus, I
lie wrapped in stifling grave clothes of self-will.
Come give me life that I to death may die.
I stink: the grave of sin is worm-filled still
despite our turning from its rotteness,
unwilling to admit that we are bound,
too proud to mention our begotteness.
Come, open sin's sarcophagus. I'm wound
in selfishness, self-satsifaction, pride,
fear of change, demands of love, greed,
self-hate, sweet sins that come in fair disguise.
Help me accept this death and open wide
the tight-closed tomb. If pain comes as we're freed,
Your daylight must have first hurt Lazarus' eyes.

LENT I:

TEMPTATION

SUNDAY

Forty days and forty nights
Thou wast fasting in the wild;
Forty days and forty nights
Tempted, and yet undefiled.

Psalm 51:1-9

1. Have mercy on me, O God,
according to your loving-kindness;
in your great compassion blot out my offences.
2. Wash me through and through from my wickedness
and cleanse me from my sin.
3. For I know my transgressions,
and my sin is ever before me.
4. Against you only have I sinned
and done what is evil in your sight.
5. And so you are justified when you speak
and upright in your judgement.
6. Indeed, I have been wicked from my birth,
a sinner from my mother's womb.
7. For behold, you look for truth deep within me,
and will make me understand wisdom secretly.
8. Purge me from my sin and I shall be pure;
wash me and I shall be clean indeed.
9. Make me hear of joy and gladness,
that the body you have broken may rejoice.

Have mercy upon me, O God

St. Augustine
In the person of Christ we were tempted

Our pilgrim life on earth cannot be without temptation for it is
through temptation that we make progress and it is only by being
tempted that we come to know ourselves. We cannot win our crown

unless we overcome, and we cannot overcome unless we enter the contest and there is no contest unless we have an enemy and the temptations he brings . . .

When he (Christ) willed to be tempted by the devil, he figuratively transferred us into himself . . . In Christ you were being tempted because Christ had his human flesh from you, just as he won salvation for you from himself. He received death from you, just as he gained life from himself for you. From you he received reproaches and from himself for you he gained glory and honour. In the same way he suffered the temptation for you and he won from himself the victory for you.

If we have been tempted in him, in him we conquer the devil. Do you notice that Christ has been tempted and fail to notice that he overcame temptation? Recognize your own self, tempted in him and conquering also in him. He might have avoided the devil completely but, had he not been tempted, he would have failed to give you the lesson of conquering when you are tempted.

Silence

Meditation

Lord our God,
you invite us to follow Christ
in his struggle in the desert.
Through our self-denial
may your Spirit make us ever strong against evil.
Hear us, you who remain faithful to us,
for ever and ever. Amen

MONDAY

Sunbeams scorching all the day;
Chilly dew-drops nightly shed;
Prowling beasts about thy way;
Stones thy pillow, earth thy bed.

Psalm 39:1-8

1. I said, 'I will keep watch on my ways;
so that I do not offend with my tongue.
2. I will put a muzzle on my mouth,
while the wicked are in my presence.'
3. So I held my tongue and said nothing;
I refrained from rash words;
but my pain became unbearable.
4. My heart was hot within me;
while I pondered, the fire burst into flame;
I spoke out with my tongue.
5. Lord, let me know my end
and the number of my days;
so that I may know how short my life is.
6. You have given me a mere handful of days,
and my lifetime is as nothing in your sight;
truly, even those who stand erect are but a puff of wind.
7. We walk about like a shadow
and in vain we are in turmoil;
we heap up riches and cannot tell who will gather them.
8. And now what is my hope?
O Lord, my hope is in you.

O Lord, my hope is in you

Luke 4:1-13

Jesus, full of the Holy Spirit, returned from the Jordan and was led by the Spirit in the desert, where for forty days he was tempted by the devil. He ate nothing during those days, and at the end of them he was hungry. The devil said to him, "If you are the Son of God, tell this stone to become bread." Jesus answered, "It is written: 'People do not live on bread alone.'" The devil led him up to a high place and showed him in an instant all the kingdoms of the world. And he said to him, "I will give you all their authority and splendour, for it has been given to me, and I can give it to anyone I want to. So if you worship me, it will all be yours." Jesus answered, "It is written: 'Worship the Lord your God and serve him only.'" The devil led him to Jerusalem and had him stand on the highest point of the temple. "If you are the Son of God," he said, "throw yourself down from here. For it is written: 'He will command his angels concerning you to guard you carefully; they will lift you up in their hands, so that you will not strike your foot against a stone.'" Jesus answered, "It says: 'Do not put the Lord your God to the test.'" When the devil had finished all this tempting, he left him until an opportune time.

Silence

Meditation

> *God of the Desert,*
> *as we follow Jesus into the unknown,*
> *may we recognise the tempter*
> *when he comes;*
> *let it be your bread we eat,*
> *your world we serve*
> *and you alone we worship.*
> .   *Amen.*

TUESDAY

> *And if Satan, vexing sore,*
> *Flesh or spirit should assail,*
> *Thou, his vanquisher before,*
> *Grant we may not faint nor fail.*

Psalm 6

1. Lord, do not rebuke me in your anger;
   do not punish me in your wrath.
2. Have pity on me, Lord, for I am weak;
   heal me, Lord, for my bones are racked.

3. My spirit shakes with terror;
how long, O Lord, how long?
4. Turn, O Lord, and deliver me;
save me for your mercy's sake.
5. For in death no one remembers you;
and who will give you thanks in the grave?
6. I grow weary because of my groaning;
every night I drench my bed
and flood my couch with tears.
7. My eyes are wasted with grief
and worn away because of all my enemies.
8. Depart from me, all evildoers;
for the Lord has heard the sound of my weeping.
9. The Lord has heard my supplication;
the Lord accepts my prayer.
10. All my enemies shall be confounded and quake with fear;
they shall turn back and suddenly be put to shame.

Have pity on me, Lord, for I am weak

Job: 2:1-10

On another day the angels came to present themselves before the
LORD, and Satan also came with them to present himself before him.
And the LORD said to Satan, "Where have you come from?" Satan
answered the LORD, "From roaming through the earth and going
back and forth in it." Then the LORD said to Satan, "Have you
considered my servant Job? There is no-one on earth like him; he is
blameless and upright, a man who fears God and shuns evil. And he
still maintains his integrity, though you incited me against him to
ruin him without any reason." "Skin for skin!" Satan replied. "A man
will give all he has for his own life. But stretch out your hand and
strike his flesh and bones, and he will surely curse you to your face."
The LORD said to Satan, "Very well, then, he is in your hands; but
you must spare his life." So Satan went out from the presence of the
LORD and afflicted Job with painful sores from the soles of his feet
to the top of his head. Then Job took a piece of broken pottery and
scraped himself with it as he sat among the ashes. His wife said to

him, "Are you still holding on to your integrity? Curse God and die!" He replied, "You are talking like a foolish woman. Shall we accept good from God, and not trouble?" In all this, Job did not sin in what he said.

Silence

Meditation

O God, who has been the refuge of my forebears
through many generations, be my refuge today
in every time and circumstance of need.
Be my guide through all that is dark and doubtful.
Be my guard against all that threatens my spirit's welfare.
Be my strength in time of testing.
. Gladden my heart with your peace. Amen

WEDNESDAY

Shall we not thy sorrows share,
And from earthly joys abstain,
Fasting with unceasing prayer,
Glad with thee to suffer pain?

Psalm 36:1-9

1. There is a voice of rebellion deep in the heart of the wicked;
    there is no fear of God before their eyes.
    2. They flatter themselves in their own eyes
    that their hateful sins will not be found out.
3. The words of their mouths are wicked and deceitful;
    they have left off acting wisely and doing good.
    4. They think up wickedness upon their beds
    and have set themselves in no good way;
    they do not abhor that which is evil.

5. Your love, O Lord, reaches to the heavens,
    and your faithfulness to the clouds.
6. Your righteousness is like the strong mountains,
        your justice like the great deep;
    you save both human and beast, O Lord.
7. How priceless is your love, O God!
Your people take refuge under the shadow of your wings.
8. They feast upon the abundance of your house;
    you give them drink from the river of your delights.

How priceless is your love, O God!

James 1:2-15

Consider it pure joy, my brothers and sisters, whenever you face
trials of many kinds, because you know that the testing of your faith
develops perseverance. Perseverance must finish its work so that you
may be mature and complete, not lacking anything. If any of you
lacks wisdom, you should ask God, who gives generously to all
without finding fault, and it will be given to you. But when you ask,
you must believe and not doubt, because the one who doubts is like a
wave of the sea, blown and tossed by the wind. Those who doubt
should not think they will receive anything from the Lord; they are
double-minded and unstable in all they do. Believers in humble
circumstances ought to take pride in their high position. But those
who are rich should take pride in their low position, because they
will pass away like a wild flower. For the sun rises with scorching
heat and withers the plant; its blossom falls and its beauty is
destroyed. In the same way, the rich will fade away even while they
go about their business. Blessed are those who persevere under trial,
because when they have stood the test, they will receive the crown of
life that God has promised to those who love him. When tempted,
no-one should say, "God is tempting me." For God cannot be
tempted by evil, nor does he tempt anyone; but each of you is
tempted when, by your own evil desire, you are dragged away and
enticed. Then, after desire has conceived, it gives birth to sin; and
sin, when it is full-grown, gives birth to death.

Silence

Meditation

Father of mercy,
alone we have no power in ourselves to help ourselves.
When we are discouraged by our weakness,
strengthen us to follow Christ,
our pattern and our hope;
who lives and reigns with you and the Holy Spirit,
One God, now and for ever. Amen.

THURSDAY

So shall we have peace divine;
Holier gladness ours shall be;
Round us too shall angels shine,
Such as ministered to thee.

Psalm 91:1-4, 9-15

1. He who dwells in the shelter of the Most High,
    abides under the shadow of the Almighty.
    2. He shall say to the Lord,
    'You are my refuge and my stronghold,
    my God in whom I put my trust.'
3. He shall deliver you from the snare of the hunter
    and from the deadly pestilence.
    4. He shall cover you with his pinions,
    and you shall kind refuge under his wings;
    his faithfulness shall be a shield and buckler.

9. Because you have made the Lord your refuge,
    and the Most High your habitation.

10. There shall no evil happen to you,
neither shall any plague come near your dwelling.
11. For he shall give his angels charge over you,
to keep you in all your ways.
12. They shall bear you in their hands,
lest you dash you foot against a stone.
13. You shall tread the lion and the adder;
you shall trample the young lion and the serpent
under your feet
14. 'Because he is bound to me in love
therefore I will deliver him;
I will protect him, because he knows my name.
15. He shall call upon me and I will answer him;
I am with him in trouble,
I will rescue him and bring him to honour.'

The Lord is my refuge, in God will I put my trust

Hebrews 4:12-16

For the word of God is living and active. Sharper than any double-edged sword, it penetrates even to dividing soul and spirit, joints and marrow; it judges the thoughts and attitudes of the heart. Nothing in all creation is hidden from God's sight. Everything is uncovered and laid bare before the eyes of him to whom we must give account. Therefore, since we have a great high priest who has gone through the heavens, Jesus the Son of God, let us hold firmly to the faith we profess. For we do not have a high priest who is unable to sympathise with our weaknesses, but we have one who has been tempted in every way, just as we are—yet was without sin. Let us then approach the throne of grace with confidence, so that we may receive mercy and find grace to help us in our time of need.

Silence

Meditation

Men and women seek you, Lord Jesus,
in the desert, in the night of suffering, in doubt and isolation,
perhaps even while they blaspheme you.
We beg you, who willed to live our life and face our death,
bestow on all
the warmth of your presence,
for you live for ever and ever.   Amen.

FRIDAY

Keep, O Keep us, Saviour dear,
Ever constant by thy side;
That with thee we may appear
At the eternal Eastertide.

Psalm 39:9-15

9. Deliver me from all my transgressions
and do not make me the taunt of the fool.
10. I fell silent and did not open my mouth,
for surely it was you that did it.
11. Take your afflictions from me;
I am worn down by the blows of your hand.
12. With rebukes for sin you punish us;
like a moth you eat away all that is dear to us;
truly, everyone is but a puff of wind.
13. Hear my prayer, O Lord, and give ear to my cry;
hold not your peace at my tears.
14. For I am but a sojourner with you,
a wayfarer, as all my forebears were.
15. Turn your gaze from me, that I may be glad again,
before I go away and am no more.

O Lord, deliver me from all my transgressions

Mark 14:32-42

They went to a place called Gethsemane, and Jesus said to his disciples, "Sit here while I pray." He took Peter, James and John along with him, and he began to be deeply distressed and troubled. "My soul is overwhelmed with sorrow to the point of death," he said to them. "Stay here and keep watch." Going a little farther, he fell to the ground and prayed that if possible the hour might pass from him. "*Abba*, Father," he said, "everything is possible for you. Take this cup from me. Yet not what I will, but what you will." Then he returned to his disciples and found them sleeping. "Simon," he said to Peter, "are you asleep? Could you not keep watch for one hour? Watch and pray so that you will not fall into temptation. The spirit is willing, but the body is weak." Once more he went away and prayed the same thing. When he came back, he again found them sleeping, because their eyes were heavy. They did not know what to say to him. Returning the third time, he said to them, "Are you still sleeping and resting? Enough! The hour has come. Look, the Son of Man is betrayed into the hands of sinners. Rise! Let us go! Here comes my betrayer!"

Silence

Meditation

> *Holy Jesus,*
> *in body, mind, and soul*
> *you faced every temptation*
> *of our common humanity.*
> *Throughout this sacred season*
> *help us to lean on you and learn from you.*
> *May we do nothing*
> *to defile our body, the temple of the Holy Spirit.*
> *May we think nothing*
> *to displace the mind of Christ in us.*
> *May we admit nothing into our souls*
> *except the goodness of God our Father.*
> *Amen.*

SATURDAY

Still nigh me, O my Saviour, stand,
And guard in fierce temptation's hour;
Hide in the hollow of thy hand,
Show forth in me thy saving power;
Still be thine arm my sure defence:
Nor earth nor hell shall pluck me thence.

Psalm 25:13-20

13. The Lord is a friend to those who fear him
and will show them his covenant.
14. My eyes are ever looking to the Lord,
for he shall pluck my feet out of the net.
15. Turn to me and have pity on me,
for I am left alone and in misery.
16. The sorrows of my heart have increased;
bring me out of my troubles.
17. Look upon my adversity and misery
and forgive me all my sin.
18. Look upon my enemies, for they are many,
and they bear a violent hatred against me.
19. Protect my life and deliver me;
let me not be put to shame, for I have trusted in you.
20. Let integrity and uprightness preserve me,
for my hope has been in you.

The Lord is a friend to those who fear him

Evelyn Underhill
Spiritual Warfare

The maturing of our personality, in its full transformation in God, could hardly be achieved unless we were left in an apparent independence; to suffer, accept, deal with circumstances as real incarnate spirits, subject to all the vicissitudes of physical life. Our courage and loyalty must be tested by a genuine experience of solitude and darkness, if all our latent possibilities are to be realized.

'O Lord, your battles *do* last a long time!' said poor Suzo, worn out by the disciplines, sufferings, and reverses through which his ardent but unsteady soul was brought into stability and peace. Certainly life is not made soft for Christians, though it is in the last resort made safe. Nor do the struggles of the spiritual life – even the most crucial and most heroic – either look or feel very glorious while they are going on. Muddy trenches, great watchfulness and weariness, a limited view, endless small duties and deprivations and no certainty as to whether we are winning or not; these are the conditions of the long struggle for the victory of disinterested love. It is often the patient defence of an unnoticed corner that decides the result. The difference between the real spiritual experiences even of sanctity, and the popular notion of them, is the difference between the real private in the trenches and the glossy photograph of the same warrior, taken when he is at home on leave.

Yet the whole power and life of the Invisible God, the divine Charity itself, stands by us in the trenches. 'As ye are the partakers of the suffering, so are ye of the support,' says St. Paul to the Corinthians.

Silence

Meditation

> *Blessed Lord, who was tempted in all things as we are,*
> *have mercy upon our frailty. Out of weakness give us strength,*
> *Support us in time of temptation. Embolden us in time of danger.*
> *Help us to do your work with good courage.*
> *Amen.*

SUNDAY

Edward Schillebeeckx
Temptations: Jesus' option in rejecting earthly power

In the story of the temptations the approach of the devil in the first two temptations begins: 'If you are the Son of God...' Certainly he is! Then it is suggested to Jesus that he should make use of his sonship to his own advantage, i.e., misuse it. Strikingly, 'if you are the son of God' is no longer used in the third temptation. The seductive suggestion becomes all the more brutal: son of God or not, with my satanic help you can just as well become a child of Satan with a guaranteed absolute rule over the world, in other words, become anti-Christ. We can (regretfully) hardly forget in this connection that in the course of church history Christianity (because of behaviour out of keeping with the gospel) has itself been called anti-Christ. Jesus' temptation remains topical!

We also hear at the crucifixion in Matthew's Gospel: 'If you are the son of God ... come down from the cross.' And after the last trial, that of his death, the risen Jesus again ascends a high mountain with his disciples and says there: 'All power is given to me in heaven and on earth' (Matt 28:16-18). The divine counterpart of the devil's suggestion! As the risen one, the powerless and vulnerable earthly Jesus becomes the Lord of history and the world. For Matthew that is ultimately the significance of being 'son of God'. According to this Gospel Jesus wants to restore the relationship of all men and women to God. Jesus is human as men and women must be human in their vulnerable positions, as 'Adam', created in the image of God: a human being as a child of God, and a child of God precisely in being human himself. Jesus does not seek his own will but the will of the Father: that makes him the unique 'messianic son of God'. Therefore we must reflect three times before we speak about the church or the people of God as a 'messianic community'; in that case we must first be subjected to the test of Jesus' three temptations.

WEEKDAY READINGS

MONDAY: Matthew 4:1-11
TUESDAY: Genesis 22:1-19
WEDNESDAY: Romans 7:15-25
THURSDAY: Hebrews 2:10-18
FRIDAY: Luke 22:39-45

SATURDAY

George Herbert
The Tempter

How should I praise thee, Lord! How should my rhymes
Gladly engrave thy love in steel,
If what my soul doth feel sometimes,
My soul might ever feel!

Although there were some fourtie heav'ns, or more,
Sometimes I peere above them all;
Sometimes I hardly reach a score,
Sometimes to hell I fall.

O rack me not to such a vast extent;
Those distances belong to thee:
The world's too little for thy tent,
A grave too big for me.

Wilt thou meet arms with man, that thou dost stretch
A crumme of dust from heav'n to hell?
Will great God measure with a wretch?
Shall he thy stature spell?

O let me, when thy roof my soul hath hid,
O let me roost and nestle there:
Then of a sinner thou art rid,
And I of hope and fear.

Yet take thy way; for sure thy way is best:
Stretch or contract me thy poore debtor:
This is but tuning of my breast,
To make the musick better.

Whether I flie with angels, fall with dust,
Thy hands made both, and I am there:
Thy power and love, my love and trust
Make one place ev'ry where.

SUNDAY

A Carthusian
Jesus in the wilderness

The temptations undoubtedly reveal the very real trials which the Messiah had to undergo in order to assume the full weight of humanity – both his and ours – in his call to accomplish its salvation. The heart which was subjected for forty days to the poverty of spirit ... was reduced to its fundamental condition: that of having to make an explicit choice, either to place complete and infinite trust in God, or to take up a stance against God as Satan did. One cannot help but recall the two analogous temptations which were the starting points for our ancestors in the flesh and in the spirit: Adam and Abraham. The first was faced with the wiles of the serpent, the second called by God to sacrifice his only son, the sole bearer of the covenant promises. Each found himself in a situation in which he has to surpass the accessory, the futile and the transient, and denude himself of all but the essential: the ability to dialogue with God and the liberty to say yes or no to him.

This is the real vocation of everyone who has attained the use of their reason. Yet we know how everyday experience brings worries, distractions and instability in its train like a fog, and makes it hard for us to see clearly the choice which lies before us. Few who are occupied with worldly affairs have the strength to enter fully into their interior desert to face up to temptation, the basic test of their dignity as creatures made in the image of God. Everyone needs help to enter their personal desert and confront what they find there.

WEEKDAY READINGS

MONDAY: Job 1:6-22
TUESDAY: Ecclesiasticus 2:1-11
WEDNESDAY: Galations 6:1-10
THURSDAY: 1 Corinthians 10:1-13
FRIDAY: Matthew 26:36-45

SATURDAY

Fénelon
Temptation

There are but two things that we can do against temptations. The first is to be faithful to the light within us, in avoiding all exposure to temptation which we are at liberty to avoid. I say, all that we are at liberty to avoid, because it does not always depend upon ourselves whether we shall escape occasions of sin. Those that belong to the situation in life in which Providence has placed us are not under our control. The other is to turn our eyes to God in the moment of temptation, to throw ourselves immediately upon the protection of heaven, as a child when in danger flies to the arms of its parent.

The habitual conviction of the presence of God is the sovereign remedy; it supports, it consoles, it calms us. We must not be surprised that we are tempted. We are placed here to be proved by temptations. Everything is temptation to us. Crosses irritate our pride and prosperity flatters it; our life is a continual warfare, but Jesus Christ combats with us. We must let temptations, like a tempest, beat upon our heads, and still move on; like a traveller surprised on the way by a storm, who wraps his cloak about him, and goes on his journey in spite of the opposing elements.

A PRAYER OF PENITENCE

Lord, when you have bidden,
I have said "I will";
– and have not done it.
Lord, forgive me.
Lord, when you have bidden,
I have said "I will not".
Lord forgive me,
and make me better than my word,
to do it, for your dear sake.
Amen.

THE PRAYERS

Lord Jesus Christ,
You refused to turn stones into bread.
Save us from using our power, however little,
to satisfy the demands of selfishness
in the face of the greater needs of others.

Lord Jesus Christ,
you refused to leap from the temple top.
Save us from displaying our skills, however modest,
to win instant popularity
in the face of noble calls on our abilities.

Lord Jesus Christ,
you refused to bend the knee to a false god.
Save us from offering our devotion, however weak,
to cheap or easy religion
in the face of the harder path
on which you bid us follow you.

Saviour of the World,
you saw Satan masquerading as an angel of light
and shunned him.
Give us wisdom to discern behind each subtle temptation
the ploy of the prince of darkness;
and in the face of all that is hellishly attractive,
help us to choose the will of God.

MEDITATIONS

SUNDAY: From the moment Christ went out into the desert to be tempted, the loneliness, the temptation and the hunger of every man and woman became the loneliness, the temptation and hunger of Christ. (Thomas Merton)

MONDAY: ... now thou hast avenged supplanted Adam, and, by vanquishing Temptation, hast regained lost Paradise. (John Milton)

TUESDAY: God wishes to test you like gold in the furnace. The dross is consumed by fire, but the pure gold remains and its value increases. (Jerome Emiliani)

WEDNESDAY: We learn by the bitter experience of temptation that the spiritual life is not a matter of devout feeling or mere desire to be good. It is through temptation that most of us comprehend how serious a matter it is – a very matter of life and death, involving struggles for survival which are fierce and primitive. (Reginald Somerset Ward)

THURSDAY: O Christ, guide and strengthen all who are tempted in this hour. (United Society for the Propogation of the Gospel)

FRIDAY: And lead us not into temptation. (Luke 11:4)

SATURDAY: The only temptation for man is to be abandoned to his own resources in the presence of evil. (Simone Weil)

A Prayer of the Venerable Bede

O God that art the only hope of the world,
The only refuge for unhappy men,
Abiding in the faithfulness of heaven,
Give me strong succour in this testing place.
O King, protect thy man from utter ruin
Lest the weak faith surrender to the tyrant,
Facing innumerable blows alone.
Remember I am dust, and wind and shadow,
And life is fleeting as the flower of grass,
But may the eternal mercy which hath shone
From time of old
Rescue thy servant from the jaws of the lion.
Thou who didst come from on high in the cloak of flesh,
Strike down the dragon with that two-edged sword
Whereby our mortal flesh can war with the winds
And beat down strongholds, with our
Captain God.

LENT II:

THE FALL

SUNDAY

Lord Jesus Christ,
Son of God,
have mercy upon me,
a sinner.

As the waves of the sea
my transgressions have risen up against me,
and as a boat alone in the deep,
I am tossed by the storm of many sins.
But guide me through repentance
to a fair haven,
O Lord and save me.

O Lord, rebuke me not in your anger

I am a barren tree, O Lord,
for I do not bear all the fruit of compunction.
I fear the axe and the fire
that shall never be quenched.
Therefore I pray to you before I am condemned:
cause me to turn back and save me.

O Lord, rebuke me not in your anger

D.M. Baillie
God was in Christ

Each person makes himself the centre of his universe, caring little for the fellowship of the whole, but seeing things from his selfish point of view; becoming his own God, and worshipping himself. That is the universal aberration symbolized in the 'myth' of the Fall of Man (it is the kind of thing that can only be described in a 'myth', since we cannot conceive it as an event that occurred at a particular date in human history on earth, but something supra-historical, infecting all our history). In the story of Eden the serpent says to the woman: 'Ye shall be as gods.' That is the temptation to which mankind has succumbed: we have put ourselves, each one individually, in the centre of our universe, where God ought to be. And when persons do that, it separates them both from God and from each other. That is what is wrong with mankind. That is original sin.

Into that heritage every new child is born, and by it he is shaped from the start, so that he grows into a self-conscious moral personality into the interplay with his human environment, he is already infected with evil. And all our actual sins are the working out of that heritage. For the very essence of sin is self-centredness, refusal of divine and human community, absorption in oneself, which kills true individuality and destroys the soul. As Martin Luther put it, the 'natural man' (i.e. man fallen from his true nature and unredeemed from his spoilt sinful nature) is *incurvatus in se*, 'bent inwards upon himself', instead of looking away from himself towards God and his fellows in love. That is what sin is, and all our sins can be reduced to that, even what we call the sins of the flesh.

Silence

Meditation

> *We kneel to you, you who are uncreated and eternal.*
> *Hold out your hand and help us to our feet.*
> *Yes, O merciful God, pull us upward.*
> *Give us the courage to stand up without shame or guilt.*
> *Revoke the death sentence against us*
> *and write our names in the book of life*
> *with all your holy prophets and apostles.*
> *Amen.*

MONDAY

Lord Jesus Christ,
Son of God,
have mercy upon me,
a sinner.

The Lord my creator took me from the dust of the earth
and formed me into a living creature,
breathing into me the breath of life and giving me a soul;
He honoured me, setting me as ruler upon earth
over all things visible,
and making me the companion of the angels.
But Satan the deceiver, using the serpent as his instrument,
enticed me by food; he parted me from the glory of God
and gave me over to the earth and to the lowest depths of death.

O Lord, in your compassion, call me back again

In my wretchedness I have cast off the robe woven by God,
disobeying your divine command, O Lord,
at the counsel of the enemy;
and I am clothed now in fig leaves and in garments of sin.
I am condemned to eat the bread of toil in the sweat of my brow,
and the earth has been cursed
so that it bears thorns and thistles for me.

O Lord, call me back again and bring me into Paradise

Let us make haste to accept the season of the Fast
and hearken to the teaching of the Gospel.

O Lord, in your compassion, call me back again

Genesis 3:1-7

Now the serpent was more crafty than any of the wild animals the
LORD God had made. He said to the woman, "Did God really say,
'You must not eat from any tree in the garden'?" The woman said to
the serpent, "We may eat fruit from the trees in the garden, but God
did say, 'You must not eat fruit from the tree that is in the middle of
the garden, and you must not touch it, or you will die.'" "You will
not surely die," the serpent said to the woman. "For God knows that
when you eat of it your eyes will be opened, and you will be like

God, knowing good and evil." When the woman saw that the fruit of the tree was good for food and pleasing to the eye, and also desirable for gaining wisdom, she took some and ate it. She also gave some to her husband, who was with her, and he ate it. Then the eyes of both of them were opened, and they realized they were naked; so they sewed fig leaves together and made coverings for themselves.

Silence

Meditation

> *O paradise, garden of delight and beauty,*
> *dwelling-place made perfect by God,*
> *unending gladness and eternal joy,*
> *the hope of prophets and the home of saints:*
> *By the music of your rustling leaves*
> *beseech the Creator to open to me the gates*
> *which my sins have closed,*
> *that I may partake of the Tree of Life*
> *which was given me in the beginning.*
> *Amen.*

TUESDAY

Lord Jesus Christ,
Son of God,
have mercy upon me,
a sinner.

The depth of my sin ever holds me fast,
and the tempest of transgressions overwhelms me.

Pilot me, O Christ my God, to the haven of life and save me,
King of glory.

I have wasted in evil living the riches which the Father gave me,
and now am brought to poverty.

I am filled with shame and enslaved to fruitless thoughts.
Therefore I cry to you who loves mankind:

Take pity on me and save me

I am wasted with hunger, deprived of every blessing,
and an exile from your presence,
O Christ supreme in loving kindness.

Take pity on me as I now return,
and save me as I sing the praises of your love for mankind

Genesis 37:3-4, 18-28

Now Israel loved Joseph more than any of his other sons, because he
had been born to him in his old age; and he made a richly
ornamented robe for him. When his brothers saw that their father
loved him more than any of them, they hated him and could not
speak a kind word to him.

But they saw him in the distance, and before he reached them,
they plotted to kill him. "Here comes that dreamer!" they said to
each other. "Come now, let's kill him and throw him into one of
these cisterns and say that a ferocious animal devoured him. Then
we'll see what comes of his dreams." When Reuben heard this, he
tried to rescue him from their hands. "Let's not take his life," he said.
"Don't shed any blood. Throw him into this cistern here in the
desert, but don't lay a hand on him." Reuben said this to rescue him
from them and take him back to his father. So when Joseph came to
his brothers, they stripped him of his robe—the richly ornamented
robe he was wearing—and they took him and threw him into the
cistern. Now the cistern was empty; there was no water in it. As they
sat down to eat their meal, they looked up and saw a caravan of
Ishmaelites coming from Gilead. Their camels were loaded with
spices, balm and myrrh, and they were on their way to take them
down to Egypt. Judah said to his brothers, "What will we gain if we
kill our brother and cover up his blood? Come, let's sell him to the
Ishmaelites and not lay our hands on him; after all, he is our brother,
our own flesh and blood." His brothers agreed. So when the
Midianite merchants came by, his brothers pulled Joseph up out of

the cistern and sold him for twenty shekels of silver to the Ishmaelites, who took him to Egypt.

Silence

Meditation

> *Have mercy on your prodigal children, O God,*
> *and teach us to acknowledge our sinfulness,*
> *so that in repentance*
> *we may come to know your forgiveness*
> *which is fulfilment of our life in your Son,*
> *Jesus Christ our Lord.*
> *Amen.*

WEDNESDAY

> **Lord Jesus Christ,**
> **Son of God,**
> **have mercy upon me,**
> **a sinner.**

Look and see that I am God,
who once for my people rained down manna
and brought water from the rock in the desert,
by my right hand alone and by my own might.

'Look and see that I am God':
let me hear the Lord when he calls,
give up my former sin
and let me fear him as judge and God.

Let me hear the Lord when he calls

I have been wounded, I have been beaten.
Look, here are the hostile weapons
which have gone through my soul and body.
Look, here are the wounds, the sores, the injuries:
I cry out to you - see the stripes inflicted
by passions willingly indulged.

Let me hear the Lord when he calls

Know and see that I am God.
I search hearts,
punish thoughts, reprove actions, burn up sins;
I protect the orphan, the humble and poor.

Amos 5:7-15

You who turn justice into bitterness and cast righteousness to the ground (he who made the Pleiades and Orion, who turns blackness into dawn and darkens day into night, who calls for the waters of the sea and pours them out over the face of the land—the LORD is his name—he flashes destruction on the stronghold and brings the fortified city to ruin), you hate the one who reproves in court and despise the one who tells the truth. You trample on the poor and force him to give you grain. Therefore, though you have built stone mansions, you will not live in them; though you have planted lush vineyards, you will not drink their wine. For I know how many are your offences and how great your sins. You oppress the righteous and take bribes and you deprive the poor of justice in the courts. Therefore the prudent keep quiet in such times, for the times are evil. Seek good, not evil, that you may live. Then the LORD God Almighty will be with you, just as you say he is. Hate evil, love good; maintain justice in the courts.

Silence

Meditation

Lord God,
In this world where goodness and evil
continue to clash with each other,
instil in us, and in all your people,
discernment to see what is right,
faith to believe what is right;
and courage to do what is right,

Keep us aware of the subtlety of sin,
and preserve us, body, mind, and soul,
through the power of the Holy Spirit. Amen

THURSDAY

Lord Jesus Christ,
Son of God,
have mercy upon me,
a sinner.

Your unbearable gentleness, Lamb of God,
Whose touch dissolves, or destroys like fire.

I am yours, I am yours – what am I in your sight?
I would know myself, but in your life-giving light.

O make haste your face on mine to impress,
That you find in me no unshapeliness.

When you judge me with your clemency
For eternity.

Jesus, Lamb of God:
have mercy on us

Jesus, bearer of our sins:
have mercy on us

Jesus, redeemer of the world:
give us your peace

Mark 7:14-23

Again Jesus called the crowd to him and said, "Listen to me, everyone, and understand this. Nothing outside you can make you 'unclean' by going into you. Rather, it is what comes out of a you that makes you 'unclean.'"

After he had left the crowd and entered the house, his disciples asked him about this parable. "Are you so dull?" he asked. "Don't you see that nothing that enters you from the outside can make you 'unclean'? For it doesn't go into your heart but into you stomach, and then out of your body." (In saying this, Jesus declared all foods "clean".)

He went on: "What comes out of you is what makes you 'unclean'. For from within, out of your hearts, come evil thoughts, sexual immorality, theft, murder, adultery, greed, malice, deceit, lewdness, envy, slander, arrogance and folly. All these evils come from inside and make you 'unclean'."

Silence

Meditation

God of love and peace,
you invite us in this time of penance
to steer our course towards self-mastery and self-giving,
but not towards sadness.
Give us the grace
to find our joy and our security in love,
through Jesus, the Christ, our Lord.
Amen

Dear God,
Be good to me,
The sea is so wide
And my boat is so small.

FRIDAY

Lord Jesus Christ,
Son of God,
have mercy upon me,
a sinner.

The Song of God's Children

In Christ Jesus the life-giving law of the Spirit
has set us free from the law of sin and death.

All who are led by the Spirit of God
are children of God.
The Spirit we have received
is not a spirit of slavery,

leading us back into a life of fear,
but a Spirit of adoption,
enabling us to cry 'Abba! Father!'

The Spirit of God affirms to our spirit
that we are God's children;
and if children, then heirs, heirs of God

and fellow-heirs with Christ;
but we must share his sufferings
if we are also to share his glory.

The sufferings we now endure
bear no comparison with the glory,
as yet unrevealed, which is in store for us.

Romans 5:12-21

Therefore, just as sin entered the world through one man, and death through sin, and in this way death came to all people, because all sinned—for before the law was given, sin was in the world. But sin is not taken into account when there is no law. Nevertheless, death reigned from the time of Adam to the time of Moses, even over those who did not sin by breaking a command, as did Adam, who was a pattern of the one to come. But the gift is not like the trespass. For if the many died by the trespass of the one man, how much more did God's grace and the gift that came by the grace of the one man, Jesus Christ, overflow to the many! Again, the gift of God is not like the result of the one man's sin: The judgment followed one sin and brought condemnation, but the gift followed many trespasses and brought justification. For if, by the trespass of the one man, death reigned through that one man, how much more will those who receive God's abundant provision of grace and of the gift of righteousness reign in life through the one man, Jesus Christ. Consequently, just as the result of one trespass was condemnation for all men, so also the result of one act of righteousness was justification that brings life for all men. For just as through the disobedience of the one man the many were made sinners, so also through the obedience of the one man the many will be made righteous. The law was added so that the trespass might increase. But where sin increased, grace increased all the more, so that, just as sin reigned in death, so also grace might reign through righteousness to bring eternal life through Jesus Christ our Lord.

Silence

Meditation

> *Almighty God, conscious of the frailty of our faith*
> *and the fickleness of our wills,*
> *we offer ourselves to you*
> *as those whose living and believing*
> *need to be better modelled on your Son,*
> *our Lord and Saviour, Jesus Christ. Amen.*

SATURDAY

Lord Jesus Christ,
Son of God,
have mercy upon me,
a sinner.

I am the prodigal:
conceived in sin,
I dare not look up to the height of heaven.
But trusting in your love for us, I cry:
God be merciful to me and save me.

O Lord, do not rebuke me in your anger,
nor chasten me in your wrath.

If the righteous scarcely shall be saved,
how will it be with me a sinner?
I have not borne the heat and burden of the day:
yet, O God, number me with those
who came at the eleventh hour,
and save me.

O Lord, do not rebuke me in your anger,
nor chasten me in your wrath.

George Herbert
The Sinner

Lord, how I am all ague, when I seek
      What I have treasur'd in my memorie!
      Since, if my soul make even with the week,
Each seventh note by right is due to thee.
I finde there quarries of pil'd vanities,
      But shreds of holinesse, that dare not venture

To shew their face, since crosse to thy decrees:
There the circumference earth is, heav'n the centre.
In so much dregs the quintessence is small:
The spirit and good extract of my heart
Comes to about the many hundreth part.
Yet Lord restore thine image, heare my call:
And though my hard heart scarce to thee can grone,
Remember that thou once didst write in stone.

Silence

Meditation

I was entrusted with a land
without sin and full of life,
but I sowed it with sin,
and with a sickle reaped the ears of idleness.
I piled up in heaps the sheaves of my deeds,
but did not spread them out on the threshing-floor
of repentance.
But I pray you, O our God,
who have tilled the soil from all eternity,
by your kind mercy's breeze
blow away the chaff of my deeds,
and grant me the harvest of forgiveness.
Gather me up in your barn in heaven and save me.

YEAR 2

SUNDAY

Karl Barth
God as Reconciler

The Word of God whose revelation is attested in Scripture tells man that he
is a rebel who has wantonly abandoned the fellowship between himself as
creature and God as Creator and set himself in a place where this fellowship

is impossible. It tells him that he wanted to be his own lord and therewith betrayed and delivered himself up to the sphere of God's wrath, the state of rejection by God, and therefore of being closed up against God. It tells him that contrary to its destiny by creation his existence is a contradiction against God, a contradiction which excludes listening to God. It thus tells him, strangely, that he cannot hear it because he will not hear it, because his life-act is disobedience and therefore, factually, in respect of the use he makes of his life, it is a refusal to listen to what God says to him. Indeed, this content of the Word of God spoken to man makes it quite inconceivable that man should even get to hear God's word, that God should turn to him at all and address him. The fact that he is closed up to what God can say to him is simply an expression of the wrath of God resting upon him ... *Nevertheless* ... If we have heard and heard again ... then we can regard this possibility of our hearing as one which is given to us as a sheer miracle ... as the Nevertheless of grace which has on our side no complement or precondition.

WEEKDAY READINGS

MONDAY: Genesis 3:8-19
TUESDAY: Luke 15:11-19
WEDNESDAY: Isaiah 59:1-5
THURSDAY: Mark 9:42-50
FRIDAY: Romans 8:1-8

SATURDAY

Maria Boulding
Two kinds of sin

There seem to be two distinct kinds of sin. One is a deliberate 'No' to God in any area whatever; this automatically cancels the simple kind of prayer, until it is repented of and a 'Yes' substituted. It is obvious why this must be so: life and prayer cannot be compartmentalized. The other kind of sinfulness makes itself felt in a global sense of being weak and shabby and in need of God's mercy, an awareness of the general slum-situation within. This kind is not an act but a state, it almost seems to help; or at least the experience of it is part of prayer. You know that you are an undeserving beggar, that you have not a leg to stand on; yet somehow it is good to be there, because it is real, and to avoid this confrontation would be to escape into untruth. The strange thing is that although prayer is often completely unsatisfying and very humbling, although you seem to fail and fail again in prayer, you dimly know that it is all-important to stay there in that emptiness, refusing to fill the void with anything that is not God.

If this is your experience, you have attained to fellowship with the tax-collector in the Gospel. He had no achievements and no claim; he could only pray from his chaos, 'O God, be merciful to me, a sinner' (cf. Luke 18.13). All he could do was to make a space for God to be merciful, for God to be God for him. You have to make a space for God to be God for you, so that he can draw you into that truth-relationship with himself. This means space in the practical sense: you need a measure of time and silence to let him do it. It also means space in the sense of personal emptiness, not clinging to any righteousness of your own, letting go of any kind of inner defence against the living God. Then just abide there under his judgement and let him love you. He is a God who delights to give himself where there is hunger and thirst of spirit.

YEAR 3

SUNDAY

Reinhold Niebuhr
Original Sin

The whole crux of the doctrine of original sin lies in the seeming absurdity of the conception of free-will which underlies it. The Pauline doctrine as elaborated by Augustine and the Reformers, insists on the one hand that the will of man is enslaved to sin and is incapable of fulfilling God's Law. It may be free, declares Augustine, only it is not free to do good ... Yet on the other hand the same Augustine insists upon the reality of free-will whenever he has cause to fear that the concept of original sin might threaten the idea of human responsibility ... One could multiply examples in the thought of theologians of the Pauline tradition in which logical consistency is sacrificed in order to maintain on the one hand that the will is free in the sense that man is responsible for his sin, and on the other hand is not free in the sense that he can, of his own will, do nothing but evil ...

The full complexity of the psychological facts which validate the doctrine of original sin must be analysed, first in terms of the relation of temptation to the inevitability of sin. Such an analysis may make it plain why man sins inevitably, yet without escaping responsibility for his sin. The temptation to sin, as observed previously, lies in the human situation itself. This situation is that man as spirit transcends the temporal and natural process in which he is involved, and also transcends himself. Thus his freedom is the basis of his creativity but it is also his temptation. Since he is involved in the contingencies and necessities of the natural process on the one hand, and since, on the other, he stands outside of them and foresees their caprices and perils, he is anxious. In his anxiety, he seeks to transmute his finiteness into infinity, his weakness into strength, his dependence into independence. He seeks in other words to escape finiteness and weakness by a quantitative rather than qualitative development of his life. The quantitative antithesis of finiteness is infinity. The qualitative possibility of human life is its obedient subjection to the will of God. This possibility is expressed in the words of Jesus: "he that loseth his life for my sake shall find it". (Matthew 10:39)

WEEKDAY READINGS

MONDAY: Genesis 4:3-16
TUESDAY: 2 Samuel 11
WEDNESDAY: Micah 6:3-8
THURSDAY: Matthew 15:1-20
FRIDAY: Romans 2:1-11

SATURDAY

The Exeter Book
Lenten Contrition

Give me, O Lord, patience and sense of purpose in each of the things you send to beset me. You know the many wicked deeds which burden my heart. But out of compassion you set aside all blame, and receive me as your own. Please protect me through the dangers and confusion of my transient life on earth, ensuring that in all things I strive for eternal life in heaven. I know that I am very slow to make amends for my sins, despite the many favours you grant me. Fix my trust, my timid hopes, upon yourself so that I may stand on a secure foundation. Lift up my thoughts with your wisdom. Take me out of this world as soon as I am fit to be received into the next.

Stand by me, Lord, and hold me upright when the gales of sin blow round me. And when the dark stormy night of wickedness closes in on me, guide my steps. My soul is already battered by the temptations to which I have submitted. My spirit is crushed by the weight of past misdeeds. My mind is stained by the memory of the evil in which I have participated. Throughout my life you have been unfailingly generous to me, although I have deserved only punishment.

The trees around me flourish and spread their branches. But I am hemmed in by the guilt which surrounds me, and I wither because of the poison of sin within me. Ah Lord, you are the only remedy. I accept that while I remain on earth I must endure hardship, and must be spiritually destitute. I may enjoy the affection of friends, and the hospitality of strangers, but these are only brief flashes of light in the darkness. Let my suffering bring me true contrition, that I may receive your forgiveness, and so be made fit for the everlasting joy of heaven.

PRAYER OF PENITENCE

It is time to repent.
I come to you, my Creator.
Remove from me the burden of sin,
and in your compassion
grant me forgiveness.

Saviour, do not reject me,
do not thrust me from you.
Remove from me the burden of sin,
and in your compassion
grant me forgiveness.

Saviour, forgive all my offences,
intentional or unintentional,
open or secret,
known or unknown.
For you are God,
have mercy and save me.

THE PRAYERS

Lord we have fallen into sin,
We have fallen into wickedness,
We have fallen into evil.
Lord, lift us up and set us free.

Lord we have fallen into rebellion,
We have fallen into disobedience,
We have fallen into unrighteousness.
Lord, lift us up and set us free.

Lord we have fallen into despair,
We have fallen into disillusionment,
We have fallen into depression.
Lord, lift us up and set us free.
Lord we have fallen into loneliness,
We have fallen into darkness,
We have fallen into hell.
Lord, lift us up and set us free.

MEDITATIONS

SUNDAY: If we claim to be without sin, we deceive ourselves and the truth is not in us. (1 John 1:8)

MONDAY: I am fallen, in your compassion have mercy on me. (*The Lenten Triodion*)

TUESDAY: O God, you know how fragile is our human nature, wounded as it is by sin. (*Italian Sacramentary*)

WEDNESDAY: To deny a people their rights before the Most High, to deprive them of justice—would not the Lord see such things? (Lamentations 3:35-36)

THURSDAY: There is a deep well inside me. And in it dwells God. Sometimes I am there too. But more often stones and grit block the well, and God is buried beneath. Then God must be dug out again. (Etty Hillesum)

FRIDAY: Sin is not a thing; it is not a mortal stain or blemish, it is a damage to a relationship, a rejection of love. It is a gap, a chasm, and those who have chosen to be far off must be brought close. (Ruth Burrows, English Carmelite Nun)

SATURDAY: For all have sinned and fall short of the glory of God (Romans 3:23)

John Milton

Paradise Lost Book XII

The brandished sword of God before them blazed,
Fierce as a comet, which with torrid heat,
And vapour as the Libyan air adust,
Began to parch that temperate clime; whereat
In either hand the hast'ning Angel caught
Our lingering parents, and to th' eastern gate
Led them direct, and down the cliff as fast
To the subjected plain; then disappeared.
They, looking back, all the eastern side beheld
Of Paradise, so late their happy seat,
Waved over by that flaming brand, the gate
With dreadful faces thronged and fiery arms:
Some natural tears they dropped, but wiped them soon;
The world was all before them, where to choose
Their place of rest, and Providence their guide:
They, hand in hand, with wondering steps and slow,
Through Eden took their solitary way.

LENT III:

THE RETURN

SUNDAY

Jesus, lover of my soul,
Let me to thy bosom fly,
While the nearer waters roll,
While the tempest still is high;
Hide me, O my Saviour, hide,
Till the storm of life is past;
Safe into the haven guide,
O receive my soul at last!

Jesus our Saviour, Lord of all the nations,
Christ our Redeemer, hear the prayers we offer,
Spare us and save us, comfort us in sorrow.

Word of the Father, key-stone of God's building,
Source of our gladness, gate-way to the kingdom,
Free us in mercy from the sins that bind us.

Humbly confessing that we have offended,
Stripped of illusions, naked in our sorrow,
Pardon, Lord Jesus, those your blood has ransomed.

Hear us, almighty Lord, show us your mercy
Sinners we stand here before you

Metropolitan Anthony of Sourozh
Repentance

Repentance must not be mistaken for remorse, it does not consist in feeling terribly sorry that things went wrong in the past; it is an active, positive attitude which consists in moving in the right direction. It is made very clear in the parable of the two sons (Mt 21:28) who were commanded by their father to go to work at his vineyard. The one said, 'I am going', but did not go. The other said, 'I am not going', and then felt ashamed and went to work. This was real repentance, and we should never lure ourselves into imagining that to lament of one's past is an act of repentance. It is part of it of course, but repentance remains unreal and barren as long as it has not led us to doing the will of the father. We have a tendency to think that is should result in fine emotions instead of real, deep changes.

When we have hurt someone and realise that we were wrong, quite often we go and express our sorrow to the person, and when the conversation has been emotionally tense, when there were a lot of tears and forgiveness and moving words, we go away with a sense of having dome everything possible. We have wept together, we are at peace and now everything is all right. It is not all right at all. We have simply delighted in our virtues and the other person, who may be goodhearted and easily moved, has reacted to our emotional scene. But this is just what conversion is not. No one asks us to shed tears, nor to have a touching encounter with the victim, even when the victim is God. What is expected is that having understood the wrong we should put it right.

Silence

Meditation

Remind me ten times more
of all that you have forgiven me–
without even waiting for my sorrow,
the very instant that I slipped and sinned.

Remind me ten thousand times more
of your endless absolution,
not even sorrow required on my part,
so broad the bounty of your love.

Yes I can – I will – forgive
as you have forgiven me.

MONDAY

Just as I am, without one plea
but that thy blood was shed for me,
and that thou bidst me come to thee,
O Lamb of God, I come.

The Song of Manasseh

1. O Lord Almighty and God of our forebears,
 you who made heaven and earth in all their glory:
2. All things tremble with awe at your presence,
 before your great and mighty power.
3. Immeasurable and unsearchable is your promise of mercy,
 for you are God, Most High.
4. You are full of compassion and very merciful,
 and you relent at human suffering.
5. O God, according to your great goodness.
 You have promised repentance and forgiveness
 to those who have sinned against you.
6. The sins I have committed against you,
 are more in number than the sands of the sea.
7. I am not worthy to look up and sea the heavens,
 because of my many sins and iniquities.
8. And now my heart bows before you,
 imploring your kindness upon me.
9. I have sinned, O God, I have sinned,
 and I have acknowledged my transgressions.
10. Unworthy as I am, I know that you will save me,
 according to your great mercy.
11. For all the host of heaven sings your praise,
 and your glory is for ever and ever.

You are full of compassion and very merciful

Hosea 14:1-7
Return, O Israel, to the LORD your God. Your sins have been your downfall! Take words with you and return to the LORD. Say to him: "Forgive all our sins and receive us graciously, that we may offer the fruit of our lips. Assyria cannot save us; we will not mount war-horses. We will never again say 'Our gods' to what our own hands have made, for in you the fatherless find compassion." "I will heal

their waywardness and love them freely, for my anger has turned away from them. I will be like the dew to Israel; he will blossom like a lily. Like a cedar of Lebanon he will send down his roots; his young shoots will grow. His splendour will be like an olive tree, his fragrance like a cedar of Lebanon. People will dwell again in his shade. He will flourish like the corn. He will blossom like a vine, and his fame will be like the wine from Lebanon.

Silence

Meditation

God of all life,
you accomplish in the humble heart
what every springtime brings about in nature.
Uproot in us the seeds of sin,
and prepare the soil of our hearts
to receive the new life
Jesus, the Christ, our Lord.
Amen.

Forgive all our sins
and receive us graciously,
that we may offer the fruit of our lips.
Amen.

TUESDAY

Just as I am, though tossed about,
with many a conflict, many a doubt,
fightings and fears within, without,
O lamb of God, I come.

10. Hide your face from my sins
    and blot out all my iniquities.
11. Create in me a clean heart, O God,
    and renew a right spirit within me.
12. Cast me not away from your presence
    and take not your holy spirit from me.
13. Give me the joy of your saving help again
    and sustain me with your bountiful spirit.
14. I shall teach your ways to the wicked,
    and sinners shall return to you.
15. Deliver me from death, O God,
    and my tongue shall sing of your righteousness,
        O God, of my salvation.
16. Open my lips, O Lord,
    and my mouth shall proclaim your praise.
17. Had you desired it, I would have offered sacrifice,
    but you take no delight in burnt-offerings.
18. The sacrifice of God is a troubled spirit;
    a broken and contrite heart, O God,
        you will not despise.

Give me the joy of your saving help

Genesis 50:1-3, 15-21

Joseph threw himself upon his father and wept over him and kissed him. Then Joseph directed the physicians in his service to embalm his father Israel. So the physicians embalmed him, taking a full forty days, for that was the time required for embalming. And the Egyptians mourned for him seventy days.

When Joseph's brothers saw that their father was dead, they said, "What if Joseph holds a grudge against us and pays us back for all the wrongs we did to him?" So they sent word to Joseph, saying, "Your father left these instructions before he died: 'This is what you are to say to Joseph: I ask you to forgive your brothers the sins and the wrongs they committed in treating you so badly.' Now please forgive the sins of the servants of the God of your father." When their message came to him, Joseph wept. His brothers then came and threw themselves down before him. "We are your slaves," they said. But Joseph said to them, "Don't be afraid. Am I in the place of God? You intended to harm me, but God intended it for good to accomplish what is now being done, the saving of many lives. So then, don't be afraid. I will provide for you and your children." And he reassured them and spoke kindly to them.

Silence

Meditation

Almighty God, have mercy upon us,
and on all who would bear us evil will and would harm us,
forgive their faults and ours together,
by such tender, merciful means
as your infinite wisdom can best devise;
amend and redress and make us saved souls in heaven together
where we may ever live and love together with you. Amen.

WEDNESDAY

Just as I am, thou wilt receive,
wilt welcome, pardon, cleanse, relieve:
because thy promise I believe,
O Lamb of God, I come.

Psalm 103:1-6

1. Bless the Lord, O my soul,
and all that is within me, bless his holy name.
2. Bless the Lord, O my soul,
and forget not all his benefits.

3. He forgives all your sins
and heals all your infirmities;
4. He redeems your life from the grave
and crowns you with mercy and loving-kindness;
5. He satisfies you with good things,
and your youth is renewed like an eagle's.
6. The Lord executes righteousness
and judgement for all who are oppressed.

Bless the Lord O my soul

Luke 7:36-50

Now one of the Pharisees invited Jesus to have dinner with him, so he went to the Pharisee's house and reclined at the table. When a woman who had lived a sinful life in that town learned that Jesus was eating at the Pharisee's house, she brought an alabaster jar of perfume, and as she stood behind him at his feet weeping, she began to wet his feet with her tears. Then she wiped them with her hair, kissed them and poured perfume on them. When the Pharisee who had invited him saw this, he said to himself, "If this man were a prophet, he would know who is touching him and what kind of woman she is—that she is a sinner." Jesus answered him, "Simon, I have something to tell you." "Tell me, teacher," he said. "Two men owed money to a certain money-lender. One owed him five hundred denarii, and the other fifty. Neither of them had the money to pay him back, so he cancelled the debts of both. Now which of them will love him more?" Simon replied, "I suppose the one who had the bigger debt cancelled." "You have judged correctly," Jesus said. Then he turned towards the woman and said to Simon, "Do you see this woman? I came into your house. You did not give me any water for my feet, but she wet my feet with her tears and wiped them with her hair. You did not give me a kiss, but this woman, from the time I entered, has not stopped kissing my feet. You did not put oil on my head, but she has poured perfume on my feet. Therefore, I tell you, her many sins have been forgiven—for she loved much. But the one who has been forgiven little loves little." Then Jesus said to her, "Your sins are forgiven". The other guests began to say among themselves, "Who is this who even forgives sins?" Jesus said to the woman, "Your faith has saved you; go in peace."

Silence

Meditation

Lord our God,
your Son lived among us as a physician
for those who came to him for healing.
Make us conscious of our sin
so that we may seek our healing in him,
Jesus our Saviour.

Amen

THURSDAY

Just as I am, poor, wretched, blind;
sight, riches, healing of the mind,
yea all I need, in thee to find,
O Lamb of God, I come.

Psalm 103:8-20

8. The Lord is full of compassion and mercy,
   slow to anger and of great kindness.
   9. He will not always accuse us,
   nor will he keep his anger for ever.
10. He has not dealt with us according to our sins,
    nor rewarded us according to our wickedness.
11. For as the heavens are high above the earth,
    so is his mercy great upon those who fear him.
    12. As far as the east is from the west,
    so far has he removed our sins from us.

13. As a father cares for his children,
so does the Lord care for those who fear him.
14. For he himself knows whereof we are made;
he remembers that we are but dust.
15. Our days are like the grass;
we flourish like a flower of the field;
16. When the wind goes over it, it is gone,
and its place shall know it no more.
17. But the merciful goodness of the Lord
endures for ever on those who fear him,
and his righteousness on children's children;
18. On those who keep his covenant
and remember his commandments to do them.
19. The Lord has set his throne in heaven,
and his kingship has dominion over all.
20. Bless the Lord, you angels of his,
you mighty ones who do his bidding,
and hearken to the voice of his word.

The Lord is full of compassion and mercy

1 Timothy 1:12-17

I thank Christ Jesus our Lord, who has given me strength, that he considered me faithful, appointing me to his service. Even though I was once a blasphemer and a persecutor and a violent man, I was shown mercy because I acted in ignorance and unbelief. The grace of our Lord was poured out on me abundantly, along with the faith and love that are in Christ Jesus. Here is a trustworthy saying that deserves full acceptance: Christ Jesus came into the world to save sinners—of whom I am the worst. But for that very reason I was shown mercy so that in me, the worst of sinners, Christ Jesus might display his unlimited patience as an example for those who would believe on him and receive eternal life. Now to the King eternal, immortal, invisible, the only God, be honour and glory for ever and ever. Amen.

Silence

Meditation

> *Here is my heart, O God,*
> *here it is with all its secrets;*
> *look into my thoughts,*
> *O my hope,*
> *and take away all my wrong feelings:*
> *let my eyes ever be on you*
> *and release my feet from the snare.*
> *Amen.*

FRIDAY

> *Just as I am (thy love unknown*
> *has broken every barrier down),*
> *now to be thine, yea, thine alone,*
> *O Lamb of God, I come.*

Psalm 15

1. Lord, who may dwell in your tabernacle?
   who may abide upon your holy hill?
2. Whoever leads a blameless life
   and does what is right,
   who speaks the truth from his heart.
3. There is no guile upon his tongue;
   he does no evil to his friend;
   he does not heap contempt upon his neighbour.
4. In his sight the wicked is rejected,
   but he honours those who fear the Lord.
5. He has sworn to do no wrong
   and does not take back his word.

6. He does not give his money in hope of gain,
   nor does he take a bribe against the innocent.
   7. Whoever does these things
   shall never be overthrown.

God opposes the proud but gives grace to the humble

James 4:1-10
What causes fights and quarrels among you? Don't they come from your desires that battle within you? You want something but don't get it. You kill and covet, but you cannot have what you want. You quarrel and fight. You do not have, because you do not ask God. When you ask, you do not receive, because you ask with wrong motives, that you may spend what you get on your pleasures. You adulterous people, don't you know that friendship with the world is hatred towards God? Anyone who chooses to be a friend of the world becomes an enemy of God. Or do you think Scripture says without reason that the spirit he caused to live in us envies intensely? But he gives us more grace. That is why Scripture says: "God opposes the proud but gives grace to the humble." Submit yourselves, then, to God. Resist the devil, and he will flee from you. Come near to God and he will come near to you. Wash your hands, you sinners, and purify your hearts, you double-minded. Grieve, mourn and wail. Change your laughter to mourning and your joy to gloom. Humble yourselves before the Lord, and he will lift you up. Brothers and sisters, do not slander one another. Anyone who speaks against his brother or sisters or judges them speaks against the law and judges it. When you judge the law, you are not keeping it, but sitting in judgment on it.

Silence

Meditation

God our Father,
you have given the good things of this day
to the upright and sinners alike;
Teach us to be merciful like you
and to forgive whole-heartedly.
So shall we be ready to receive your salvation,
through Jesus, the Christ, our Lord.
                                        Amen.

SATURDAY

Plenteous grace with thee is found,
Grace to cover all my sin;
Let the healing streams abound,
Make and keep me pure within.
Thou of life the fountain art;
Freely let me take of thee;
Spring thou up within y heart,
Rise to all eternity.

Psalm 32:1-9

1. Happy are they whose transgressions are forgiven,
   and whose sin is put away!
2. Happy are they to whom the Lord imputes no guilt,
   and in whose spirit there is no guile.
3. While I held my tongue, my bones withered away,
   because of my groaning all day long.
4. For your hand was heavy upon me day and night;
   my moisture was dried up as in the heat of summer.
5. Then I acknowledged my sin to you,
   and did not conceal my guilt.
6. I said, 'I will confess my transgressions to the Lord':
   then you forgave the guilt of my sin;

7. Therefore, all the faithful will make their prayer to you
in time of trouble;
when the great waters overflow, they shall not reach them.
8. You are my hiding place; you preserve me from trouble;
you surround me with shouts of deliverance.
9. I will instruct you and teach you
in the way that you should go; I will guide you with my eye.

Happy are they whose sins are forgiven!

John Donne
A Hymn to God the Father

Wilt thou forgive that sin where I begun,
　Which is my sin, though it were done before?
Wilt thou forgive those sins through which I run,
　And do them still, though still I do deplore?
When thou hast done, thou hast not done,
　For I have more.

Wilt thou forgive that sin by which I won
　Others to sin, and made my sin their door?
Wilt thou forgive that sin which I did shun
　A year or two, but wallowed in a score?
When thou hast done, thou hast not done,
　For I have more.

I have a sin of fear, that when I've spun
　My last thread, I shall perish on the shore;
Swear by thyself that at my death thy sun
　Shall shine as it shines now, and heretofore;
And having done that, thou hast done,
　I have no more.

Silence

Meditation

> *When I look back upon my life nigh spent,*
> *Nigh spent, although the stream as yet flows on,*

I more of follies than of sins repent,
Less for offence than love's shortcomings moan.
With self, O Father, leave me not alone –
Leave not with the beguiler the beguiled;
Besmirched and ragged, Lord, take back thine own:
A fool I bring thee to be made a child.

YEAR 2

SUNDAY

John Keble
Conversion and amendment

True and full repentance is a greater work than some of us may have imagined. It is two great works in one: the first is hating the evil, 'casting away all our transgressions', and the other is loving the good, 'making us a new heart and a new spirit'. The same work, which in the psalm the penitent David prays God to accomplish for him, God himself, here in the prophet, calls upon the penitent to accomplish for himself. That is, conversion and amendment is in some mysterious way both God's work and our work; and being God's work, it is compared to creation: it is like making a world out of nothing, light out of darkness, order out of confusion.

What must we do, that we may work this great work of God? Turn your souls and bodies away from your sins, towards Jesus Christ crucified for you, with a sincere desire to love and please him; and as often as you overcome yourself in any way for his sake, he will he ready with his gracious help: until at last the new heart and the new spirit, which he gave you first in baptism, is thoroughly awakened and enlivened within you. Come to him thus, and you shall prove in your own person the mercy which he offers to all: 'He will in no wise cast you out.'

WEEKDAY READINGS

MONDAY: Job 42:1-6
TUESDAY: Luke 15:20-32
WEDNESDAY: Matthew 21:28-32
THURSDAY: 1 John 3:1-10
FRIDAY: Matthew 18:21-35

SATURDAY

Simone Weil
"And forgive us our debts, as we also forgive our debtors"

To remit debts is to renounce our own personality. It means that we renounce everything which goes to make up our own ego, without any exception. It means knowing that in the ego there is nothing whatever, no psychological element, which external circumstances could not do away with. It means accepting that truth. It means being happy that things should be so.

The words "Thy will be done" imply this acceptance, if we say a few moments later: "We forgive our debtors."

The forgiveness of debts is spiritual poverty, spiritual nakedness, death. If we accept death completely, we can ask god to make us live again, purified from the evil which is in us. Pardon is purification. God himself has not the power to forgive the evil in us while it remains there. God will have forgiven our debts when he has brought us to the state of perfection.

Until then God forgives our debts partially in the same measure as we forgive our debtors.

YEAR 3

SUNDAY

William Temple
The Conditions of Forgiveness

There seems to me to be a very surprising feature in most of the books that I have read and the sermons that I have heard on this subject. Over and over again it is said that Our Lord promises forgiveness to those who repent; there is often some discussion of the question how far His Death was a necessary condition of forgiveness on the side of God; but there is almost complete agreement that the one condition required on our side is repentance. Of course there is in the Gospels an immense insistence on the need for repentance. Also there is the reference to repentance in Our Lord's teaching about our duty to forgive others. But when He is actually speaking about God's forgiveness of us it is not 'repentance' that He mentions; it is our own forgiveness of those who have injured us. Only one petition in the Lord's prayer has any condition attached to it: it is the petition for forgiveness; and the condition attached to it is this. No doubt if by repentance we mean all that the word means in the New Testament, it will include a forgiving spirit;

for to repent is to change one's outlook and to regard men and the world as God regards them. But every one can feel that the emphasis would be quite different if the words were, 'Forgive us our trespasses, for we do truly repent of them.' This would be like saying, 'I am so sorry; and I won't do it again do forgive me.' In other words, the plea for forgiveness would rest on an apology and a promise made to God; and that is not the basis on which Our Lord bids us rest our plea. It is to rest on our attitude, not towards God, but towards His other children. He always ready and eager to forgive; but how can He restore us the freedom and intimacy of the family life if there are other members of the family towards whom we refuse to be friendly?

WEEKDAY READINGS

MONDAY: Ezekiel 18:20-24
TUESDAY: 2 Samuel: 12:1-13
WEDNESDAY: Luke 19:1-10
THURSDAY: Acts 2:36-42
FRIDAY: Luke 6:27-38

SATURDAY

Madeleine L'Engle
Forgiveness

There is only one purpose for punishment, and that is to teach a lesson, and there is only one lesson to be taught, and that is love. Perfect love banishes fear, and when we are not afraid we know that love which includes forgiveness. When the lesson to be learned is not love, that is not punishment; it is revenge or retribution. Probably the lesson of love is the most terrible punishment of all – an almost intolerable anguish – for it means that the sinner has to realize what has been done, has to be truly sorry, to repent, to turn to God. And most of us are too filled with outrage at rape and murder to want the sinner to repent. We want the sinner to feel terrible, but not to turn to God and be made whole and be forgiven. And so we show that we do not know the meaning of forgiveness any more than Jonah did in his vindictive outrage at the people of Nineveh.

PRAYER OF PENITENCE

O God, our Redeemer,
in our weakness we have failed
to be the messengers of forgiveness and hope:
renew us by your Holy Spirit,
that we may follow your commands
and proclaim your reign of love;
through Jesus Christ our Lord.
Amen.

THE PRAYERS

Lord our God, be gracious to us,
show compassion to us, and turn to us.

When heavy burdens oppress us, and our spirits grow faint,
and the gloom of failure settles upon us,
help us to see through the darkness to the light beyond.
To You, O Lord, we turn for light;
turn to us and help us.

When we come to doubt the value of life
because suffering blinds us to life's goodness,
give us the understanding to bear pain without despair.
To You, O God, we turn for understanding;
turn to us and help us.

When we are tempted to suppress the voice of conscience,
to call evil good and good evil,
turn our hearts to the rights of others,
and make us more responsive to their needs.
To You, O Lord, we turn for guidance;
turn to us and help us.

And when we become immersed in material cares
and worldly pleasures, forgetting You,
may we find that all things bear witness to You, O God,
and let them lead us back to Your presence.
To You, O God, we turn for meaning;
turn to us and help us.

MEDITATIONS

SUNDAY: Open to me the doors of repentance (Orthodox)

MONDAY: Create in me a pure heart, O God, and renew a steadfast spirit within me. Do not cast me from your presence or take your Holy Spirit from me. (Psalm 51:10, 11)

TUESDAY: Genuine forgiveness is participation, reunion overcoming the powers of estrangement. And only because this is so does forgiveness make love possible. (Paul Tillich)

WEDNESDAY: Where a penitent sinner stands, even the wholly righteous may not stand. (*Gates of Prayer*)

THURSDAY: God has given me the power to change my ways. (Mechtild of Magdeburg)

FRIDAY: Only one petition in the Lord's Prayer has any condition attached to it: it is the petition for forgiveness. (William Temple)

SATURDAY: Lord, you return gladly and lovingly to lift up the one who offends you and I do not turn to raise up and honour the one who angers me. (St. John of the Cross)

John Milton
Paradise Regained
The Fourth Book

The Son of God, with Godlike force endued
Against th'attempter of thy Father's throne
And thief of paradise! Him long of old
Thou didst debel, and down from heaven cast
With all his army; now thou hast avenged
Supplanted Adam, and by vanquishing
Temptation, hast regained lost Paradise,
And frustrated the conquest fraudulent.
He never more henceforth will dare set foot
In Paradise to tempt; his snares are broke.
For, though that seat of earthly bliss be failed,
A fairer Paradise is founded now

For Adam and his chosen sons, whom thou,
A Saviour, art come down to reinstall;
Where they shall dwell secure, when time shall be,
Of tempter and temptation without fear.
But thou, Infernal Serpent, shalt not long
Rule in the clouds; like an autumnal star,
Or lightening, thou shalt fall from Heaven, trod down
Under his feet: for proof, ere this thou feel'st
Thy wound (yet not thy last and deadliest wound)
By this repulse received, and hold'st in Hell
No triumph; in all her gates Abaddon rues
Thy bold attempt; Hereafter learn with awe
To dread the Son of God: he, all unarmed,
Shall chase thee, with the terror of his voice,
From thy demonic holds, possession foul,
Thee and thy legions; yelling they shall fly,
And beg to hide them in a herd of swine,
Lest he command them down into the Deep,
Bound, and to torment sent before their time.
Hail, Son of the Most High, heir of both worlds,
Queller of Satan! On thy glorious work
Now enter, and begin to save mankind.

Thus they the Son of God, our Saviour meek,
Sung Victor, and, from heavenly feast refreshed,
Brought on his way with joy; he, unobserved,
Home to his mother's house private returned.

LENT IV:

THE COST

SUNDAY

And can it be that I should gain
An int'rest in the Saviour's blood!
Dy'd he for me? – who caus'd his pain?
For me? – who Him to Death pursued?
Amazing love! How can it be
That Thou, my God, shouldst die for me?

Psalm 107:1-9

1. Give thanks to the Lord, for he is good,
    and his mercy endures for ever.
2. Let all those whom the Lord has redeemed proclaim
    that he redeemed them from the hand of the foe.
3. He gathered them out of the lands,
    from the east and from the west,
    from the north and from the south.
4. Some wandered in desert wastes;
    they found no way to a city where they might dwell.
5. They were hungry and thirsty;
    their spirits languished within them
6. Then they cried to the Lord in their trouble,
    and he delivered them from their distress.
7. He put their feet on a straight path
    to go to a city where they might dwell.
8. Let them give thanks to the Lord for his mercy
    and the wonders he does for his children.
9. For he satisfies the thirsty
    and fills the hungry with good things.

Let us give thanks to the Lord,
for he has redeemed us

George Herbert
Redemption

Having been a tenant long to a rich Lord,
   Not thriving, I resolved to be bold,
   And make a suit unto him, to afford
A new small-rented lease, and cancelled th'old.

In heaven at his manour I him sought:
   They told me there, that he was lately gone
   About some land, which he had dearly bought,
Long since on earth, to take possession.

I straight return'd, and knowing his great birth,
   Sought him accordingly in great resorts;
   In cities, theatres, gardens, parks, and courts:
At length I heard a ragged noise and mirth

   Of theeves and muderers: there I him espied,
   Who straight, *Your suit is granted*, said & died.

Silence

Meditation

Almighty God,
the Redeemer of all who trust in you;
give heed to the cry of your people,
deliver us from the bondage of sin
that we may serve you in perfect freedom
and rejoice in your unfailing love;
through Jesus Christ our Saviour,
Amen.

MONDAY

'Tis mystery all! Th'Immortal dies!
Who can explore his strange Design?
In vain the first-born Seraph tries
To sound the Depths of Love divine.
'Tis mercy all! Let earth adore;
Let Angel Minds Inquire no more.

Isaiah 52:2-6

Shake off your dust; rise up, sit enthroned, O Jerusalem.
Free yourself from the chains on your neck,
O captive Daughter of Zion.

For this is what the LORD says:
"You were sold for nothing,
and without money you will be redeemed."

For this is what the Sovereign LORD says:
"At first my people went down to Egypt to live;
lately, Assyria has oppressed them.

"And now what do I have here?" declares the LORD.

"For my people have been taken away for nothing,
and those who rule them mock," declares the LORD.
"And all day long my name is constantly blasphemed.
Therefore my people will know my name;
therefore in that day they will know that it is I who foretold it.
Yes, it is I."

The Lord will redeem his people

Ruth 4:1-6, 9-10

Boaz went up to the town gate and sat there. When the kinsman-redeemer came along, Boaz said, "Come over here, my friend, and sit down." So he went over and sat down. Boaz took ten of the elders of the town and said, "Sit here," and they did so. Then he said to the kinsman-redeemer, "Naomi, who has come back from Moab, is selling the piece of land that belonged to our brother Elimelech. I thought I should bring the matter to your attention and suggest that you buy it in the presence of these seated here and in the presence of the elders of my people. If you will redeem it, do so. But if you will not, tell me, so I will know. For no-one has the right to do it except you, and I am next in line." "I will redeem it," he said. Then Boaz said, "On the day you buy the land from Naomi and from Ruth the Moabitess, you acquire the dead man's widow, in order to maintain the name of the dead with his property." At this, the kinsman-redeemer said, "Then I cannot redeem it because I might endanger my own estate. You redeem it yourself. I cannot do it." Then Boaz announced to the elders and all the people, "Today you are witnesses that I have bought from Naomi all the property of Elimelech, Kilion and Mahlon. I have also acquired Ruth the Moabitess, Mahlon's widow, as my wife, in order to maintain the name of the dead with his property, so that his name will not disappear from among his family or from the town records. Today you are witnesses!"

Silence

Meditation

> *O Lord,*
> *at great cost you have redeemed us,*
> *you have called us out by name,*
> *we are yours.*

TUESDAY

He left his Father's throne above
(So free, so infinite his grace!)
Empty'd himself of All but Love,
And bled for Adam's *helpless Race.*
'Tis Mercy all, immense and free,
For, O my God! It found out Me!

Psalm 77:11-end

11. I will remember the works of the Lord,
and call to mind your wonders of old time.
12. I will meditate on all your acts
and ponder your mighty deeds.
13. Your way, O God, is holy;
who is so great a god as our God?
14. You are the God who works wonders
and have declared your power among the peoples.
15. By your strength you have redeemed your people,
the children of Jacob and Joseph.
16. The waters saw you, O God;
the waters saw you and trembled;
the very depths were shaken.
17. The clouds poured out water; the skies thundered;
your arrows flashed to and fro;
18. The sound of your thunder was in the whirlwind;
your lightenings lit up the world;
the earth trembled and shook
19. Your way was in the sea,
and your paths in the great waters,
yet your footsteps were not seen.
20. You led your people like a flock
by the hand of Moses and Aaron.

I will remember the works of the Lord

Deuteronomy 7:7-12

The LORD did not set his affection on you and choose you because you were more numerous than other peoples, for you were the fewest of all peoples. But it was because the LORD loved you and kept the oath he swore to your ancestors that he brought you out with a mighty hand and redeemed you from the land of slavery, from the power of Pharaoh king of Egypt. Know therefore that the LORD your God is God; he is the faithful God, keeping his covenant of love to a thousand generations of those who love him and keep his commands. But those who hate him he will repay to their face by destruction; he will not be slow to repay to their face those who hate him. Therefore, take care to follow the commands, decrees and laws I give you today. If you pay attention to these laws and are careful to follow them, then the LORD your God will keep his covenant of love with you, as he swore to your forefathers.

Silence

Meditation

*God of all faithfulness
you showed your power
on the night you rescued your people from slavery.
Show that same power now to us;
deliver us from sin,
and on the holy night which we await with all your children
we will be able, in full freedom, to sing your glory
through Jesus, the Christ, our Lord.*
Amen.

WEDNESDAY

*Long my imprison'd Spirit lay,
Fast bound in Sin and Natures' Night
Thine Eye diffus'd a quickning Ray;*

I woke; the Dungoen flamed with Light.
My chains fell off, My heart was free,
I rose, went forth, and follow'd Thee.

Song: Job 33:23-30

"Yet if there is an angel on their side as a mediator,
      one out of a thousand,
        to tell them what is right for them.

"To be gracious to them and say,
    'Spare them from going down to the pit;
      I have found a ransom for them'—

"Then their flesh is renewed like a child's;
    it is restored as in the days of their youth.

"They pray to God and find favour with him,
    they see God's face and shout for joy;
they are restored by God to their righteous state.

"Then they come to people and say,
    'I sinned, and perverted what was right,
      but I did not get what I deserved.

"'He redeemed my soul from going down to the pit,
    and I will live to enjoy the light.'
"God does all these things to people—twice,
even three times—to turn back their souls from the pit,
    that the light of life may shine on them."

May the light of life shine upon us

1 Peter 1:18-25
For you know that it was not with perishable things such as silver or
gold that you were redeemed from the empty way of life handed

down to you from your ancestors, but with the precious blood of Christ, a lamb without blemish or defect. He was chosen before the creation of the world, but was revealed in these last times for your sake. Through him you believe in God, who raised him from the dead and glorified him, and so your faith and hope are in God. Now that you have purified yourselves by obeying the truth so that you have sincere mutual affection, love one another deeply, from the heart. For you have been born again, not of perishable seed, but of imperishable, through the living and enduring word of God. For, "All human beings are like grass, and all their glory is like the flowers of the field; the grass withers and the flowers fall, but the word of the Lord stands for ever." And this is the word that was preached to you.

Silence

Meditation

Blessed be the name of Jesus, who died to save us.
Blessed be Jesus, who had compassion on us.
Blessed be Jesus, who suffered loneliness,
rejection and pain, for our sakes.
Blessed be Jesus, through whose cross I am forgiven.
Lord Jesus, deepen my understanding of your suffering and death.

THURSDAY

Still the small inward Voice I hear,
That whispers all my Sins forgiv'n;
Still the atoning Blood is near,
That quench'd the Wrath of hostile Heav'n:
I feel the Life his wounds impart;
I feel my Saviour in my Heart.

Psalm 20

1. May the Lord answer you in the day of trouble,
   the name of the God of Jacob defend you;
2. Send you help from his holy place
   and strengthen you out of Zion;
3. Remember all your offerings
   and accept your burnt sacrifice;
4. Grant your heart's desire
   and prosper all your plans.
5. We will shout for joy at your victory
   and triumph in the name of our God;
   may the Lord grant all your requests.
6. Now I know that the Lord gives victory to his anointed;
   he will answer him out of his holy heaven,
   with the victorious strength of his right hand.
7. Some put their trust in chariots and some in horses,
   but we will call upon the name of the Lord our God.
8. They collapse and fall down,
   but we will arise and stand upright.
9. O Lord, give victory to the king
   and answer us when we call.

O Lord, answer us when we call

Colossians 1:13-20

For he has rescued us from the dominion of darkness and brought us into the kingdom of the Son he loves, in whom we have redemption, the forgiveness of sins. He is the image of the invisible God, the firstborn over all creation. For by him all things were created: things in heaven and on earth, visible and invisible, whether thrones or powers or rulers or authorities; all things were created by him and for him. He is before all things, and in him all things hold together. And he is the head of the body, the church; he is the beginning and the firstborn from among the dead, so that in everything he might have the supremacy. For God was pleased to have all his fullness dwell in him, and through him to reconcile to himself all things, whether things on earth or things in heaven, by making peace through his blood, shed on the cross.

Silence

Meditation

> *Christ our Redeemer,*
> *you have crushed the serpent's head;*
> *you have freed us from our sin;*
> *rescue all your suffering world from the evil*
> *that attracts us still.*
> *Amen.*

> *God of compassion,*
> *deepen and increase our love for you*
> *so that we may leave behind the sins*
> *from which you have redeemed us,*
> *and serve you in perfect freedom.*
> *Amen.*

FRIDAY

> *No Condemnation now I dread,*
> *Jesus, and all in Him, is mine.*
> *Alive in Him, my Living Head,*
> *And clothed in Righteousness Divine,*
> *Bold I approach th'Eternal Throne,*
> *And claim the Crown, thro' CHRIST my own.*

Song: Job 19:23-27

"Oh, that my words were recorded,
that they were written on a scroll.

"That they were inscribed with an iron tool on lead,
or engraved in rock forever!

"I know that my Redeemer lives,
and that in the end he will stand
upon the earth.

"And after my skin has been
destroyed,
yet in my flesh I will see God;

"I myself will see him
with my own eyes—I,
and not another.
How my heart yearns within me!"

I know that my Redeemer lives

Hebrews 9:11-15

When Christ came as high priest of the good things that are already here, he went through the greater and more perfect tabernacle that is not made with human hands, that is to say, not a part of this creation. He did not enter by means of the blood of goats and calves; but he entered the Most Holy Place once for all by his own blood, having obtained eternal redemption. The blood of goats and bulls and the ashes of a heifer sprinkled on those who are ceremonially unclean sanctify them so that they are outwardly clean. How much more, then, will the blood of Christ, who through the eternal Spirit offered himself unblemished to God, cleanse our consciences from acts that lead to death, so that we may serve the living God!

For this reason Christ is the mediator of a new covenant, that those who are called may receive the promised eternal inheritance—now that he has died as a ransom to set them free from the sins committed under the first covenant.

Silence

Meditation

Merciful God,
your Son came to free us from sin,
overcoming death and rising in triumph:
may we, who are redeemed by his blood
be made ready to meet you face to face;
this we ask for Jesus' sake.
Amen.

SATURDAY

'Although the road be rough and steep,
I go to the desert to find my sheep.'
But none of the ransomed ever knew
How deep were the waters crossed,
Nor how dark was the night that the Lord passed through
Ere he found the sheep that was lost.

Psalm 130

1. Out of the depths have I called to you, O Lord;
Lord, hear my voice;
let your ears consider well the voice of my supplication.
2. If you, Lord, were to note what is done amiss,
O Lord, who could stand?
3. For there is forgiveness with you;
therefore you shall be feared.
4. I wait for the Lord; my soul waits for him;
in his word is my hope.
5. My soul waits for the Lord,
more than the night-watch for the morning,
more than the night-watch for the morning.

6. O Israel, wait for the Lord,
for with the Lord there is mercy;
7. With him there is plenteous redemption,
and he shall redeem Israel from all their sins.

For with the Lord there is mercy

D. M. Baillie
Why Atonement?

But God loves me perfectly knows me perfectly far better than I can
know or love myself. If I have been disloyal to Him, as I have in all
my misdeeds, I have been disloyal to the infinite Love which is the
heart of the universe, which is the source and end of my existence,
and the very meaning of the 'moral law' which I have broken. There
can be nothing more inexorable than such a love. If I have betrayed
it, that is the ultimate betrayal. That is what has to be wiped out, and
such an 'atonement' must be the most difficult, the most
supernatural, the costliest thing in the world.

But also – if we may follow the analogy farther – it is God that
bears the cost. Our reconciliation is infinitely costly to Him. Not in
the sense that it is difficult for Him to forgive us, as it would be
difficult for a Shylock, who has to be induced not to insist upon his
pound of flesh; not in the sense that He is inhibited from forgiving,
by some hard necessity outside His own nature, so that there has to
be an 'expiation' before God can act mercifully. It is His very nature
to love and to forgive. He could do no other, and He has to wait for
nothing but our response. Yet the forgiveness is not an easy amnesty,
such as a good-natured tyrant might give with a stroke of his pen. It
comes from the heart of a love that has borne our sins, and because
the love is infinite, the passion is infinite too. 'Who suffers more
than God?' asks Piers Plowman. There is an atonement, an expiation,
in the heart of God Himself, and out of this comes the forgiveness of
our sin.

Silence

Meditation

Fashion in me, Lord,
eyes within my eyes, so that with new eyes,
I may contemplate your divine sacrifice.
Create in me a pure heart,
so that, through the power of your Spirit,
I may inhale your salvation.

YEAR 2

SUNDAY

John Donne
Holy Sonnets XV

Wilt thou love God, as he thee! then digest,
My Soule, this wholsome meditation,
How God the Spirit, by Angels waited on
In heaven, doth make his Temple in thy brest.
The Father having begot a Sonne most blest;
And still begetting, (for he ne'r begonne)
Hath deign'd to chuse thee by adoption,
Coheire to 'his glory, 'and Sabbaths endlesse rest.
And as a robb'd man which by search doth finde
His stolne stuffe sold, must lose or buy'it againe:
The Sonne of glory came downe, and was slaine,
Us whom he'had made, and Satan stolne, to unbinde.
Twas much, that man was made like God before,
But, that God should be made like man, much more.

WEEKDAY READINGS

MONDAY: Exodus 13:11-16
TUESDAY: Isaiah 43:1-8
WEDNESDAY: Romans 3:21-31
THURSDAY: John 10:11-18
FRIDAY: Colossians 2:6-15

SATURDAY

Irenaeus
Againt the Heresies V.i.1

Thus the powerful Word and true human being, ransoming us by his own blood in a rational manner, gave himself as a ransom for those who have been led into captivity. The apostate one unjustly held sway over us though we were by nature the possession of Almighty God, we had been alienated from our proper nature, making us instead his own disciples. Therefore the almighty Word of God, who did not lack justice, acted justly even in the encounter with the apostate one, ransoming from him the things which were his own, not by force, in the way in which [the apostate one] secured his dominion over us at the beginning, by greedily snatching what was not his own. Rather, it was appropriate that God should obtain what he wished through persuasion, not by the use of force, so that the principles of justice might not be infringed, and, at the same time, that God's original creation might not perish. The Lord therefore ransomed us by his own blood and gave his life for our life, his flesh for our flesh; and he poured out the Spirit of the Father to bring about the union and fellowship of God and humanity, bringing God down to humanity through the Spirit while raising humanity to God through his incarnation, and in his coming surely and truly giving us incorruption through the fellowship which we have with him.

YEAR 3

SUNDAY

Peter Abelard
The Love of Christ in Redemption

Love is increased by the *faith* which we have concerning Christ because, on account of the belief that God in Christ has united our human nature to himself and by suffering in that same nature has demonstrated to us that Supreme love of which Christ himself speaks: "Greater love has no-one than this" (John 15:13). We are thus joined through his grace to him and our neighbour by an unbreakable bond of love ... Just as all have sinned, so they are justified without respect of person by this supreme grace which has been made known to us by God. And this is what [Paul] declares: "For all have sinned, and all need the grace of God" (Romans 3:23), that is, they need to glorify the Lord as a matter of obligation ... Now it seems to me that we have been justified by the blood of Christ and reconciled to God in this way: through this singular act of grace made known in us (in that his Son has taken our nature on himself, and persevered in this nature, and taught us by both his word and his example, even to the point of death) he has more fully bound us to himself by love. As a result, our hearts should be set on fire by such a gift of divine grace, and true love should not hold back from suffering anything for his sake ... Therefore, our redemption through the suffering of Christ is that deeper love within us which not only frees us from slavery to sin, but also secures for us the true liberty of the children of God, in order that we might do all things out of love rather than out of fear – love for him who has shown us such grace that no greater can be found.

WEEKDAY READINGS

MONDAY: Leviticus 25:47-54
TUESDAY: Isaiah 60:15-22
WEDNESDAY: John 10:11-18
THURSDAY: Galations 3:6-14
FRIDAY: 2 Corinthians 5:11-20

SATURDAY

Clement of Alexandria
Christ's Death as an Example of Love

Consider the mysteries of love, and you will then have a vision of the bosom of the Father, whom the only-begotten God alone has declared. God himself is love, and for the sake of this love he made himself known. And while the unutterable nature of God is Father, his sympathy with us is Mother. It was in his love that the Father became the nature which derives from woman, and the great proof of this is the Son whom he begot from himself, and the love that was the fruit produced from his love. For this he came down, for this he assumed human nature, for this he willingly endured the sufferings of humanity, that by being reduced to the measure of our weakness, he might raise us to the measure of his power. And just before he poured out his offering, when he gave himself as a ransom, he left us a new testament: "I give you my love" (John 13:34). What is the nature and extent of this love? For each of us he laid down his life, the life which was worth the whole universe, and he requires in return that we should do the same for each other.

A PRAYER OF PENITENCE

O Saviour of the world,
who by thy Cross and precious Blood
hast redeemed us,
Save us, and help us,
we humbly beseech thee, O Lord.

THE PRAYERS

Holy Father, Lord God of Truth,
as I cannot create myself,
no more can I redeem myself;
that power, that gift, is yours alone.
You who have made me can alone remake me.

Remake, redeem me, O my Father!
What else do I need?
What righteousness have I of myself?
How can I forgive myself?
How myself be the propitiation of my sins?
But what we cannot do ourselves,
you have done for us
through your Son our Saviour Jesus Christ.

Christ has taken our flesh upon him,
faced and felt our flesh and sorrows.
Christ has borne my sins in his body on the Tree.
Gift, all is gift; boasting is excluded,
but not gratitude, not joy, not praise.
For all my foolishness and sin,
you accept me through HIM;
you forgive, cleanse, recreate, and renew me in HIM.
Complete your mercy, O Father; to-day
and ever make me a new creature in Christ.
For the old things are passed away;
behold, all things are become new,
through Christ our Lord. Amen.

MEDITATIONS

SUNDAY: Greater love has no-one than this, to lay down one's life for one's friends. (John 15:13)

MONDAY: No man can redeem the life of another or give to God a sufficient ransom—the ransom for a life is costly, no payment is ever enough. (Psalm 49:7-8)

TUESDAY: ... for with the LORD is unfailing love and with him is full redemption. (Psalm 130:7)

WEDNESDAY: For even the Son of Man did not come to be served, but to serve, and to give his life as a ransom for many." (Mark 10:45)

THURSDAY: You were bought at a price; do not become slaves of people. (1 Corinthians 7:23)

FRIDAY: In Christ we have redemption through his blood, the forgiveness of sins, in accordance with the riches of God's grace ... (Ephesians 1:7)

SATURDAY: When you pass through the waters, I will be with you; and when you pass through the rivers, they will not sweep over you. When you walk through the fire, you will not be burned; the flames will not set you ablaze. (Isaiah 43:2)

John Donne
Good Friday, 1613. Riding Westward

Let man's soul be a sphere, and then, in this,
The intelligence that moves, devotion is,
And as the other Spheres, by being grown,
Subject to foreign motions, lose their own,
And being by others hurried every day,
Scarce in a year their natural form obey;
Pleasure or business, so, our souls admit
For their first mover, and are whirl'd by it.
Hence is't, that I am carried towards the west
This day, when my soul's form bends toward the east.
There I should see a sun, by rising set,
And by that setting endless day beget;
But that Christ on this cross, did rise and fall,

Sin had eternally benighted all.
Yet dare I almost be glad, I do not see
That spectacle of too much weight for me.
Who sees God's face, that is self life, must die;
What a death were it then to see God die?
It made his own lieutenant, Nature, shrink,
It made his footstool crack, and the sun wink.
Could I behold those hands which span the poles,
And turn all sphere at once, pierced with those holes?
Could I behold that endless height which is
Zenith to us, and our Antipodes,
Humbled below us? Or that blood which is
The seat of our souls, if not of his,
Made dirt of dust, or that flesh which was worn
By God, for his apparel, ragg'd and torn?
If on these things I durst not look, durst I
Upon his miserable mother cast mine eye,
Who was God's partner here, and furnished thus
Half of that sacrifice, which ransomed us?
Though these things, as I ride, be from my eye,
They are present yet to my memory,
For that looks towards them; and thou look'st towards me,
O Saviour, as thou hang'st upon the tree;
I turn my back to thee, but to receive
Corrections, till thy mercies bid thee leave.
O think me worth thine anger, punish me,
Burn off my rusts, and my deformity,
Restore thine image, so much, by thy grace,
That thou may'st know me, and I'll turn my face.

LENT V:

THE NARROW GATE

SUNDAY

My song is love unknown,
My Saviour's love to me,
love to the loveless shown,
that they might lovely be.
O who am I,
That for my sake
My Lord would take
Frail flesh, and die?

Song: Isaiah 42:1-4

"Here is my servant, whom I uphold,
my chosen one in whom I delight;
I will put my Spirit on him
and he will bring justice to the nations.

"He will not shout or cry out,
or raise his voice in the streets.

"A bruised reed he will not break,
and a smouldering wick
he will not snuff out.
In faithfulness he will bring forth justice;

"he will not falter or be discouraged
till he establishes justice on earth.
In his law the islands will put their hope."

Here is my servant, whom I uphold,
my chosen one is whom I delight

Jacques LeClerq
A Year with the Liturgy

Jesus is going to Jerusalem to fulfill his destiny. He knows it. From the beginning he has before his eyes all our sins which he will redeem. Now, little by little, day by day, their weight lies on him more heavily, for the moment approaches when he must pay.

The cross. And he alone; all the others are busy with silly dreams.

We too; there is our business and the stock exchange which is not going well and which is worrying us. Or else it is working out all right and our worries are no less. There are clients and there is the price of butter. All that is so much more important than the cross of Jesus.

Silence

Meditation

Holy God,
holy and strange,
holy and intimate,
have mercy on us.

I brooded over the abyss,
with my words I called forth creation:
but you have brooded on destruction,
and manufactured the means of chaos

O my people, what have I done to you?
How have I offended you?
Answer me?

MONDAY

He came from his blest throne,
Salvation to bestow;
But men made strange, and none
The longed-for Christ would know.
But O, my Friend,
My friend indeed,
Who at my need
His life did spend!

Song: Isaiah 53:1-3

Who has believed our message
and to whom has the arm of the LORD been revealed?

He grew up before him
like a tender shoot,
and like a root out of dry ground.
He had no beauty or majesty to attract us to him,
nothing in his appearance
that we should desire him.

He was despised and rejected by others,
a man of sorrows, and familiar with suffering.
Like one from whom people hide their faces
he was despised,
and we esteemed him not.

He was despised and we esteemed him not

John 5:16-27

So, because Jesus was doing these things on the Sabbath, the Jews
persecuted him. Jesus said to them, "My Father is always at his work
to this very day, and I, too, am working." For this reason the Jews
tried all the harder to kill him; not only was he breaking the Sabbath,
but he was even calling God his own Father, making himself equal
with God. Jesus gave them this answer: "I tell you the truth, the Son

can do nothing by himself; he can do only what he sees his Father doing, because whatever the Father does the Son also does. For the Father loves the Son and shows him all he does. Yes, to your amazement he will show him even greater things than these. For just as the Father raises the dead and gives them life, even so the Son gives life to whom he is pleased to give it. Moreover, the Father judges no-one, but has entrusted all judgment to the Son, that all may honour the Son just as they honour the Father. He who does not honour the Son does not honour the Father, who sent him. "I tell you the truth, whoever hears my word and believes him who sent me has eternal life and will not be condemned; he has crossed over from death to life. I tell you the truth, a time is coming and has now come when the dead will hear the voice of the Son of God and those who hear will live. For as the Father has life in himself, so he has granted the Son to have life in himself. And he has given him authority to judge because he is the Son of Man.

Silence

Meditation

> I breathed life into your bodies,
> and carried you tenderly in my arms:
> but you have armed yourselves for war,
> breathing out threats of violence.

> *O my people, what have I done to you?*
> *How have I offended you?*
> *Answer me?*

TUESDAY

> *Sometimes they strew his way,*
> *And his sweet praises sing;*
> *Resounding all the day*
> *Hosannas to their King.*

Then 'Crucify!'
Is all their breath,
And for his death
They thirst and cry.

Isaiah 53:4-9

Surely he took up our infirmities and carried our sorrows,
yet we considered him stricken by God,
smitten by him, and afflicted.

But he was pierced for our transgressions,
he was crushed for our iniquities;
the punishment that brought us peace was upon him,
and by his wounds we are healed.

We all, like sheep, have gone astray,
each of us has turned to his own way;
and the LORD has laid on him the iniquity of us all.

He was oppressed and afflicted, yet he did not open his mouth;
he was led like a lamb to the slaughter,
and as a sheep before her shearers is silent,
so he did not open his mouth.

By oppression and judgment he was taken away.
And who can speak of his descendants?
For he was cut off from the land of the living;
for the transgression of my people he was stricken.
He was assigned a grave with the wicked,
and with the rich in his death,
though he had done no violence,
nor was any deceit in his mouth.

Surely he has borne our infirmities and carried our sorrows

Matthew 23:29, 33-39

"Woe to you, teachers of the law and Pharisees, you hypocrites!
"You snakes! You brood of vipers! How will you escape being
condemned to hell? Therefore I am sending you prophets and wise

men and teachers. Some of them you will kill and crucify; others you will flog in your synagogues and pursue from town to town. And so upon you will come all the righteous blood that has been shed on earth, from the blood of righteous Abel to the blood of Zechariah son of Berekiah, whom you murdered between the temple and the altar. I tell you the truth, all this will come upon this generation. "O Jerusalem, Jerusalem, you who kill the prophets and stone those sent to you, how often I have longed to gather your children together, as a hen gathers her chicks under her wings, but you were not willing. Look, your house is left to you desolate. For I tell you, you will not see me again until you say, 'Blessed is he who comes in the name of the Lord.'"

Silence

Meditation

> I have laboured to deliver you,
> as a woman delights to give life:
> but you have delighted in bloodshed,
> and laboured to bereave the world.

> *O my people, what have I done to you?*
> *How have I offended you?*
> *Answer me?*

WEDNESDAY

> *Why, what hath my Lord done?*
> *What makes this rage and spite?*
> *He made the lame to run,*
> *He gave the blind their sight.*
> *Sweet injuries!*
> *Yet they at these*
> *Themselves displease,*
> *And 'gainst him rise.*

Song: Isaiah 49:1-6

Listen to me, you islands; hear this, you distant nations:
   Before I was born the LORD called me;
   from my birth he has made mention of my name.

He made my mouth like a sharpened sword,
   in the shadow of his hand he hid me;
   he made me into a polished arrow
   and concealed me in his quiver.

He said to me, "You are my servant, Israel,
   in whom I will display my splendour."

But I said, "I have laboured to no purpose;
   I have spent my strength in vain and for nothing.
Yet what is due me is in the LORD's hand,
   and my reward is with my God."

And now the LORD says—
he who formed me in the womb to be his servant to bring Jacob back
to him and gather Israel to himself, for I am honoured in the eyes of
the LORD and my God has been my strength—

he says: "It is too small a thing for you to be my servant to restore
   the tribes of Jacob and bring back those of Israel I have kept.
   I will also make you a light for the Gentiles,
   that you may bring my salvation to the ends of the earth."

He will bring salvation to the ends of the earth

Mark 11:27-33

They arrived again in Jerusalem, and while Jesus was walking in the
temple courts, the chief priests, the teachers of the law and the elders
came to him. "By what authority are you doing these things?" they
asked. "And who gave you authority to do this?" Jesus replied, "I
will ask you one question. Answer me, and I will tell you by what
authority I am doing these things. John's baptism—was it from
heaven, or of human origin? Tell me!" They discussed it among

themselves and said, "If we say, 'From heaven,' he will ask, 'Then why didn't you believe him?' But if we say, 'Of human origin' ... " (They feared the people, for everyone held that John really was a prophet.) So they answered Jesus, "We don't know." Jesus said, "Neither will I tell you by what authority I am doing these things."

Silence

Meditation

> I have torn the veil of my glory,
> transfiguring the earth:
> but you have disfigured my beauty,
> and turned away your face.

> *O my people, what have I done to you?*
> *How have I offended you?*
> *Answer me?*

THURSDAY

> *They rise, and needs will have*
> *My dear Lord made away;*
> *A murderer they save,*
> *The Prince of Life they slay.*
> *Yet cheerful he*
> *To suffering goes,*
> *That he his foes*
> *From thence might free.*

Song: Isaiah 50:4-11

The Sovereign LORD has given me an instructed tongue,
to know the word that sustains the weary.

He wakens me morning by morning,
wakens my ear to listen like one being taught.

The Sovereign LORD has opened my ears,
and I have not been rebellious;
I have not drawn back.

I offered my back to those who beat me,
my cheeks to those who pulled out my beard;
I did not hide my face from mocking and spitting.

Because the Sovereign LORD helps me,
I will not be disgraced.
Therefore have I set my face like flint,
and I know I will not be put to shame.

It is the Sovereign Lord who helps me

John 7:14-24

Not until halfway through the Feast of Tabernacles did Jesus go up
to the temple courts and begin to teach. The Jews were amazed and
asked, "How did this man get such learning without having studied?"
Jesus answered, "My teaching is not my own. It comes from him
who sent me. Anyone who chooses to do the will of God, will find
out whether my teaching comes from God or whether I speak on my
own. Those who speak on their own do so to gain honour for
themselves, but he who works for the honour of the one who sent
him is a man of truth; there is nothing false about him. Has not
Moses given you the law? Yet not one of you keeps the law. Why
are you trying to kill me?" "You are demon-possessed," the crowd
answered. "Who is trying to kill you?" Jesus said to them, "I did one
miracle, and you are all astonished. Yet, because Moses gave you
circumcision (though actually it did not come from Moses, but from
the patriarchs), you circumcise a child on the Sabbath. Now if a child
can be circumcised on the Sabbath so that the law of Moses may not
be broken, why are you angry with me for healing the whole man on

the Sabbath? Stop judging by mere appearances, and make a right judgment."

Silence

Meditation

> I abandoned my power like a garment,
> choosing your unprotected flesh:
> but you have robed yourselves in privilege
> and chosen to despise the abandoned.

> *O my people, what have I done to you?*
> *How have I offended you?*
> *Answer me?*

FRIDAY

> *In life, no house, no home*
> *My Lord on earth might have;*
> *In death, no friendly tomb*
> *But what a stranger gave.*
> *What may I say?*
> *Heaven was his home;*
> *But mine the tomb*
> *Wherein he lay.*

Song: Isaiah 53:10-12

Yet it was the LORD's will to crush him and cause him to suffer,
and though the LORD makes his life a guilt offering,
he will see his offspring and prolong his days,
and the will of the LORD will prosper in his hand.

After the suffering of his soul,
he will see the light of life and be satisfied;

by his knowledge my righteous servant will justify many,
and he will bear their iniquities.

Therefore I will give him a portion among the great,
and he will divide the spoils with the strong,
because he poured out his life unto death,
and was numbered with the transgressors.
For he bore the sin of many,
and made intercession for the transgressors.

For he has carried our sins

John 11:45-57

Therefore many of the Jews who had come to visit Mary, and had seen what Jesus did, put their faith in him. But some of them went to the Pharisees and told them what Jesus had done. Then the chief priests and the Pharisees called a meeting of the Sanhedrin. "What are we accomplishing?" they asked. "Here is this man performing many miraculous signs. If we let him go on like this, everyone will believe in him, and then the Romans will come and take away both our place and our nation." Then one of them, named Caiaphas, who was high priest that year, spoke up, "You know nothing at all! You do not realise that it is better for you that one man die for the people than that the whole nation perish." He did not say this on his own, but as high priest that year he prophesied that Jesus would die for the Jewish nation, and not only for that nation but also for the scattered children of God, to bring them together and make them one. So from that day on they plotted to take his life. Therefore Jesus no longer moved about publicly among the Jews. Instead he withdrew to a region near the desert, to a village called Ephraim, where he stayed with his disciples. When it was almost time for the Jewish Passover, many went up from the country to Jerusalem for their ceremonial cleansing before the Passover. They kept looking for Jesus, and as they stood in the temple area they asked one another, "What do you think? Isn't he coming to the Feast at all?" But the chief priests and Pharisees had given orders that if anyone found out where Jesus was, he should report it so that they might arrest him.

Silence

Meditation

> I have followed you with the power of my spirit,
> to seek truth and heal the oppressed:
> but you have followed a lie,
> and returned to your own comfort.

> *My people, what have I done to you?*
> *How have I offended you?*
> *Answer me?*

SATURDAY

> *Here might I stay and sing.*
> *No story so divine,*
> *Never was love, dear King,*
> *Never was grief like thine!*
> *This is my Friend,*
> *In whose sweet praise*
> *I all my days*
> *Could gladly spend.*

Song: Isaiah 52:13-15

> See, my servant will act wisely;
> he will be raised and lifted up and highly exalted.

> Just as there were many who were appalled at him—
> his appearance was so disfigured beyond that of any human being
> and his form marred beyond human likeness—

> so will he sprinkle many nations,
> and kings will shut their mouths because of him.
> For what they were not told, they will see,
> and what they have not heard, they will understand.

My servant will be raised and lifted up

Does this mean that Jesus never thought that he might lose his life? This is a different question. Would he have been so naive as not to have had any presentiment of what finally happened to him? A Christological interest must be allowed for everywhere in the Gospels but historical scepticism can become uncritical. No supernatural knowledge was required to recognize the *danger of a violent end,* only a sober view of reality. His radical message raised doubts about the pious self reliance of; individuals and of society and about the traditional religious system as a whole and created opposition from the very beginning. Consequently Jesus was bound to expect serious conflicts and violent reactions on the part of the religious and perhaps also the political authorities, particularly at the centre of power. Accusations of infringing the Sabbath, contempt for the law, blasphemy, had to be taken seriously The move of the heretical "prophet" from the province to the capital, confusing and upsetting the credulous people, in any case meant a challenge to the ruling circles. Even as late as John's Gospel we can read: "Search and you will find that no prophet comes from Galilee." The entry into Jerusalem, interpreted symbolically and given a legendary touch with the reference to the peaceable mount used on that occasion, perhaps did not have the triumphal character subsequently attributed to it. But anyone who was suspected of working miracles by demonic power, of being a false prophet or a blasphemer, had to reckon with the possibility of the death penalty. To incur the death penalty it was sufficient deliberately to break the Sabbath after a single warning in the presence of witnesses (this comes out clearly in Mark where there is a warning after the first infringement of the Sabbath and plans to kill him immediately after the second).

Silence

Meditation

> *Saviour of the world, though easier paths beckoned*
> *and friends pleaded for you to stay with them,*

you turned your face resolutely towards Jerusalem,
determined to go all the way to Calvary.
Take us with you now Lord, and show us how
through your sufferings evil is conquered and the world is saved.

YEAR 2

SUNDAY

Cyril of Jerusalem
The Narrow Gate

We have to eat bitter herbs. These stand for the bitter sufferings we must undergo, and we should greatly value the endurance they demand. It would indeed be quite absurd if those desiring to serve God imagined they could achieve great virtue, and glory in the supreme reward, without having first contended for it and given proof of the most steadfast courage. The approach to this goal is rugged and steep, and it is inaccessible to most people. It becomes easy only for those whose desire to arrive is so strong that they are dismayed by nothing and are ready to face hardship and toil. Christ's own words urge us to do this. Enter by the narrow gate, for the gate is wide and the road easy that leads to damnation, and those who enter by it are many. The gate is narrow and the road hard that leads to life, and those who find it are few."

WEEKDAY READINGS

MONDAY: Mark 6:1 6
TUESDAY: Luke 13:22-35
WEDNESDAY: Mark 12:13-17
THURSDAY: John 7:25-44
FRIDAY: Luke 21:37-22:6

SATURDAY

Karl Barth
The Suffering Servant

In all four Gospels the story of Jesus' life is described as one which, strictly speaking, is from the very first a story of self-declaring and increasingly self-actualising death ... It is as the High-priest of the new covenant who is

Himself the victim that the author of Hebrews understands Him. His obedience is an obedience of suffering (Heb. 5:8) ... For this reason God has highly exalted Him and given Him the name *Lord Jesus Christ* (Phil. 2:11). The Lamb that was slain is worthy to receive power and riches and wisdom and strength and honour and glory and praise (Rev. 5:12). This is why the continuation of His life is unthinkable. He is the grain of wheat that must fall into the ground and die in order to bring forth much fruit (Jn. 12:24). Beyond the death of the man Jesus of Nazareth lies the place from which there falls on Him the light that makes Him the revelation of God the Father. He is instituted as the Son of God (Rom. 14). God the Father acts on Him and through Him by raising Him from the dead ... He who sees Jesus sees this Father (Jn. 14: 7f.). The Jesus "who was delivered for our offences and was raised again for our justification" (Rom. 4:25) is the One to whom this applies. And since faith is faith in Jesus it is itself faith in the will and work of this Father. Being baptised into Christ is being baptised into His death, "being planted together in the likeness of his death" (Rom. 6:3, cf. Phil. 3:10), being crucified and dead with Him in His crucifixion. Already in the Synoptics, then, following Jesus is identical with self-denial and taking up one's cross (Mk. 8:34) and one can save one's life only by losing it for Jesus' sake (Mk. 8:35). Beyond this strait gate lies absolutely everything the New Testament can say about *new life* (Rom. 6:4) in the baptised and believing. And the One who deals thus with men in Christ, who leads them along this way to this goal, is called by believers "Father" and "Father of the Lord Jesus Christ." He is the Father of the Son who was dead and is alive again, who was lost and is found (Lk. 15:29).

YEAR 3

SUNDAY

Leonardo Boff
Way of the Cross, Way of Justice

There are countless prophets of sacred causes that espouse the rights of the poor. Some are known; the vast majority are anonymous. They all share the impotence and helplessness of Jesus on the cross. They are asked to accept the most difficult assignment: to hope against hope, to love what does not seem to be present to them, and to believe in what they cannot see. They are asked to endure the worst plight a human being can experience: to die feeling abandoned by the God for whom they lived and sacrificed their lives.

Still, they do not abandon God. They surrender themselves to God in complete confidence. In total inner emptiness they cling to the nameless mystery that is infinitely beyond them. For this mysterious God holds the secret meaning of all their failed quests, of all the absurdities of history. To die like that is to share Jesus' death on the cross. It is to share his redeeming mystery, which will go on through history until the world reaches its end and fulfillment in the liberation of the last sinner who opens to God's mercifulness.

WEEKDAY READINGS

MONDAY: Matthew 12:1-8
TUESDAY: Luke 11:37-53
WEDNESDAY: Mark 12:28-34
THURSDAY: John 7:45-53
FRIDAY: John 10:22-42

SATURDAY

Herbert Butterfield
We Did It

One of the most solemn facts in all history – one of the most significant for anybody who cares to ponder over it – is the fact that Jesus Christ was not merely murdered by hooligans in a country road; He was condemned by everything that was most respectable in that day, everything that pretended to be most righteous – the religious leaders of the time, the authority of the Roman government, and even the democracy itself which shouted to save Barabbas rather than Christ ... In a profound sense we may say that the Crucifixion, however else we may interpret it, accuses human nature, accuses all of us in the very things that we think are our righteousness. If we followed the twentieth-century forms of moralizing, which have run so quickly to the national sort, we might imagine that the Jews of the time of Christ were particularly bad sinners, worse than the rest of human nature. Our attitude to the Crucifixion must be that of self-identification with the rest of human nature – we must say '*We* did it'; and the inability to adopt something of the same attitude in the case of twentieth-century events has caused our phenomenal failure to deal with the problem of evil in our time. So the Crucifixion challenges the prestige and power of the Pharisaical notion of upright living, challenges the old Roman respectabilities, and supersedes the pre-Christian notion of a righteous man. In the light of it the claim that '*our* conscience is clear' is the ugliest pretence of all. Indeed, if we call to mind that high-and-mighty kind of righteousness which congeals into moral rectitude and seems to close up the windows of the soul and sometimes makes good men so intolerable – in all the world's literature there is no place where it is attacked more persistently and more profoundly than in the Bible.

A PRAYER OF PENITENCE

Almighty and most merciful Father,
we have strayed from your ways like lost sheep
we have followed too much
the devices and desires of our own hearts,
we have offended against your holy laws.
We have left undone what we ought to have done,
and we have done what we ought not to have done.
Yet, good Lord, have mercy on us;
restore those who are penitent,
according to your promises declared
in Jesus Christ our Lord.
Grant, most merciful Father, for his sake,
that we may live godly, righteous and sober lives
to the glory of your holy name. Amen.

THE PRAYERS

Brother Jesus,
help us to follow you
deep into the waters of baptism
to break the chains of past wrongs;
to become fit to face the coming age:
Jesus, our brother, help us to follow.

Help us to follow you into the desert,
with you to fast, denying false luxury values,

refusing the tempting ways of self-indulgence,
the ways of success at all costs,
the ways of coercive persuasion.
Jesus, our brother, help us to follow.

Help us to follow you into the place of quiet retreat,
to intercede for the confused, the despairing, the anxiety driven,
to prepare ourselves for costly service.
Jesus, our brother, help us to follow you.

Help us to follow you on the road to Jerusalem,
to set our faces firmly against friendly suggestions
to live a safe, expedient life;
to embrace boldly the way of self-offering.
Jesus, our brother, help us to follow.

Help us to follow you even to the cross,
to see our hope in self-spending love;
to die to all within us not born of your love.
Jesus, our brother, help us to follow.

MEDITATIONS

SUNDAY: Let us strive to enter by the narrow gate. Just as trees, if they have not stood before the winter's storms cannot bear fruit, so it is with us: this present age is a storm and it is only through many trials and temptations that we can obtain an inheritance in the kingdom of heaven. (Theodora, desert mother)

MONDAY: For I desire mercy, not sacrifice, and acknowledgment of God rather than burnt offerings. (Hosea 6:6)

TUESDAY: "Is that you, you troubler of Israel?" (1 Kings 18:17)

WEDNESDAY: For the Lord of all will not stand in awe of anyone, or show deference to greatness; because he himself made both small and great, and he takes thought for all alike. (Wisdom 6:7, *NRSV*)

THURSDAY: "But a time is coming, and has come, when you will be scattered, each to his own home. You will leave me all alone. Yet I am not alone, for my Father is with me." (John 16:31)

FRIDAY: So they did away with God in the name of peace and quietness. (Dorothy L. Sayers)

SATURDAY: "Enter through the narrow gate. For wide is the gate and broad is the road that leads to destruction, and many enter through it." (Matthew 7:13)

Michel Quoist
It's too late

Lord, it's too late for you to be quiet, you have spoken too much;
    you have fought too much;
You were not sensible, you know, you exaggerated, it was
    bound to happen.
You called the better people a brood of vipers;
You told them that their hearts were black sepulchres with fine
    exteriors;
You kissed the decaying lepers;
You spoke fearlessly with unacceptable strangers;
You ate with notorious sinners, and you said that street-walkers
    would be the first in paradise;
You got on well with the poor, the tramps, the crippled;
You belittled the religious regulations;
Your interpretation of the Law reduced it to one little commandment:
    to love.
Now they are avenging themselves.
They have taken steps against you; they have approached the
authorities and action will follow.

HOLY WEEK

It is Holy Week. A time of great contrasts; of joy and grief, of feasting and fasting, of song and dirge. A place of paradox, where love and sorrow meet, and where there is life in death.

We know the story, and the ending of it; those who knew Jesus during his last days did not. He had told them, repeatedly, what was to come. And yet, surely it could not end like this? They had seen, they had heard, and they had believed — Jesus of Nazareth, the Messiah. Surely not?

The events of Holy Week reveal the darker side of human nature. Jesus, betrayed and deserted by his friends and the crowd, who had cried 'hosanna', now baying for his blood, goes alone to the Cross.

Holy Week is difficult. It is a working week. We are full of our own concerns and the tasks of the day; it is hard to turn our hearts and minds towards Jesus, and to walk with him to the Cross.

But are we not islands of faith in a world which does not seem to care? And the cry from Lamentations echoes through our busy lives:

'Is it nothing to you, all you who pass by?'

INDIFFERENCE

When Jesus came to Golgotha they hanged him on a tree,
They drave great nails though hands and feet, and made a Calvary;
They crowned him with a crown of thorns, red were his wounds and deep,
For those were crude and cruel days, the human flesh was cheap.

When Jesus came to Birmingham, they simply passed him by,
They never hurt a hair of him, they only let him die;
For men had grown more tender, and they would not give him pain,
They only passed down the street, and left him in the rain.

Still Jesus cried, 'Forgive them, for they know not what they do',
And still it rained the winter rain that drenched him through and through;
The crowds went home and left the streets without a soul to see,
And Jesus crouched against a wall and cried for Calvary.

G. A. Studdert Kennedy[1]

---

[1] *The Lion Christian Poetry Collection*, compiled by Mary Batchelor, Oxford, 1995, p. 126.

PALM SUNDAY

Ride on! Ride on in majesty!
Hark! All the tribes Hosanna cry!
O Saviour meek, pursue thy road
With palms and scattered garments strowed.

Zechariah 9:9-12

Rejoice greatly, O Daughter of Zion!
Shout, Daughter of Jerusalem!
See, your king comes to you, righteous and having salvation,
gentle and riding on a donkey, on a colt, the foal of a donkey.

I will take away the chariots from Ephraim
and the war-horses from Jerusalem,
and the battle bow will be broken.
He will proclaim peace to the nations.
His rule will extend from sea to sea
and from the River to the ends of the earth.

As for you, because of the blood of my covenant with you,
I will free your prisoners from the waterless pit.

Return to your fortress, O prisoners of hope;
even now I announce that I will restore twice as much to you.

Blessed is he who comes in the name of the Lord!

St. Andrew of Crete
Blessed is he who comes in the name of the Lord,
the King of Israel

Come, come, let us go up together to the Mount of Olives. Together
let us meet Christ, who is returning today from Bethany and going of
his own accord to that holy and blessed passion to complete the
mystery of our salvation.

... it is ourselves that we must spread under Christ's feet, not coats or lifeless branches or shoots of trees, matter which wastes away and delights the eye only for a few brief hours. But we have clothed ourselves with Christ's grace, or with the whole Christ – 'for as many of you as were baptized into Christ have put on Christ' – so let us spread ourselves like coats under his feet.

As those who were formerly scarlet from sin but became white as wool through the purification of saving baptism, let us offer not palm branches but the prizes of victory to the conqueror of death.

Today let us too give voice with the children to that sacred chant, as we wave the spiritual branches of our soul: 'Blessed is he who comes in the name of the Lord, the King of Israel.'

Silence

Meditation

Jesus King of the universe, ride on in humble majesty.
Ride on, through conflict and debate,
ride on through sweaty prayer and betrayal of friends.
Lord, this Palm Sunday forgive my evasion of truth,
my carelessness of your honour; my weakness which leaves
me sleeping while in others you suffer and are anguished;
my cowardice that does not risk the consequences of
publicly acknowledging you as Lord.

Ride on to the empty tomb and your rising in triumph,
Ride on to raise up your Church, a new body for your service;
Ride on, King Jesus, to renew the whole earth in your image,
in compassion come to help us.

MONDAY

A stranger once did bless the earth
who never caused a heart to mourn,
whose very voice gave sorrow mirth;
and how did earth his worth return?
it spurned him from his lowliest lot:
the meanest station owned him not.

Silence

O my people, O my Church,
What have I done to you,
or in what have I offended you?
Testify against me.
I led you from the land of Egypt,
and delivered you by the waters of baptism,
but you have prepared a cross for your Saviour.

Holy God, holy and mighty,
holy and immortal, have mercy on us.

I led you through the desert forty years,
and fed you with manna.
I brought you through tribulation and penitence,
and gave you my body, the bread of heaven,
but you have prepared a cross for your Saviour.

Holy God, holy and mighty,
holy and immortal, have mercy on us.

Mark 11:11-19
The next day as they were leaving Bethany, Jesus was hungry.
Seeing in the distance a fig-tree in leaf, he went to find out if it had
any fruit. When he reached it, he found nothing but leaves, because it

was not the season for figs. Then he said to the tree, "May no-one ever eat fruit from you again." And his disciples heard him say it.

On reaching Jerusalem, Jesus entered the temple area and began driving out those who were buying and selling there. He overturned the tables of the money changers and the benches of those selling doves, and would not allow anyone to carry merchandise through the temple courts. And as he taught them, he said, "Is it not written: "'My house will be called a house of prayer for all nations' ? But you have made it 'a den of robbers.'"

The chief priests and the teachers of the law heard this and began looking for a way to kill him, for they feared him, because the whole crowd was amazed at his teaching. When evening came, they went out of the city.

Silence

Meditation

> *O God, the source of our passion,*
> *who took upon you our unprotected flesh,*
> *kindle in us*
> *your anger and desire;*
> *that in suffering we may not be consumed,*
> *but hold fast to you*
> *through Jesus Christ,*
> *Amen.*

TUESDAY

> *An outcast thrown in sorrow's way,*
> *a fugitive that knew no sin,*
> *yet in lone places forced to stray;*
> *men would not take the stranger in.*
> *Yet peace, though much himself he mourned,*
> *was all to others he returned.*

What more could I have done for you
that I have not done?
I planted you, my chosen and fairest vineyard,
I made you the branches of my vine;
but when I was thirsty, you gave me vinegar to drink,
and pierced with a spear the side of your Saviour.

Holy God, holy and mighty,
holy and immortal, have mercy on us.

I went before you in a pillar of cloud,
and you have led me to the judgement hall of Pilate.
I scourged your enemies and brought you
to a land of freedom,
but you have scourged, mocked, and beaten me.
I gave you the water of salvation from the rock,
but you have given me gall and left me to thirst.

Holy God, holy and mighty,
holy and immortal, have mercy on us.

Mark 11:20-33

In the morning, as they went along, they saw the fig-tree withered from the roots. Peter remembered and said to Jesus, "Rabbi, look! The fig-tree you cursed has withered!" "Have faith in God," Jesus answered. "I tell you the truth, if you say to this mountain, 'Go, throw yourself into the sea,' and do not doubt in your heart but believe that what you say will happen, it will be done for you. Therefore I tell you, whatever you ask for in prayer, believe that you have received it, and it will be yours. And when you stand praying, if you hold anything against anyone, forgive them, so that your Father in heaven may forgive you your sins."

They arrived again in Jerusalem, and while Jesus was walking in the temple courts, the chief priests, the teachers of the law and the elders came to him. "By what authority are you doing these things?" they asked. "And who gave you authority to do this?" Jesus replied,

"I will ask you one question. Answer me, and I will tell you by what authority I am doing these things. John's baptism—was it from heaven, or of human origin? Tell me!" They discussed it among themselves and said, "If we say, 'From heaven,' he will ask, 'Then why didn't you believe him?' But if we say, 'Of human origin' ... " (They feared the people, for everyone held that John really was a prophet.) So they answered Jesus, "We don't know." Jesus said, "Neither will I tell you by what authority I am doing these things."

Silence

Meditation

Who are you Jesus, that you speak with such authority?
Not like scholars and teachers, simply repeating each other,
you speak the Word of God to us and all who will listen. The power
of God living within you shines through everything you say.
Lord Jesus, help us to hear what you are saying,
to understand what you are teaching,
to know God's power in our lives
and in the words we speak of you.

WEDNESDAY

His presence was a peace to all,
he bade the sorrowful rejoice.
Pain turned to pleasure at his call,
health lived and issued from his voice;
he healed the sick, and sent abroad
the dumb rejoicing in the Lord.

Silence

I grafted you into the tree of my chosen Israel,
and you turned on them with persecution
and mass murder.

I made you joint heirs with them of my covenants,
but you made them scapegoats of your own guilt.

Holy God, holy and mighty,
holy and immortal, have mercy on us.

I came to you as the least of your brothers and sisters;
I was hungry and you gave me no food,
I was thirsty and you gave me no drink,
I was a stranger and you did not welcome me,
sick and in prison and you did not visit me.

Holy God, holy and mighty,
holy and immortal, have mercy on us.

Mark 14:1-10

Now the Passover and the Feast of Unleavened Bread were only two
days away, and the chief priests and the teachers of the law were
looking for some sly way to arrest Jesus and kill him. "But not
during the Feast," they said, "or the people may riot."

While he was in Bethany, reclining at the table in the home of
Simon the Leper, a woman came with an alabaster jar of very
expensive perfume, made of pure nard. She broke the jar and poured
the perfume on his head. Some of those present were saying
indignantly to one another, "Why this waste of perfume? It could
have been sold for more than a year's wages and the money given to
the poor." And they rebuked her harshly. "Leave her alone," said
Jesus. "Why are you bothering her? She has done a beautiful thing to
me. The poor you will always have with you, and you can help them
any time you want. But you will not always have me. She did what
she could. She poured perfume on my body beforehand to prepare
for my burial. I tell you the truth, wherever the gospel is preached
throughout the world, what she has done will also be told, in memory
of her."

Then Judas Iscariot, one of the Twelve, went to the chief priests to
betray Jesus to them. They were delighted to hear this and promised
to give him money. So he watched for an opportunity to hand
him over.

Meditation

God our pain-bearer,
Give us the courage of this unknown woman,
to speak the gospel with authority from the place of no authority;
to break open all our resources from the place of no resource;
to break open and pour out even the pain we want to hold on to;
so that we can dare to name the truth about our world,
and truthfully stand with the one who made himself nothing
for our sake, Jesus Christ, our Lord. Amen.

THURSDAY

Here in Christ, we gather, love of Christ our calling;
Christ, our love, is with us, gladness be his greeting;
Let us revere and love him, God eternal:
Loving him, let us love Christ in all his brothers.

God is love, and where true love is, God himself is there.

Silence

My peace I gave, which the world cannot give,
and washed your feet as a sign of my love,
but you draw the sword to strike in my name,
and seek high places in my kingdom.
I offer you my body and blood,
but you scatter and deny and abandon me.

Holy God, holy and mighty,
holy and immortal, have mercy on us.

I sent the spirit of truth to guide you,
and you close your hearts to the Counsellor,

I pray that all may be as one in the Father and me,
    but you continue to quarrel and divide.
I call you to go and bring forth fruit,
    but you cast lots for my clothing.

*Holy God, holy and mighty,
holy and immortal, have mercy on us.*

Mark 14:17-31

When evening came, Jesus arrived with the Twelve. While they were reclining at the table eating, he said, "I tell you the truth, one of you will betray me—one who is eating with me." They were saddened, and one by one they said to him, "Surely not I?" "It is one of the Twelve," he replied, "one who dips bread into the bowl with me. The Son of Man will go just as it is written about him. But woe to that man who betrays the Son of Man! It would be better for him if he had not been born."

While they were eating, Jesus took bread, gave thanks and broke it, and gave it to his disciples, saying, "Take it; this is my body." Then he took the cup, gave thanks and offered it to them, and they all drank from it. "This is my blood of the covenant, which is poured out for many," he said to them. "I tell you the truth, I will not drink again of the fruit of the vine until that day when I drink it anew in the kingdom of God."

When they had sung a hymn, they went out to the Mount of Olives. "You will all fall away," Jesus told them, "for it is written: "'I will strike the shepherd, and the sheep will be scattered.' But after I have risen, I will go ahead of you into Galilee." Peter declared, "Even if all fall away, I will not." "I tell you the truth," Jesus answered, "today—yes, tonight—before the cock crows twice you yourself will disown me three times." But Peter insisted emphatically, "Even if I have to die with you, I will never disown you." And all the others said the same.

Silence

Meditation

> *Infinite, intimate God;*
> *this night you kneel before your friends*
> *and wash our feet.*
> *Bound together in your love,*
> *trembling, we drink your cup,*
> *and watch.*

THE WATCH

Silence

Mark 14:32-42

They went to a place called Gethsemane, and Jesus said to his disciples, "Sit here while I pray." He took Peter, James and John along with him, and he began to be deeply distressed and troubled. "My soul is overwhelmed with sorrow to the point of death," he said to them. "Stay here and keep watch." Going a little farther, he fell to the ground and prayed that if possible the hour might pass from him. "Abba, Father," he said, "everything is possible for you. Take this cup from me. Yet not what I will, but what you will." Then he returned to his disciples and found them sleeping. "Simon," he said to Peter, "are you asleep? Could you not keep watch for one hour? Watch and pray so that you will not fall into temptation. The spirit is willing, but the body is weak." Once more he went away and prayed the same thing. When he came back, he again found them sleeping, because their eyes were heavy. They did not know what to say to him. Returning the third time, he said to them, "Are you still sleeping and resting? Enough! The hour has come. Look, the Son of Man is betrayed into the hands of sinners. Rise! Let us go! Here comes my betrayer!"

Psalm 22:1-2 (NIV)

Why are you so far from saving me,
so far from the words of my groaning?
O my God, I cry out by day, but you do not answer,
by night, and am not silent.

Silence

Mark 14:43-52

Just as he was speaking, Judas, one of the Twelve, appeared. With him was a crowd armed with swords and clubs, sent from the chief priests, the teachers of the law, and the elders. Now the betrayer had arranged a signal with them: "The one I kiss is the man; arrest him and lead him away under guard." Going at once to Jesus, Judas said, "Rabbi!" and kissed him. The men seized Jesus and arrested him. Then one of those standing near drew his sword and struck the servant of the high priest, cutting off his ear. "Am I leading a rebellion," said Jesus, "that you have come out with swords and clubs to capture me? Every day I was with you, teaching in the temple courts, and you did not arrest me. But the Scriptures must be fulfilled." Then everyone deserted him and fled. A young man, wearing nothing but a linen garment, was following Jesus. When they seized him, he fled naked, leaving his garment behind.

Psalm 22:19-21 (NIV)

O LORD, be not far off; O my Strength,
come quickly to help me.
Deliver my life from the sword,
my precious life from the power of the dogs.
Rescue me from the mouth of the lions.

Silence

Mark 14:53-65

They took Jesus to the high priest, and all the chief priests, elders and teachers of the law came together. Peter followed him at a distance, right into the courtyard of the high priest. There he sat with the guards and warmed himself at the fire. The chief priests and the whole Sanhedrin were looking for evidence against Jesus so that they could put him to death, but they did not find any. Many testified falsely against him, but their statements did not agree. Then some stood up and gave this false testimony against him: "We heard him say, 'I will destroy this temple made with human hands and in three days will build another, not made with hands.'" Yet even then their testimony did not agree. Then the high priest stood up before them and asked Jesus, "Are you not going to answer? What is this testimony that these men are bringing against you?" But Jesus remained silent and gave no answer. Again the high priest asked him, "Are you the Christ, the Son of the Blessed One?" "I am," said Jesus. "And you will see the Son of Man sitting at the right hand of the Mighty One and coming on the clouds of heaven." The high priest tore his clothes. "Why do we need any more witnesses?" he asked. "You have heard the blasphemy. What do you think?" They all condemned him as worthy of death. Then some began to spit at him; they blindfolded him, struck him with their fists, and said, "Prophesy!" And the guards took him and beat him.

Psalm 31:11-13 (NIV)

Because of all my enemies,
I am the utter contempt of my neighbours;
I am a dread to my friends--
those who see me on the street flee from me.
I am forgotten by them as though I were dead;
I have become like broken pottery.
For I hear the slander of many;
there is terror on every side;
they conspire against me and plot to take my life.

Silence

Mark 14:66-72
While Peter was below in the courtyard, one of the servant girls of the high priest came by. When she saw Peter warming himself, she looked closely at him. "You also were with that Nazarene, Jesus," she said. But he denied it. "I don't know or understand what you're talking about," he said, and went out into the entrance. When the servant girl saw him there, she said again to those standing around,

"This fellow is one of them." Again he denied it. After a little while, those standing near said to Peter, "Surely you are one of them, for you are a Galilean." He began to call down curses on himself, and he swore to them, "I don't know this man you're talking about." Immediately the cock crowed the second time. Then Peter remembered the word Jesus had spoken to him: "Before the cock crows twice you will disown me three times." And he broke down and wept.

Psalm 55:12-14, 16 (NIV)

If an enemy were insulting me,
I could endure it;
if a foe were rising against me,
I could hide.
But it is you, one like myself,
my companion, my close friend,
with whom I once enjoyed sweet fellowship
as we walked with the throng at the house of God.

But I call to God, and the LORD saves me.

Silence

GOOD FRIDAY

Silence

Is it nothing to you, all you who pass by?
Look and see if there is any sorrow like my sorrow
which was brought upon me,
which the Lord inflicted on the day of his fierce anger.

Holy God, holy and mighty,
holy and immortal one, have mercy upon us.

Mark 15:1-15

Very early in the morning, the chief priests, with the elders, the
teachers of the law and the whole Sanhedrin, reached a decision.
They bound Jesus, led him away and handed him over to Pilate. "Are
you the king of the Jews?" asked Pilate. "Yes, it is as you say," Jesus
replied. The chief priests accused him of many things. So again
Pilate asked him, "Aren't you going to answer? See how many
things they are accusing you of." But Jesus still made no reply, and
Pilate was amazed. Now it was the custom at the Feast to release a
prisoner whom the people requested. A man called Barabbas was in
prison with the insurrectionists who had committed murder in the
uprising. The crowd came up and asked Pilate to do for them what he
usually did. "Do you want me to release to you the king of the
Jews?" asked Pilate, knowing it was out of envy that the chief priests
had handed Jesus over to him. But the chief priests stirred up the
crowd to have Pilate release Barabbas instead. "What shall I do,
then, with the one you call the king of the Jews?" Pilate asked them.
"Crucify him!" they shouted. "Why? What crime has he
committed?" asked Pilate. But they shouted all the louder, "Crucify
him!" Wanting to satisfy the crowd, Pilate released Barabbas to
them. He had Jesus flogged, and handed him over to be crucified.

Since you are my rock and my fortress,
for the sake of your name lead and guide me.
Free me from the trap that is set for me,
for you are my refuge.

Silence

Mark 15:16-20

The soldiers led Jesus away into the palace (that is, the Praetorium) and called together the whole company of soldiers. They put a purple robe on him, then twisted together a crown of thorns and set it on him. And they began to call out to him, "Hail, king of the Jews!" Again and again they struck him on the head with a staff and spat on him. Falling on their knees, they paid homage to him. And when they had mocked him, they took off the purple robe and put his own clothes on him. Then they led him out to crucify him.

Isaiah 50:6-7

I offered my back to those who beat me,
my cheeks to those who pulled out my beard;
I did not hide my face from mocking and spitting.
Because the Sovereign LORD helps me,
I will not be disgraced.
Therefore have I set my face like flint,
and I know I will not be put to shame.

Silence

Mark 15:21-32

A certain man from Cyrene, Simon, the father of Alexander and Rufus, was passing by on his way in from the country, and they forced him to carry the cross. They brought Jesus to the place called Golgotha (which means The Place of the Skull). Then they offered him wine mixed with myrrh, but he did not take it. And they crucified him. Dividing up his clothes, they cast lots to see what each would get. It was the third hour when they crucified him. The written notice of the charge against him read: THE KING OF THE JEWS. They crucified two robbers with him, one on his right and one on his left. Those who passed by hurled insults at him, shaking their heads and saying, "So! You who are going to destroy the temple and build it in three days, come down from the cross and save yourself!" In the same way the chief priests and the teachers of the law mocked him among themselves. "He saved others," they said, "but he can't save himself! Let this Christ, this King of Israel, come down now from the cross, that we may see and believe." Those crucified with him also heaped insults on him.

Psalm 22:6-8, 16-18 (NIV)

But I am a worm and not a human being,
scorned by everyone and despised by the people.
All who see me mock me;
they hurl insults, shaking their heads:
"He trusts in the LORD; let the LORD rescue him.
Let him deliver him, since he delights in him."

Dogs have surrounded me;
a band of evil people have encircled me,
they have pierced my hands and my feet.
I can count all my bones; people stare and gloat over me.
They divide my garments among them
and cast lots for my clothing.

My God, my God, why have you forsaken me?

Silence

Mark 15:33-41

At the sixth hour darkness came over the whole land until the ninth hour. And at the ninth hour Jesus cried out in a loud voice, *"Eloi, Eloi, lama sabachthani?"*—which means, "My God, my God, why have you forsaken me?" When some of those standing near heard this, they said, "Listen, he's calling Elijah." Someone ran, filled a sponge with wine vinegar, put it on a stick, and offered it to Jesus to drink. "Now leave him alone. Let's see if Elijah comes to take him down," he said. With a loud cry, Jesus breathed his last. The curtain of the temple was torn in two from top to bottom. And when the centurion, who stood there in front of Jesus, heard his cry and saw how he died, he said, "Surely this man was the Son of God!"

Some women were watching from a distance. Among them were Mary Magdalene, Mary the mother of James the younger and of Joses, and Salome. In Galilee these women had followed him and cared for his needs. Many other women who had come up with him to Jerusalem were also there.

Psalm 31:5 (NIV)

Into your hands I commit my spirit;
redeem me, O LORD, the God of truth.

Silence

Mark 15:42-47
It was Preparation Day (that is, the day before the Sabbath). So as evening approached, Joseph of Arimathea, a prominent member of the Council, who was himself waiting for the kingdom of God, went boldly to Pilate and asked for Jesus' body. Pilate was surprised to hear that he was already dead. Summoning the centurion, he asked him if Jesus had already died. When he learned from the centurion that it was so, he gave the body to Joseph. So Joseph bought some linen cloth, took down the body, wrapped it in the linen, and placed it in a tomb cut out of rock. Then he rolled a stone against the entrance of the tomb. Mary Magdalene and Mary the mother of Joses saw where he was laid.

Psalm 88:1-10 (NIV)

1. O LORD, the God who saves me,
day and night I cry out before you.

2. May my prayer come before you;
   turn your ear to my cry.

3. For my soul is full of trouble
   and my life draws near the grave.
4. I am counted among those who go down to the pit;
   I am like one without strength.
5. I am set apart with the dead,
   like the slain who lie in the grave,
whom you remember no more, who are cut off from your care.

6. You have put me in the lowest pit,
   in the darkest depths.
7. Your wrath lies heavily upon me;
   you have overwhelmed me with all your waves.
8. You have taken from me my closest friends
   and have made me repulsive to them.
   I am confined and cannot escape;
9. my eyes are dim with grief.

I call to you, O LORD, every day; I spread out my hands to you.
10. Do you show your wonders to the dead?
    Do those who are dead rise up and praise you?

Silence

Joseph of Arimathea

Give me that Stranger
Who since his youth
Had wandered as a stranger

Give me that Stranger
Killed in hatred by his own people
As a Stranger.

Give me that Stranger
Upon whom I look with wonder,
Seeing Him a Guest of Death.

Give me that Stranger
Whom envious men
Estranged from this world.

Give me that Stranger
That I may bury Him in a tomb,
Who being a stranger has no place
Whereon to lay his head.

And sleeps my Lord in silence yet,
within the darkness laid away;
where none remember nor forget,
where breaks no more the sunlit day?
And sleeps my Lord in silence yet,
where cold his lifeless body lay?

And does the sting of death remain
to work unchanged its bitter will?
Were cross and passion all in vain,
no battle won on Calvary's hill?
And does the sting of death remain,
and gapes the grave in triumph still?

SATURDAY

THE VIGIL

Silence

What keeps us from sleeping
is that
they have threatened us with resurrection.

Accompany us, then,
on this vigil
and you will know
how marvellous it is
to live
threatened with resurrection

Something strange is happening – there is a great silence on earth today, a great silence and stillness. The whole earth keeps silence because the king is asleep. The earth trembles and is still because God has fallen asleep in the flesh and he has raised up all who have slept ever since the world began. God has died in the flesh and hell trembles with fear . . .

Silence

Isaiah 54:5-14

For your Maker is your husband—the LORD Almighty is his name—the Holy One of Israel is your Redeemer; he is called the God of all the earth. The LORD will call you back as if you were a wife deserted and distressed in spirit—a wife who married young, only to be rejected," says your God. "For a brief moment I abandoned you, but with deep compassion I will bring you back. In a surge of anger I hid my face from you for a moment, but with everlasting kindness I will have compassion on you," says the LORD your Redeemer. "To me this is like the days of Noah, when I swore that the waters of Noah would never again cover the earth. So now I have sworn not to be angry with you, never to rebuke you again. Though the mountains be shaken and the hills be removed, yet my unfailing love for you will not be shaken nor my covenant of peace be removed," says the LORD, who has compassion on you. "O afflicted city, lashed by storms and not comforted, I will build you with stones of turquoise, your foundations with sapphires. I will make your battlements of rubies, your gates of sparkling jewels, and all your walls of precious stones. All your children will be taught by the LORD, and great will be your children's peace. In righteousness you will be established: Tyranny will be far from you; you will have nothing to fear. Terror will be far removed; it will not come near you.

Psalm 30:1-4 (NIV)

1. I will exalt you, O LORD,
for you lifted me out of the depths
and did not let my enemies gloat over me.
2. O LORD my God,
I called to you for help and you healed me.
3. O LORD, you brought me up from the grave ;
you spared me from going down into the pit.

4. Sing to the LORD, you saints of his;
praise his holy name.

Silence

Job 14:1-14

"Mortals, born of woman, are of few days and full of trouble. They spring up like flowers and wither away; like fleeting shadows, they do not endure. Do you fix your eye on such as these? Will you bring them before you for judgment? Who can bring what is pure from the impure? No-one! The days of mortals are determined; you have decreed the number of their months and have set limits they cannot exceed. So look away from us and let us alone, till we have put in our time like a hired workers. At least there is hope for a tree: If it is cut down, it will sprout again, and its new shoots will not fail. Its roots may grow old in the ground and its stump die in the soil, yet at the scent of water it will bud and put forth shoots like a plant. But human beings die and are laid low; they breathe their last and are no more. As water disappears from the sea or a river bed becomes parched and dry, so they lie down and do not rise; till the heavens are no more, they will not awake or be roused from their sleep. If only you would hide me in the grave and conceal me till your anger has passed! If only you would set me a time and then remember me! If human beings die, will they live again? All the days of my hard service I will wait for my renewal to come."

Psalm 18:4-6 (NIV)

4. The cords of death entangled me;
the torrents of destruction overwhelmed me.
5. The cords of the grave coiled around me;
the snares of death confronted me.
6. In my distress I called to the LORD;
I cried to my God for help.
From his temple he heard my voice;
my cry came before him, into his ears.

Silence

Ezekiel 37:1, 11-14

The hand of the LORD was upon me, and he brought me out by the Spirit of the LORD and set me in the middle of a valley; it was full of bones.

Then he said to me: "Son of man, these bones are the whole house of Israel. They say, 'Our bones are dried up and our hope is gone; we are cut off.' Therefore prophesy and say to them: 'This is what the Sovereign LORD says: O my people, I am going to open your graves and bring you up from them; I will bring you back to the land of Israel. Then you, my people, will know that I am the LORD, when I open your graves and bring you up from them. I will put my Spirit in you and you will live, and I will settle you in your own land. Then you will know that I the LORD have spoken, and I have done it, declares the LORD.'"

Psalm 143:7-10 (NIV)

7. Answer me quickly, O LORD; my spirit fails.
Do not hide your face from me
or I will be like those who go down to the pit.

8. Let the morning bring me word of your unfailing love,
    for I have put my trust in you.
    Show me the way I should go,
    for to you I lift up my soul.
    9. Rescue me from my enemies, O LORD,
        for I hide myself in you.
    10. Teach me to do your will, for you are my God;
    may your good Spirit lead me on level ground.

Silence

John 2:18-22

Then the Jews demanded of him, "What miraculous sign can you show us to prove your authority to do all this?" Jesus answered them, "Destroy this temple, and I will raise it again in three days." The Jews replied, "It has taken forty-six years to build this temple, and you are going to raise it in three days?" But the temple he had spoken of was his body. After he was raised from the dead, his disciples recalled what he had said. Then they believed the Scripture and the words that Jesus had spoken.

Psalm 30:8-12 (NIV)

8. To you, O LORD, I called;
    to the Lord I cried for mercy:
9. "What gain is there in my destruction,
    in my going down into the pit?
    Will the dust praise you?
    Will it proclaim your faithfulness?
10. Hear, O LORD, and be merciful to me;
    O LORD, be my help."

11. You turned my wailing into dancing;
you removed my sackcloth and clothed me with joy,
12. that my heart may sing to you and not be silent.
O LORD my God, I will give you thanks forever.

Silence

From an ancient homily

Rise, let us leave this place. The enemy led you out of the earthly paradise. I will not restore you to that paradise, but I will enthrone you in heaven. I forbade you the tree that was only a symbol of life, but see, I who am life itself am now one with you. I appointed the cherubim to guard you as slaves are guarded, but now I make them worship you as God. The throne formed by cherubim awaits you, its bearers swift and eager. The bridal chamber is adorned, the banquet is ready, the eternal dwelling places are prepared, the treasure houses of all good things lie open. The kingdom of heaven has been prepared for you from all eternity.

YEAR 2

PALM SUNDAY

Giles Fletcher
Palm Sunday: Good Friday

It was but now their sounding clamours sung,
'Blessed is he that comes from the Most High',
And all the mountains with 'Hosanna' rung,
And now, 'Away with him, away,' they cry,
And nothing can be heard but 'Crucify'!
    It was but now the crown itself they save,
    And golden name of King unto him gave,
And now no King but only Caesar they will have.

It was but now they gathered blooming May,
And of his arms disrobed the branching tree,
To strew with boughs and blossoms all thy way,
And now, the branchless trunk a cross for thee,
And May, dismayed, thy coronet must be:
    It was but now they were so kind to throw
    Their own best garments where thy feet should go,
And now, thyself they strip, and bleeding wounds they show.

See where the author of all life is dying.
O fearful day! He dead, what hope of living?
See where the hopes of all our lives are buying.
O cheerful day! They bought, what fear of grieving?
Love love for hate, and death for life is giving:
   Lo, how his arms are stretched abroad to grace thee,
   And, as they open stand, call to embrace thee.
Why stay'st thou then my open soul; O fly, fly thither haste thee.

WEEKDAY READINGS

MONDAY: Matthew 21:12-17
TUESDAY: Matthew 22:34-46
WEDNESDAY: Matthew 26:1-16
THURSDAY: John 13
THE WATCH: John 18:1-11; 18:12-18; 18:19-24; 18:25-27.
FRIDAY: John 18:28-40; 19:1-3; 19:1-27; 19:28-37; 19:38-42
SATURDAY: THE VIGIL as for Year 1

YEAR 3

PALM SUNDAY

Dietrich Bonhoeffer
Sorrow And Joy

Sorrow and Joy:
striking suddenly on our startled senses
seem, at the first approach, all but impossible
of just distinction one from the other:
even as frost and heat at the first keen contact
burn us alike.

Joy and Sorrow,
hurled from the height of heaven in meteor fashion,
flash in an arc of shining menace o'er us.
Those they touch are left
stricken amid fragments
of their colourless, usual lives.

Imperturbable, mighty,
ruinous and compelling,

Sorrow and Joy,
– summoned or all unsought for –
processionally enter.

Those they encounter
they transfigure, investing them
with strange gravity
and a spirit of worship.

Joy is rich in fears:
Sorrow has its sweetness.
Undistinguishable from each other
they approach us from eternity,
equally potent in their power and terror.

From every quarter
mortals come hurrying:
part envious, part awe-struck,
swarming and peering
into the portent;
where the mystery sent from above us
is transmuting into the inevitable
order of earthly human drama.

What then is Joy? What then is Sorrow?
Time alone can decide between them,
when the immediate poignant happening
lengthens out to continuous wearisome suffering,
when laboured creeping moments of daylight
slowly uncover the fulness of our disaster
Sorrow's unmistakable features.
Then do most of our kind
sated, if only by the monotony
of unrelieved unhappiness,
turn away from the drama, disillusioned,
uncompassionate.

O ye mothers, and loved ones – then, ah, then
comes your hour, the hour of true devotion.
Then your hour comes, ye friends and brothers!
Loyal hearts can change the face of Sorrow,
softly encircle it with love's most gentle
unearthly radiance.

MONDAY: Luke 19:41-48
TUESDAY: Luke 20:20-26
WEDNESDAY: John 12:1-11
THURSDAY: Luke 22:14-38
THE WATCH: Luke 22:39-48; 22:47-53; 22:54-62; 22:63-65
FRIDAY: Luke 22:66-23:12; 23:13-25; 23:26-43; 23:44-49; 23:50-56.
SATURDAY: THE VIGIL as for Year 1

AN ALTERNATIVE COURSE OF READINGS FOR HOLY WEEK

Some users may wish to follow the events of Holy Week in a semi-continuous narrative in one of the gospels.

	Matthew	Mark	Luke	John
Sun p.m.	21:1-11	11:1-11	19:28-40	12:1-19
Mon a.m.	21:12-17	11:12-19	19:41-48	12:20-26
Mon p.m.	21:18-21	11:20-25	20:9-18	12:27-36
Tues a.m.	21:23-27	12:13-17	20:41-47	12:37-50
Tues p.m.	23:23-33	12:28-34	21:1-19	13
Wed a.m.	24:1-14	13:14-37	21:20-38	14
Wed p.m.	26:1-13	14:1-11	22:1-6	15
Thurs a.m.	26:17-19	14:12-16	22:7-13	16
Thurs p.m.	26:20-35	14:17-31	22:14-38	17
The Watch	26:36-75	14:32-72	22:39-65	18:1-27
Fri a.m.	27:1-44	15:1-32	22:66-23:43	18:28-19:27
Fri p.m.	27:45-66	15:33-47	23:44-56	19:28-42

PRAYER OF PENITENCE

Saviour of the world,
to the mystery of undeserved suffering,
you bring the deeper mystery of unmerited love.
Forgive us for not knowing what we have done;
open our eyes to see what you are doing now,
as, through wood and nails,
you disempower our depravity
and transform us by your grace.

Amen.

THE PRAYERS

Jesu, by your wounded feet,
Direct our paths aright:

Jesu, by your nailed hands,
Move ours to deeds of love:

Jesu, by your pierced side,
Cleanse our desires:

Jesu, by your crown of thorns,
Annihilate our pride:

Jesu, by your silence,
Shame our complaints:

Jesu, by your parched lips,
Curb our cruel speech:

Jesu, by your closing eyes,
Look on our sin no more:

Jesu, by your broken heart,
Knit ours to you.

By this sweet and saving Sign,
Lord, draw us to your peace.

A Time Between Times

Lord, it is a time between times:
a time of chaos and uncertainty
a time of fear and frustration
a time of solitude and suffering;
our own sense of powerlessness confines and constricts us
leaving our spirits scarred, our wills unwilling,
our bodies broken;
defeated to death we ask your mercy.

Lord, it is a time between times:
a time when dreams die
and the gaunt ground grows no grass;
a time when power proves profligate

and our connection with one another severed;
a time when darkness dominates
and hope is only a halting halo of light.

Lord, it is a time between times:
a time when the breaking seems fatal
and the mending seems remote;
when blood stains several soils
and the blunt bullets of the terrorist and liberator alike
seem the only reasoned response to noon's midnight;
a time when even our prayers for mercy
mumble in the silent shadow of Calvary

MEDITATIONS

SUNDAY: No palm, no palm, no thorn, no throne. (William Penn)

MONDAY: Now as Jesus was going up to Jerusalem, he took the twelve disciples aside and said to them, "We are going up to Jerusalem, and the Son of Man will be betrayed to the chief priests and the teachers of the law. They will condemn him to death and will turn him over to the Gentiles to be mocked and flogged and crucified. On the third day he will be raised to life!" (Matthew 20:17-19)

The one and only thing that seems to have roused the 'meek and mild' Son of God to a display of outright violence was precisely the assumption that 'business is business'. (Dorothy L. Sayers)

TUESDAY: "Can you drink the cup I drink or be baptised with the baptism I am baptised with?" (Mark 10:39)

Men never do evil so completely and cheerfully as when they do it from religious conviction. (Blaise Pascal)

WEDNESDAY: Jesus said "I tell you the truth, wherever the gospel is preached throughout the world, what she has done will also be told, in memory of her." (Mark 14:9)

Our Lord does not care so much for the importance of our works as for the love with which they are done. (Teresa of Avila)

THURSDAY: Jesus said to them, "I tell you the truth, unless you eat the flesh of the Son of Man and drink his blood, you have no life in you. Those who eat my flesh and drink my blood have eternal life, and I will raise them up at the last day." (John 6:53-54)

The last supper was not a political event. It was a meal of redemption prepared by the compassionate God. (Choan-Seng Song)

THE WATCH: "Couldn't you keep watch with me for one hour?" (Matthew 26:40)

Waiting can be the most intense and poignant of all human experiences – the experience which, above all others, strips us of our needs, our values, and ourselves. (W. H. Vanstone)

FRIDAY: Jesus was crucified not in a cathedral between two candles, but on a cross between two thieves. (George Mcleod)

A cross is not just a piece of wood, it is everything that makes life difficult (Leonardo Boff)

We all wish to be God with God. But, God knows, there are few enough of us who want to live as men and women with his humanity or to bear his cross, and be crucified with him in order to pay for the sins of the world. (Hadewijch of Brabant)

SATURDAY:

> And fire from fire our candles take the light,
> As we take fire from the eternal flame,
> And flame from flame we walk down the dark aisle,
> Each flame a glory gold against the night,
> That trembles at the whisper of the name
> That burns through all the empty halls of hell.
> (Marion Pitman)

THE WAY OF THE CROSS

PRELUDE

Mark 8:34
Then he called the crowd to him along with his disciples and said: "Those who would come after me must deny themselves and take up their cross and follow me."

1. JESUS IS CONDEMNED TO DEATH

Matthew 27:20-6

But the chief priests and the elders persuaded the crowd to ask for Barabbas and to have Jesus executed.

"Which of the two do you want me to release to you?" asked the governor.

"Barabbas," they answered.

"What shall I do, then, with Jesus who is called Christ?" Pilate asked.

They all answered, "Crucify him!"

"Why? What crime has he committed?" asked Pilate.

But they shouted all the louder, "Crucify him!"

When Pilate saw that he was getting nowhere, but that instead an uproar was starting, he took water and washed his hands in front of the crowd. "I am innocent of this man's blood," he said. "It is your responsibility!"

All the people answered, "Let his blood be on us and on our children!"

Then he released Barabbas to them. But he had Jesus flogged, and handed him over to be crucified.

Reflection: 1 Peter 2:21-23

To this you were called, because Christ suffered for you, leaving you an example, that you should follow in his steps. "He committed no sin, and no deceit was found in his mouth." When they hurled their insults at him, he did not retaliate; when he suffered, he made no threats. Instead, he entrusted himself to him who judges justly.

Lord, I know that if I try to live a little like you,
I shall be condemned.
And yet, Lord I know you are right. Help me to fight, help me to speak,
help me to live your Gospel, to the end, to the folly of the Cross.

Silence

2. JESUS RECEIVES THE CROSS

Mark 15:16-20

The soldiers led Jesus away into the palace (that is, the Praetorium) and called together the whole company of soldiers. They put a purple robe on him, then twisted together a crown of thorns and set it on him. And they began to call out to him, "Hail, king of the Jews!" Again and again they struck him on the head with a staff and spat on him. Falling on their knees, they paid homage to him. And when they had mocked him, they took off the purple robe and put his own clothes on him. Then they led him out to crucify him.

Reflection: 1 Peter 2:24

He himself bore our sins in his body on the tree, so that we might die to sins and live for righteousness; by his wounds you have been healed.

Silence

> *Lord, I would rather fight the Cross; to bear it is hard.*
> *But since you want this long way of the Cross for me,*
> *at the dawning of each day, help me to set forth.*

3. CAN YOU DRINK MY CUP?

Mark 10:38-40

Jesus said. "Can you drink the cup I drink or be baptised with the baptism I am baptised with?" "We can," James and John answered. Jesus said to them, "You will drink the cup I drink and be baptised with the baptism I am baptised with, but to sit at my right or left is not for me to grant. These places belong to those for whom they have been prepared."

Reflection: Acts 12:1-3

It was about this time that King Herod arrested some who belonged to the church, intending to persecute them. He had James, the brother of John, put to death with the sword. When he saw that this pleased the Jews, he proceeded to seize Peter also. This happened during the Feast of Unleavened Bread.

Silence

> *Lord, help me not only to follow after you but to keep steadily on.*
> *Keep me from all sudden weaknesses that leave me stupefied and empty,*
> *far from the place where you are shaping the world.*

4. THE MOTHER OF JESUS

Luke 2:33-35

The child's father and mother marvelled at what was said about him. Then Simeon blessed them and said to Mary, his mother: "This child is destined to cause the falling and rising of many in Israel, and to be a sign that will be spoken against, so that the thoughts of many hearts will be revealed. And a sword will pierce your own soul too."

Reflection

How can I bear it?
I see you, my son,
staggering, weighed down
by the cruel burden of the cross
and the jeering of the crowd.

I want to hide my eyes.
But I step from the crowd,
and reach out my hand
to offer my love, my strength, my pain.
God knows how I can bear it.

(Jan Sutch Pickard)

Silence

O Lord, may I never avert my eyes.
May I never close my heart,
that in welcoming the sufferings of the world, with Mary, your Mother,
I may suffer and redeem.

5. SIMON OF CYRENE IS FORCED TO CARRY THE CROSS

Mark 15:21

A certain man from Cyrene, Simon, the father of Alexander and Rufus, was passing by on his way in from the country, and they forced him to carry the cross.

Reflection: Philippians 3:10

I want to know Christ and the power of his resurrection and the fellowship of sharing in his sufferings.

Silence

Lord, I need others, but I avoid the hands outstretched to help me.
And yet it is together that we shall save the world.
Lord, even if they are requisitioned, grant that I may see,
that I may accept, all the Simons on my road.

6. AND WERE YOU THERE?

Matthew 25:31-40

"When the Son of Man comes in his glory, and all the angels with him, he will sit on his throne in heavenly glory. All the nations will be gathered before him, and he will separate the people one from another as a shepherd separates the sheep from the goats. He will put the sheep on his right and the goats on his left. Then the King will say to those on his right, 'Come, you who are blessed by my Father; take your inheritance, the kingdom prepared for you since the creation of the world. For I was hungry and you gave me something to eat, I was thirsty and you gave me something to drink, I was a stranger and you invited me in, I needed clothes and you clothed me, I was sick and you looked after me, I was in prison and you came to visit me.' Then the righteous will answer him, 'Lord, when did we see you hungry and feed you, or thirsty and give you something to drink? When did we see you a stranger and invite you in, or needing clothes and clothe you? When did we see you sick or in prison and go to visit you?' The King will reply, 'I tell you the truth, whatever you did for one of the least of these brothers and sisters of mine, you did for me.'"

Reflection: 2 Corinthians 4:8-11

We are hard pressed on every side, but not crushed; perplexed, but not in despair; persecuted, but not abandoned; struck down, but not destroyed. We always carry around in our body the death of Jesus, so that the life of Jesus may also be revealed in our body. For we who are alive are always being given over to death for Jesus' sake, so that his life may be revealed in our mortal body.

Silence

Lord, forgive my body, eager for pleasures;
it does not bring your presence to others.
Forgive my clouded eyes: in them others cannot see your light.
Forgive my encumbered heart: in it others do not see your light.
Nevertheless, Lord, come to me; my door is open.

7. COME TO ME

Matthew 11:28-30

"Come to me, all you who are weary and burdened, and I will give you rest. Take my yoke upon you and learn from me, for I am gentle and humble in heart, and you will find rest for your souls. For my yoke is easy and my burden is light."

Reflection: Isaiah 53:3-5

He was despised and rejected by others, a man of sorrows, and familiar with suffering. Like one from whom people hide their faces he was despised, and

we esteemed him not. Surely he took up our infirmities and carried our
sorrows, yet we considered him stricken by God, smitten by him, and
afflicted. But he was pierced for our transgressions, he was crushed for our
iniquities; the punishment that brought us peace was upon him, and by his
wounds we are healed.

Silence

> *O Lord, give us to bear your easy yoke,*
> *ever mindful of the burden you have borne for us.*

8. THE WOMEN OF JERUSALEM

Luke 23:27-31
A large number of people followed him, including women who mourned and
wailed for him. Jesus turned and said to them, "Daughters of Jerusalem, do
not weep for me; weep for yourselves and for your children. For the time
will come when you will say, 'Blessed are the barren women, the wombs
that never bore and the breasts that never nursed!' Then 'they will say to the
mountains, "Fall on us!" and to the hills, "Cover us!"'"

Reflection: **Isaiah 53:6**
We all, like sheep, have gone astray, each of us has turned to our own way;
and the LORD has laid on him the iniquity of us all.

Silence

> *Lord, you have seen them, you have heard them.*
> *But you said: 'Weep first for your sins.'*
> *I manage very well, Lord to pity your sufferings*
> *and the sufferings of the world.*
> *But to weep for my own sins, that's another matter.*
> *Lord, teach me that I am a sinner.*

9. THE HOUR HAS COME

John 12:23-24
Jesus replied, "The hour has come for the Son of Man to be glorified. I tell
you the truth, unless a kernel of wheat falls to the ground and dies, it remains
only a single seed. But if it dies, it produces many seeds."

Reflection: **Psalm 69:1-4**

Save me, O God, for the waters have come up to my neck. I sink in the miry depths, where there is no foothold. I have come into the deep waters; the floods engulf me. I am worn out calling for help; my throat is parched. My eyes fail, looking for my God. Those who hate me without reason outnumber the hairs of my head; many are my enemies without cause, those who seek to destroy me. I am forced to restore what I did not steal.

Silence

> *How demanding you are! I give and you want more.*
> *But if you want all, Lord, take all. Strip me, yourself, of my last garment.*
> *For well I know that we must die to deserve life,*
> *as the seed must die to turn into the golden grain.*

10. JESUS IS CRUCIFIED

Mark 15:22-24

They brought Jesus to the place called Golgotha (which means The Place of the Skull). Then they offered him wine mixed with myrrh, but he did not take it. And they crucified him. Dividing up his clothes, they cast lots to see what each would get.

Reflection: **Colossians 2:13-15**

When you were dead in your sins and in the uncircumcision of your sinful nature, God made you alive with Christ. He forgave us all our sins, having cancelled the written code, with its regulations, that was against us and that stood opposed to us; he took it away, nailing it to the cross. And having disarmed the powers and authorities, he made a public spectacle of them, triumphing over them by the cross.

Silence

> *Lord, I must gather my body, my heart, my spirit,*
> *and stretch myself at full length on the Cross of the present moment.*
> *I haven't the right to choose the wood of my passion.*
> *The Cross is ready, to my measure. You present it to me each day,*
> *each minute and I must lie on it. It isn't easy.*
> *And, yet, Lord, I can meet you nowhere else. It's where you await me.*
> *It's there that together we shall save our brothers and sisters.*

11. FATHER, FORGIVE

Luke 23:33-34
When they came to the place called the Skull, there they crucified him, along with the criminals--one on his right, the other on his left. Jesus said, "Father, forgive them, for they do not know what they are doing."

Reflection: **Galations 2:20**
I have been crucified with Christ and I no longer live, but Christ lives in me. The life I live in the body, 1 live by faith in the Son of God, who loved me and gave himself for me.

Silence

> *O Lord Jesus Christ, touch me with those hands*
> *which the sins of men and sins of mine pierced with the nails;*
> *and forgive my ignorance; for, Lord, I knew not,*
> *I know not, what I did in sinning against you.*
> *Touch me to forgive and to bless,*
> *O Lord, for your endless mercies' sake.*

12. THE DEATH OF JESUS

Luke 23:44-46
It was now about the sixth hour, and darkness came over the whole land until the ninth hour, for the sun stopped shining. And the curtain of the temple was torn in two. Jesus called out with a loud voice, "Father, into your hands I commit my spirit." When he had said this, he breathed his last.

Reflection: **Philippians 2:6-8**
Christ Jesus who, being in very nature God, did not consider equality with God something to be grasped, but made himself nothing, taking the very nature of a servant, being made in human likeness. And being found in appearance as a human being, he humbled himself and became obedient to death—even death on a cross!

Silence

> *Mankind is there, waiting unknowingly for the cry of its Saviour.*
> *Your brothers and sisters are there; they need you.*
> *Your Father bends over you, already holding out his arms.*
> *Lord save us.*
> *Christ has just died for us.*
> *Lord, help me to die for you.*
> *Help me to die for them.*

13. JESUS IS TAKEN DOWN FROM THE CROSS

Luke 23:50-53

Now there was a man named Joseph, a member of the Council, a good and upright man, who had not consented to their decision and action. He came from the Judean town of Arimathea and he was waiting for the kingdom of God. Going to Pilate, he asked for Jesus' body. Then he took it down, and wrapped it in linen cloth.

Reflection: **Psalm 88:6-7**

I am set apart with the dead, like the slain who lie in the grave, whom you remember no more, who are cut off from your care. You have put me in the lowest pit, in the darkest depths.

Silence

Lord, it is not over.
'You are in agony to the end of time,' I know.
Men tread the Way of the Cross in relays.
It would be a lie to weep before your lifeless image,
if I did not follow you, living, on the road that men and women travel.

14. THE BURIAL OF JESUS

Luke 23:53-56

Then Joseph of Arimathea placed the body of Jesus in a tomb cut in the rock, one in which no-one had yet been laid. It was Preparation Day, and the Sabbath was about to begin. The women who had come with Jesus from Galilee followed Joseph and saw the tomb and how his body was laid in it. Then they went home and prepared spices and perfumes. But they rested on the Sabbath in obedience to the commandment.

Reflection: **Psalm 16:9-10**

Therefore my heart is glad and my tongue rejoices; my body also will rest secure, because you will not abandon me to the grave, nor will you let your Holy One see decay.

Silence

Lord, it is not over.
There is not a fraction of my little suffering that you have not already
lived and transformed into infinite redemption.
When the road is hard and monotonous, when it leads to the grave,
I know that beyond the grave you are waiting for me in your glory.
Lord, help be to travel along my road faithfully.
Help me above all to recognize you and to help you in all
my pilgrim brothers and sisters. Amen.

THE SEVEN WORDS FROM THE CROSS

PRELUDE

Zechariah 12:10

"And I will pour out on the house of David and the inhabitants of Jerusalem a spirit of grace and supplication. They will look on me, the one they have pierced, and they will mourn for him as one mourns for an only child, and grieve bitterly for him as one grieves for a firstborn son."

THE FIRST WORD

"Father, forgive them,
for they do not know what they are doing."

Reflection: Isaiah 53:11-12

After the suffering of his soul, he will see the light of life and be satisfied; by his knowledge my righteous servant will justify many, and he will bear their iniquities. Therefore I will give him a portion among the great, and he will divide the spoils with the strong, because he poured out his life unto death, and was numbered with the transgressors. For he bore the sin of many, and made intercession for the transgressors.

Silence

Grant us, O Lord, the glory of praying with our Master, the Crucified,
by praying for our enemies,
by forgiving them that wrong or spitefully use us:
that we may better deserve the gift of your glorious pardon;
through Jesus Christ our Lord. Amen

THE SECOND WORD

"I tell you the truth, today you will be with me in paradise."

Reflection: Roman 8:31-end

What, then, shall we say in response to this? If God is for us, who can be against us? He who did not spare his own Son, but gave him up for us all—how will he not also, along with him, graciously give us all things? Who will bring any charge against those whom God has chosen? It is God who justifies. Who is he that condemns? Christ Jesus, who died—more than that, who was raised to life—is at the right hand of God and is also interceding for us. Who shall separate us from the love of Christ? Shall trouble or hardship or persecution or famine or nakedness or danger or sword? As it is written: "For your sake we face death all day long; we are considered as sheep to be slaughtered." No, in all these things we are more than conquerors through him who loved us. For I am convinced that neither death nor life, neither angels nor demons, neither the present nor the future, nor any powers, neither height nor depth, nor anything else in all creation, will be able to separate us from the love of God that is in Christ Jesus our Lord.

Silence

> *'If thou be Christ, then save us now';*
> *Blame not the pain-racked thief who cried:*
> *He saves us all, this Lamb of God,*
> *Who for our sins was crucified.*

THE THIRD WORD

When Jesus saw his mother there, and the disciple whom he loved standing nearby, he said to his mother, "Dear woman, here is your son," and to the disciple, "Here is your mother." From that time on, this disciple took her into his home.

Reflection: 2 Corinthians 5:16-19

So from now on we regard no one from a worldly point of view. Though we once regarded Christ in this way, we do so no longer. Therefore, if anyone is in Christ, there is a new creation; the old has gone, the new has come! All this is from God, who reconciled us to himself through Christ and gave us the ministry of reconciliation: that God was reconciling the world to himself in Christ, not counting people's sins against them. And he has committed to us the message of reconciliation.

Silence

O come and stand beneath the cross,
Come, and be at the Saviour's side,
With sword-pierced Mary and with John,
Jesus, our Love, is crucified.

THE FOURTH WORD

Jesus cried out in a loud voice,
"Eloi, Eloi, lama sabachthani?"—
which means,
"My God, my God, why have you forsaken me?"

Reflection: Hebrews 5:7-9
During the days of Jesus' life on earth, he offered up prayers and petitions
with loud cries and tears to the one who could save him from death, and he
was heard because of his reverent submission. Although he was a son, he
learned obedience from what he suffered and, once made perfect, he became
the source of eternal salvation for all who obey him

Silence

O Lord Jesus Christ, fill me with that faith of yours
wherewith in the last agony you did cry to the Father, My God, my God:
That no suffering, no sin, no shadow of doubt
may darken my trust in God,
not separate me from your Father and mine, now or ever.

THE FIFTH WORD

Jesus said, "I am thirsty."

Reflection: Psalm 42:1-3
As the deer pants for streams of water, so my soul pants for you, O God. My
soul thirsts for God, for the living God. When can I go and meet with God?
My tears have been my food day and night, while men say to me all day
long, "Where is your God?"

Silence

Pierced by the spear, from thence there flow
Water and blood from out his side:
Baptise me in that cleansing stream,
Jesus, my Lord, the crucified.

THE SIXTH WORD

Jesus said, "It is finished."
With that, he bowed his head and gave up his spirit.

Reflection: **Psalm 40:1-3**

I waited patiently for the LORD; he turned to me and heard my cry. He lifted me out of the slimy pit, out of the mud and mire; he set my feet on a rock and gave me a firm place to stand. He put a new song in my mouth, a hymn of praise to our God. Many will see and fear and put their trust in the LORD.

Silence

> *'All is accomplished' – hear his word*
> *Who on that wondrous cross has died:*
> *The travail of his soul is done;*
> *Victor, he reigns, the crucified.*

THE SEVENTH WORD

Jesus called out with a loud voice,
"Father, into your hands I commit my spirit."

Reflection: **Philippians 1:20-23**

I eagerly expect and hope that I will in no way be ashamed, but will have sufficient courage so that now as always Christ will be exalted in my body, whether by life or by death. For to me, to live is Christ and to die is gain. If I am to go on living in the body, this will mean fruitful labour for me. Yet what shall I choose? I do not know! I am torn between the two: I desire to depart and be with Christ, which is better by far.

Silence

> *Rent is the veil, the way revealed,*
> *Where heaven's gate he opens wide*
> *Through death to life his own shall rise,*
> *Through him, their Lord, once crucified.*

> When I survey the wondrous Cross
> On which the Prince of Glory died,
> My richest gain I count but loss,
> And pour contempt on all my pride.

Forbid it, Lord, that I should boast
Save in the Cross of Christ my God;
All the vain things that charm me most,
I sacrifice them to his Blood.

See from his head, his hands, his feet,
Sorrow and love flow mingling down;
Did e'er such love and sorrow meet,
Or thorns compose so rich a crown?

His dying crimson like a robe,
Spreads o'er his body on the Tree;
Then I am dead to all the globe,
And all the globe is dead to me.

Forbid it, Lord, that I should boast
Save in the Cross of Christ my God;
All the vain things that charm me most,
I sacrifice them to his Blood.

Edwin Muir
The Killing

That was the day they killed the Son of God
On a squat hill-top by Jerusalem.
Zion was bare, her children from their maze
Sucked by demon curiosity
Clean through the gates, The very halt and blind
Had somehow got themselves up to the hill.

After the ceremonial preparation,
The scourging, nailing, nailing against the wood,
Erection of the main-trees with their burden,
While from the hill rose an orchestral wailing,
They were there at last, high up in the soft spring day.
We watched the writhings, heard the moanings, saw
The three heads turning on their separate axles
Like broken wheels left spinning. Round his head
Was loosely bound a crown of plaited thorn
That hurt at random, stinging temple and brow
As the pain swung into its envious circle.

In front the wreath was gathered in a knot
That as he gazed looked like the last stump left
Of a death-wounded deer's great antlers. Some
Who came to stare grew silent as they looked,
Indignant or sorry. But the hardened old
And the heard-hearted young, although at odds
From the first morning, cursed him with one curse,
Having prayed for a Rabbi or an armed Messiah
And found the Son of God. What use to them
Was a God or a Son of God? Of what avail
For purposes such as theirs? Beside the cross-foot
Alone, four women stood and did not move
All day. The sun revolved, the shadow wheeled,
The evening fell. His head lay on his breast,
But in his breast they watched his heart move on
By itself alone, accomplishing its journey.
Their taunts grew louder, sharpened by the knowledge
That he was walking in the park of death,
Far from their rage. Yet all grew stale at last,
Spite, curiosity, envy, hate itself.
They waited only for death and death was slow
And came so quietly they scarce could mark it.
They were angry then with death and death's deceit.

I was a stranger, could not read these people
Or this outlandish deity. Did a God
Indeed in dying cross my life that day
By chance, he on his road and I on mine?

EASTER:

CHRIST
IS
RISEN!

EASTER

Two thousand years after the event, it is not easy to understand how Jesus' followers must have felt on that first Easter day. The images of Good Friday like a raw wound in their minds, the shock, the disillusionment, and the numbing grief. Then, against all reason, the unthinkable happens – he is risen! What bewilderment, what confusion, and what joy they experienced!

Many of us have lived with these stories all our lives. They are woven into the fabric of our faith. We tend to celebrate Easter Day, one day, in what is a celebration of fifty days culminating in the great feast of the Holy Spirit. How can we rediscover a sense of the wonder and awe of the season?

At Passover, Jews down the centuries have rehearsed the mighty redeeming acts of God in word and song. This is our heritage too. So the resurrection of Jesus is not the end of a story or even a beginning. It is a pivotal event in the great history of salvation, and we should proclaim:
Christ yesterday and today and for all eternity!

Christ is risen!
He is risen indeed!
Alleluia!

FOLLOW THE LAMB

For Philip

We have followed him, the Lamb,
from his star-bright night of birth
across the plains of Palestine
to Golgotha: and down,
down into Saturn's night of death.
Here at the edge of darkness do we stand,
halt before the grave. (Whose heart
does not halt here?) – Yet,
see how the Lamb is laid within the tomb,
see how they wind him, white, in linen bands:
gaze upon his silent fallen form,
gaze: do not flee the face of death.
Let sorrow softly soften.
The Lamb but sweetly waits
until our shadowed inward eyes,
grown quiet,
gently waken, bathed
in Resurrection's radiant dawn.
See how the way of Love leads on!

Melissa Kay[1]

---

[1] *Liturgy: Journal of the Liturgical Conference*, Volume II, No. 4, October 1994,
p. 27, Maryland, USA.

EASTER SUNDAY

Jesus Christ is risen today, Alleluia!
Our triumphant holy day, Alleluia!
Who did once, upon the Cross, Alleluia!
Suffer to redeem our loss, Alleluia!

Gerd Theissen
The Shadow of the Galilean

I got up from my bed, went out into the open air and looked at the sea from the upper story of our house ... The city shyly reflected the first brightness. The buildings emerged increasingly clearly from the shadow of the streets. Temple and synagogue, the houses of Jews and Gentiles, all bathed in the dawning light. The sun rose on good and evil, just and unjust. I felt it, bright and warm.

The chaotic monsters of the night had been overcome. My anguish at the harshness of life was over. In me the rule of the beasts had come to an end. The true man had appeared to me. And I had recognised the features of Jesus in him. He had given me back the earth. It had not got better since the previous day. Today, as yesterday, the struggle for a chance to live would continue. But that wasn't everything. The battle need not dominate all my action and thought. I made a new covenant with life.

I could clearly feel a voice coming to me from all things, a voice which offered me this covenant with life. Never again would I wish the earth away, never again deny life. Never again would I allow myself to be overcome by beasts from the abyss. I hear the voice of Jesus. I had the certainty that wherever I went it would always accompany me. I could not escape it anywhere.

Silence

Christ is risen!

Come, O faithful:
let us drink a new drink,
produced miraculously not from a barren rock,
but springing from the tomb which is a fountain of immortality:
the tomb of Christ by which we are strengthened.

Glory to your holy resurrection, O Lord!

Today the whole creation, heaven and earth
and the deepest abyss of the earth are filled with joy.
Let the whole universe celebrate the resurrection
by which we are strengthened.

Glory to your holy resurrection, O Lord!

Yesterday I was buried with You, O Christ!
Today I rise with You in your resurrection.
Yesterday I was crucified with You:
glorify me with You in your kingdom.

Christ is risen from the dead!
He has crushed death by his death
and bestowed life upon those who lay in the tomb.

Today we rejoice in the salvation of the world.
Christ is risen; let us rise in him!
Christ enters new life, let us live in him!
Christ has come forth from the tomb,
let us shake off the fetters of evil!
The gates of hell are open, the powers of evil are overcome!
In Christ a new creation is coming to birth,
Alleluia!
Lord, make us new,
Alleluia!

MONDAY

Jesus lives! thy terrors now
Can no more, O death, appal us;
Jesus lives! by this we know
Thou, O grave, canst not enthral us.
Alleluia!

Mark 16:1-8

When the Sabbath was over, Mary Magdalene, Mary the mother of James, and Salome bought spices so that they might go to anoint Jesus' body. Very early on the first day of the week, just after sunrise, they were on their way to the tomb and they asked each other, "Who will roll the stone away from the entrance of the tomb?" But when they looked up, they saw that the stone, which was very large, had been rolled away. As they entered the tomb, they saw a young man dressed in a white robe sitting on the right side, and they were alarmed. "Don't be alarmed," he said. "You are looking for Jesus the Nazarene, who was crucified. He has risen! He is not here. See the place where they laid him. But go, tell his disciples and Peter, 'He is going ahead of you into Galilee. There you will see him, just as he told you.'" Trembling and bewildered, the women went out and fled from the tomb. They said nothing to anyone, because they were afraid.

Silence

He is not here

Psalm 118:17-26

17. I shall not die, but live,
and declare the works of the Lord.
18. The Lord has punished me sorely,
but he did not hand me over to death.
19. Open for me the gates of righteousness;
I will enter them; I will offer thanks to the Lord.
20. This is the gate of the Lord;
he who is righteous may enter.

21. I will give thanks to you, for you answered me
and have become my salvation.
22. The same stone which the builders rejected
has become the chief corner stone.
23. This is the Lord's doing,
and it is marvellous in our eyes.
24. On this day the Lord has acted;
we will rejoice and be glad in it.
25. Hosanna, Lord, hosanna!
Lord, now send us success.
26. Blessed is he who comes in the name of the Lord;
we bless you from the house of the Lord.

I will offer thanks to the Lord

Jesus Christ, we greet you!
Your hands still have holes in them,
your feet are wet from the dew;
and with the memory of our names
undimmed by three days of death
you meet us,
risen from the grave.

We fail to understand how; we puzzle the reason why.
But you have come:
not to answer our questions, but to show us your face.
You are alive, and the world can rejoice again.
Hallelujah!

TUESDAY

Jesus lives! Henceforth is death
But the gate of life immortal:
This shall calm our trembling breath
When we pass its gloomy portal.
Alleluia!

John 20:10-18

Then the disciples went back to their homes, but Mary stood outside the tomb crying. As she wept, she bent over to look into the tomb and saw two angels in white, seated where Jesus' body had been, one at the head and the other at the foot. They asked her, "Woman, why are you crying?" "They have taken my Lord away," she said, "and I don't know where they have put him." At this, she turned around and saw Jesus standing there, but she did not realise that it was Jesus. "Woman," he said, "why are you crying? Who is it you are looking for?" Thinking he was the gardener, she said, "Sir, if you have carried him away, tell me where you have put him, and I will get him." Jesus said to her, "Mary." She turned toward him and cried out in Aramaic, "Rabboni!" (which means Teacher). Jesus said, "Do not hold on to me, for I have not yet returned to the Father. Go instead to my brothers and tell them, 'I am returning to my Father and your Father, to my God and your God.'" Mary Magdalene went to the disciples with the news: "I have seen the Lord!" And she told them that he had said these things to her.

Silence

Jesus said to her, "Mary."

O Faithful,
let us rise at the break of dawn;
let us bring our hymns of praise to the Master
instead of ointments:
then shall we look upon Christ, the Sun of Justice,
handing out life to all.

Jesus is risen indeed;
he has given us eternal life and abundant mercy.

O Christ,
When those who were bound in the chains of Hades
experienced your boundless love,
they ran to the Light with great joy,
clapping their hands for You, the eternal Passover.

Jesus is risen indeed;
he has given us eternal life and abundant mercy.

With lamps in hand,
let us go forth to Christ rising from the tomb,
as we would go to a bridegroom,
and with the feasting multitude,
let us celebrate the saving Passover of our God.

Jesus is risen indeed;
he has given us eternal life and abundant mercy.

Lord Jesus Christ, we greet you.
The cross has not defeated you, the grave has not kept you silent.
At the first dew of the morning, you met our sister, Mary,
and called her by her name.
O Lord, meet us as you met Mary,
with gentleness and resolution,
speak our names quietly in our hearts,
that we may proclaim your name boldly on our lips.

WEDNESDAY

Love's redeeming work is done;
Fought the fight, the battle won:
Lo, our Sun's eclipse is o'er!
Lo, he sets in blood no more!

John 20:24-29

Now Thomas (called Didymus), one of the Twelve, was not with the disciples when Jesus came. So the other disciples told him, "We have seen the Lord!" But he said to them, "Unless I see the nail marks in his hands and put my finger where the nails were, and put my hand into his side, I will not believe it." A week later his disciples were in the house again, and Thomas was with them. Though the doors were locked, Jesus came and stood among them and said, "Peace be with you!" Then he said to Thomas, "Put your finger here; see my hands. Reach out your hand and put it into my side. Stop doubting and believe." Thomas said to him, "My Lord and my God!" Then Jesus told him, "Because you have seen me, you have believed; blessed are those who have not seen and yet have believed."

Silence

My Lord and my God!

Psalm 18:1-8

1. I love you, O Lord my strength,
   O Lord my stronghold, my crag and my haven,
2. My God, my rock in whom I put my trust,
   my shield, the horn of my salvation and my refuge;
   you are worthy of praise.
3. I will call upon the Lord,
   and so shall I be saved from my enemies.
4. The breakers of death rolled over me,
   and the torrents of oblivion made me afraid.
5. The cords of hell entangle me,
   and the snares of death were set for me.
6. I called upon the Lord in my distress
   and cried out to my God for help.
7. He heard my voice from his heavenly dwelling;
   my cry of anguish came to his ears.

17. He reached down from on high and grasped me;
    he drew me out of great waters.
18. He delivered me from my strong enemies
    and from those who hated me;
    for they were too mighty for me.
19. They confronted me in the day of my disaster;
    but the Lord was my support.

20. He brought me out into an open place;
    he rescued me because he delighted in me.

I will call upon the Lord and so I shall be saved

If you were not risen, Lord Christ, to whom would we go
to discover a radiance on the face of God?

If you were not risen, we would not be together
seeking your communion.
We would not find your presence in forgiveness,
wellspring of a new beginning.

If you were not risen, where would we draw the energy
for following you right to the end of our existence,
for choosing you again and anew?

THURSDAY

Vain the stone, the watch, the seal!
Christ has burst the gates of hell;
Death in vain forbids his rise;
Christ has opened Paradise.

Matthew 28:11-20

While the women were on their way, some of the guards went into
the city and reported to the chief priests everything that had
happened. When the chief priests had met with the elders and
devised a plan, they gave the soldiers a large sum of money, telling
them, "You are to say, 'His disciples came during the night and stole
him away while we were asleep.' If this report gets to the governor,
we will satisfy him and keep you out of trouble." So the soldiers took
the money and did as they were instructed. And this story has been
widely circulated among the Jews to this very day.

Then the eleven disciples went to Galilee, to the mountain where Jesus had told them to go. When they saw him, they worshipped him; but some doubted. Then Jesus came to them and said, "All authority in heaven and on earth has been given to me. Therefore go and make disciples of all nations, baptising them in the name of the Father and of the Son and of the Holy Spirit, and teaching them to obey everything I have commanded you. And surely I am with you always, to the very end of the age."

Silence

Surely I am with you always, to the very end of the age

Psalm 66:1-9

1. Be joyful in God, all you lands;
   sing the glory of his name;
   sing the glory of his praise.
2. Say to God, 'How awesome are your deeds!
   Because of your great strength
   your enemies cringe before you.
3. 'All the earth bows down before you,
   sings to you, sings out your name.'
4. Come now and see the works of God,
   how wonderful he is in his doing towards all people.
5. He turned the sea into dry land,
   so that they went through the water on foot,
   and there we rejoiced in him.
6. In his might he rules for ever;
   his eyes keep watch over the nations;
   let no rebel rise up against him.
7. Bless our God, you peoples;
   make the voice of his praise to be heard.
8. Who holds our souls in life,
   and will not allow our feet to slip.
9. For you, O God, have proved us;
   you have tried us just as silver is tried.

Be joyful in God, sing the glory of his name

When you appeared to your disciples,
risen Lord,
you delivered them from fear
and made them the heralds of your victory.
Grant that your Church
may always remain faithful to their proclamation,
you who live for ever and ever.
Amen.

FRIDAY

Lives again our glorious King;
Where, O death, is now thou sting?
Dying once, he all doth save;
Where thy victory, O grave?

1 Corinthians 15:1-11

Now, brothers and sisters, I want to remind you of the gospel I preached to you, which you received and on which you have taken your stand. By this gospel you are saved, if you hold firmly to the word I preached to you. Otherwise, you have believed in vain. For what I received I passed on to you as of first importance: that Christ died for our sins according to the Scriptures, that he was buried, that he was raised on the third day according to the Scriptures, and that he appeared to Peter, and then to the Twelve. After that, he appeared to more than five hundred of the brothers and sisters at the same time, most of whom are still living, though some have fallen asleep. Then he appeared to James, then to all the apostles, and last of all he appeared to me also, as to one abnormally born. For I am the least of the apostles and do not even deserve to be called an apostle, because I persecuted the church of God. But by the grace of God I am what I am, and his grace to me was not without effect. No, I worked harder than all of them—yet not I, but the grace of God that was with me.

Whether, then, it was I or they, this is what we preach, and this is what you believed.

Silence

By this gospel you are saved

Psalm 17:1-8

1. Hear my plea of innocence, O Lord;
   give heed to my cry;
   listen to my prayer,
   which does not come from lying lips.
2. Let my vindication come forth from your presence;
   let your eyes be fixed on justice.
3. Weigh my heart, summon me by night,
   melt me down; you will find no impurity in me.
4. I give no offence with my mouth as others do;
   I have heeded the words of your lips.
5. My footsteps hold fast to the ways of your law;
   in your paths my feet shall not stumble.
6. I call upon you, O god, for you will answer me;
   incline your ear to me and hear my words.
7. Show me your marvellous loving-kindness;
   O Saviour of those who take refuge at your right hand
   from those who rise up against them.
8. Keep me as the apple of your eye;
   hide me under the shadow of your wings.

**Keep me as the apple of your eye,
hide me under the shadow of your wings**

*Brightness of God's glory,
whom death could not conquer nor the tomb imprison:
as you have shared our frailty in human flesh,
help us to share your immortality in the Spirit;
let no shadow of the grave terrify us,
and no fear of darkness turn our hearts from you.*

Reveal yourself to us this day and all our days,
as the First and the Last,
the Living One, our immortal Saviour and Lord. Amen.

SATURDAY

Soar we now where Christ has led,
Following our exalted Head;
Made like him, like him we rise;
Ours the cross, the grave, the skies.

Karl Rahner
A Faith that Loves the Earth

It is difficult in well-worn human words to do justice to the joy of Easter. Not simply because all the mysteries of the Gospel have difficulty in penetrating the narrow limits of our being and because it is even more difficult for our language to contain them. The message of Easter is the most human news brought by Christianity. That is why we have most difficulty in understanding it. It is most difficult to be, do and believe what is truest, closest and easiest. For we of today live by the tacitly assumed and therefore to us all the more self-evident prejudice that what is religious is purely a matter of the innermost heart and the highest point of the mind, something which we have to do for ourselves alone and which therefore has the difficulty and unreality of the thoughts and moods of the heart. But Easter says that God has done something. God himself. And his action has not merely lightly touched the heart of some human being here and there, so that it trembles at the inexpressible and nameless. God has raised his Son from the dead. God has called flesh to life. He has conquered death. He has done something and triumphed where it is not at all a question merely of interior sensibility but where, despite all our praise of mind, we are most really ourselves, in the reality of the earth, far from all that is purely thought and feeling, where we learn what we are – mortal children of the earth.

... One thing is needed, it is true, for his *(Jesus')* action, which we can never undo, to become the benediction of our human reality. He must break open the tomb of our hearts.

Silence

God has raised his Son from the dead

Psalm 150

1. Alleluia!
Praise God in his holy temple;
praise him in the firmament of his power.
2. Praise him for his mighty acts;
praise him for his excellent greatness.
3. Praise him with the blast of the ram's-horn;
praise him with lyre and harp.
4. Praise him with timbrel and dance;
praise him with strings and pipe.
5. Praise him with resounding cymbals;
praise him with loud clanging cymbals.
6. Let everything that has breath
praise the Lord.
Alleluia!

Let the whole earth sing the praises of the Lord!

Christ yesterday and today,
the beginning and the end,
Alpha and Omega,
all time belongs to him, and all ages,
to him be glory and power,
through every age and for ever. Amen.

SUNDAY

Oscar Cullman
Immortality of the Soul or Resurrection Of the Dead?

Only he who apprehends with the first Christians the horror of death, who takes death seriously as death, can comprehend the Easter exultation of the primitive Christian community and understand that the whole thinking of the New Testament is governed by belief in the Resurrection. Belief in the immortality of the soul is not belief in a revolutionary event. Immortality, in fact, is only a *negative*, assertion: the soul does *not* die, but simply lives on. Resurrection is a *positive* assertion: the whole man, who has really died, is recalled to life by a new act of creation by God. Something has happened – a miracle of creation! For something has also happened previously, something fearful: life formed by God has been destroyed.

Silence

Something has happened – a miracle of creation!

WEEKDAY READINGS

MONDAY: Luke 24:1-12
Why do you look for the living among the dead?

TUESDAY: Luke 24:13-27
Did not the Christ have to suffer these things and then enter his glory?

WEDNESDAY: Luke 24:28-35
Were not our hearts burning within us?

THURSDAY: Luke 24:36-49
Why are you troubled, and why do doubts rise in your minds?
FRIDAY: 1 Corinthians 15:12-19
And if Christ has not been raised, our preaching is useless and so is your faith.

SATURDAY

Dylan Thomas

And death shall have no dominion.
Dead men naked they shall be one
With the man in the wind and the west moon;
When their bones are picked clean and the clean bones gone,
They shall have stars at elbow and foot;
Though they go mad they shall be sane,
Though they sink through the sea they shall rise again;
Though lovers be lost love shall not;
And death shall have no dominion.

And death shall have no dominion.
Under the windings of the sea
They lying long shall not die windily;
Twisting on racks when sinews give way,
Strapped to a wheel, yet they shall not break;
Faith in their hands shall snap in two,
And the unicorn evils run them through;
Split all ends up they shan't crack;
And death shall have no dominion.

And death shall have no dominion.
No more may gulls cry at their ears
Or waves break loud on the seashores;
Where blew a flower may a flower no more
Lift its head to the blows of rain;
Though they be mad and dead as nails,
Heads of the characters hammer through daisies;
Break in the sun till the sun breaks down,
And death shall have no dominion.

Silence

They shall rise again

SUNDAY

Janet Morley
I Never Meant You To Roll Back The Stone

I never meant you to roll back the stone
before I was ready to ask.
I had not even fingered
the roughness and edge of it,
tested my shoulder against its painful weight,
stood contemplating its massive shadow,
or wept in the half dark for a miracle
I would not have accepted.

How can I want what I wanted
and never believed in?
Despair was at least articulate, unstrange:
I knew what the repeated question was,
endlessly safe from an answer.
Not this open grave,
this violation of my certainty, this
chill ecstasy I can no longer refuse,
this fear I flee from without hope
it will leave me behind;
this large, gratuitous terror
I cannot now seek refuge from
without complete betrayal.

You, beloved,
for whom I stretched my heart with grief,
rudely announce its irrelevance;
arising to my unreadiness
not with a comfortable word,
but to a world appalled.

Silence

I never meant you to roll back the stone

WEEKDAY READINGS

MONDAY: John 20:1-9
They still did not understand

TUESDAY: John 20:19-23
Jesus came and stood among them

WEDNESDAY: John 21:1-14
It is the Lord!

THURSDAY: John 21:15-25
Do you love me?

FRIDAY: 1 Corinthians 15:20-33
For as in Adam all die, so in Christ will all be made alive

SATURDAY

Jacques LeClercq
Death and Resurrection

My faith in the resurrection doesn't come from my instincts. It isn't biological. It is rooted in the contemplation of the God of whom I believe passionately that he is the human dimension.

My faith in the resurrection doesn't depend on reasoning, or on a form of education, or on a theological culture.

I started to believe that I will rise again, like any good Christian, because that is what we were taught from our earliest years. But I challenge the Good Christian to face the mystery of his own death to its furthest limits and be reassured by what he has been taught about the resurrection.

In any case, my faith in the resurrection doesn't reassure me. It frees me, and that is quite different. It is in my faith that I make my death my own.

My death is no longer destiny, it is liberty ...

My faith in the resurrection accepts humbly all the distress of death. It does not originate from me. It does not originate in me.

It is the fruit of an infinite tenderness in which the relation of man to God ... reaches its culminating point: our God is the God of the living.

He is living.

He is life.

The seed of divinity has been planted in me, and my passion for life, so pure and so tortured, surrounded by anxieties and with the obsession of death constantly gnawing at it, a great soaring wave in which tenderness and joy are nevertheless feasting and dancing, wild flames of my desires, this passion of mine for life suddenly becomes intoxicated with infinity because I have raised my eyes and met the transfigured face of Jesus risen.

Silence

He is living

PRAYER OF PENITENCE

God of life,
forgive our denial of life,
our destruction of its hopes,
our denial of its needs,
our distorting of its possibilities.
Fill us with your Spirit of life,
that we might be people of life,
servants of life, encouragers of life,
signs of Christ, the life of the world,
in his name we pray.

Amen.

THE PRAYERS

O risen Lord,
who in your first appearance to Mary
was mistaken for the gardener:
be present with us,
and show yourself to us in all our mistakes and uncertainties.

O risen Lord,
who appeared to your dejected disciples on the road to Emmaus,
and opened to them the scriptures,
so that their hearts burned within them:
be present with us,
and set our hearts on fire with love for you.

O risen Lord,
who gave to your distraught followers
the assurance of healing and forgiveness:
be present with us,
and bring together all Christians in peace and harmony.

O risen Lord,
who mindful of the needs of your disciples,
prepared a meal by the Sea of Galilee:
be present with us,
and make yourself known to us in all acts
of hospitality and sharing.

O risen Lord,
who in your final appearance on the Mount of Olives,
lifted up hands of blessing on all people:
be present with us,
and grant that our prayers may be taken up with yours
on behalf of the whole world.

MEDITATIONS

John 11: 25

I am the resurrection and the life

Jacques LeClercq

It seems to me to be dishonest to talk about the resurrection in a way that makes it look like an easy excuse for getting round the reality of biological death. It is a way – in my view the only way – of accepting the absurdity of death with the maximum of freedom. The implacable violence of death makes my life a destiny.

The hope of the resurrection makes my life freedom

Michael Ramsey

No resurrection. No Christianity.

EASTER I:

THE
PASSOVER

SUNDAY

The God of Abraham Praise
Who reigns enthroned above,
Ancient of everlasting Days,
and God of love:
Jehovah, great I AM,
By earth and heaven confest;
We bow and bless the sacred name
For ever blest.

Michele Guinness
A Festival of Freedom

Then came the moment of compromise with Christian tradition. Just as Jesus had gone out from that great feast of joy into Gethsemane, we were asked to leave the upper room in silence, walk done several flights of stairs in single file into a darkened church, where a solitary, rough hewn cross was illuminated by a single candle. It was one of the most moving experiences of my life. The contrast was immense. Bleary-eyed children who, a moment earlier, lay slouched with sleeping-sickness in their chairs, walked up to the cross and instinctively knelt, wide eyed, as if they were seeing it for the first time. Adults sat motionless in the pews. The intense, profound silence, after so much noise and celebration, drove home, as nothing ever had before, the overwhelming desolation of Jesus in the garden, having said goodbye to his loved ones, now facing the unbearable, alone. No one wanted to leave the building. Never was any Maundy Thursday vigil so compelling. "You've danced and sang and laughed with me, now won't you stay with me in my sorrow?"

... I learned more that Easter than the starkness of contrast Jesus must have experienced that terrible night. When two great traditions appear to clash it doesn't necessarily mean one is right and the other wrong. Each may have the insight the other lacks. Put the two together, and a far richer picture is painted. What began as a compromise became a revelation.

Silence

Christ our Passover is sacrificed for us

Psalm 114:1-7

1. Alleluia! When Israel came out of Egypt,
the house of Jacob came from a people of strange speech,
2. Judah became God's sanctuary
and Israel his dominion.
3. The sea beheld it and fled;
Jordan turned and went back.
4. The mountains skipped like rams,
and the little hills like young sheep.
5. What ailed you, O sea, that you fled?
O Jordan, that you turned back?
6. You mountains, that you skipped like rams?
You little hills like young sheep?
7. Tremble, O earth, at the presence of the Lord,
at the presence of the God of Jacob.

The God of Abraham praise!

O Christ,
great and all-holy Passover,
Wisdom of God
and his Word and Strength:
grant that we may partake perfectly
of the everlasting day of your kingdom.
Amen.

MONDAY

O God our help in ages past,
Our hope for years to come,
Our shelter from the stormy blast,
And our eternal home.

Exodus 1:1-14; 6:1

These are the names of the sons of Israel who went to Egypt with
Jacob, each with his family: Reuben, Simeon, Levi and Judah;
Issachar, Zebulun and Benjamin; Dan and Naphtali; Gad and Asher.
The descendants of Jacob numbered seventy in all; Joseph was
already in Egypt. Now Joseph and all his brothers and all that
generation died, but the Israelites were fruitful and multiplied greatly
and became exceedingly numerous, so that the land was filled with
them. Then a new king, who did not know about Joseph, came to
power in Egypt. "Look," he said to his people, "the Israelites have
become much too numerous for us. Come, we must deal shrewdly
with them or they will become even more numerous and, if war
breaks out, will join our enemies, fight against us and leave the
country." So they put slave masters over them to oppress them with
forced labour, and they built Pithom and Rameses as store cities for
Pharaoh. But the more they were oppressed, the more they multiplied
and spread; so the Egyptians came to dread the Israelites and worked
them ruthlessly. They made their lives bitter with hard labour in
brick and mortar and with all kinds of work in the fields; in all their
hard labour the Egyptians used them ruthlessly.

The LORD said to Moses, "Now you will see what I will do to
Pharaoh: Because of my mighty hand he will let them go; because of
my mighty hand he will drive them out of his country."

Silence

Let my people go

Psalm 113

1. Give praise, you servants of the Lord;
     praise the name of the Lord.
2. Let the name of the Lord be blessed,
     from this time forth for evermore.
3. From the rising of the sun to its going down
     let the name of the Lord be praised.
4. The Lord is high above all nations,
     and his glory above the heavens.
5. Who is like the Lord our God, who sits enthroned on high,
     but stoops to behold the heavens and the earth?
6. He takes up the weak out of the dust
     and lifts up the poor from the ashes.
7. He sets them with the princes,
     with the princes of his people.
8. He makes the woman of a childless house
     to be the joyful mother of children.

The Lord hears the cry of his people

God whose holy name
defies our definition,
but whose will is known
in freeing the oppressed:
make us to be one
with all who cry for justice;
that we who speak your praise
may struggle for your truth,
through Jesus Christ,
      Amen.

TUESDAY

If only He had brought us out of Egypt,
And not brought judgements upon them!
It would have been enough!

If only he had brought judgements upon them
And not defeated their gods!
It would have been enough!

Exodus 7:14-24

Then the LORD said to Moses, "Pharaoh's heart is unyielding; he refuses to let the people go. Go to Pharaoh in the morning as he goes out to the water. Wait on the bank of the Nile to meet him, and take in your hand the staff that was changed into a snake. Then say to him, 'The LORD, the God of the Hebrews, has sent me to say to you: Let my people go, so that they may worship me in the desert. But until now you have not listened. This is what the LORD says: By this you will know that I am the LORD: With the staff that is in my hand I will strike the water of the Nile, and it will be changed into blood. The fish in the Nile will die, and the river will stink; the Egyptians will not be able to drink its water.'" The LORD said to Moses, "Tell Aaron, 'Take your staff and stretch out your hand over the waters of Egypt—over the streams and canals, over the ponds and all the reservoirs'—and they will turn to blood. Blood will be everywhere in Egypt, even in the wooden buckets and stone jars." Moses and Aaron did just as the LORD had commanded. He raised his staff in the presence of Pharaoh and his officials and struck the water of the Nile, and all the water was changed into blood. The fish in the Nile died, and the river smelled so bad that the Egyptians could not drink its water. Blood was everywhere in Egypt. But the Egyptian magicians did the same things by their secret arts, and Pharaoh's heart became hard; he would not listen to Moses and Aaron, just as the LORD had said. Instead, he turned and went into his palace, and did not take even this to heart. And all the Egyptians dug along the Nile to get drinking water, because they could not drink the water of the river.

Silence

Let my people go

Psalm 115:1-9

1. Not to us, O Lord, not to us,
but to your name give glory;
because of your love and because of your faithfulness.
2. Why should the heathen say,
'Where then is their God?'
3. Our God is in heaven;
whatever he wills to do he does.
4. Their idols are silver and gold,
the work of human hands.
8. Those who make them are like them,
and so are all who put their trust in them.
9. O Israel, trust in the Lord;
he is their help and their shield.

O Israel, trust in the Lord

O God almighty,
who in your enduring goodness
recall your erring children to unending life:
spare us who declare the mighty acts of your salvation,
for we have sinned, as all our forebears;
this we ask through Jesus Christ our Lord.
Amen.

WEDNESDAY

If only He had defeated their gods,
And not slain their first born!
It would have been enough!

If only He had slain their firstborn,
And not given us their wealth!
It would have been enough!

Exodus 11

Now the LORD said to Moses, "I will bring one more plague on Pharaoh and on Egypt. After that, he will let you go from here, and when he does, he will drive you out completely. Tell the people that men and women alike are to ask their neighbours for articles of silver and gold." (The LORD made the Egyptians favourably disposed toward the people, and Moses himself was highly regarded in Egypt by Pharaoh's officials and by the people.) So Moses said, "This is what the LORD says: 'About midnight I will go throughout Egypt. Every firstborn son in Egypt will die, from the firstborn son of Pharaoh, who sits on the throne, to the firstborn son of the slave girl, who is at her hand mill, and all the firstborn of the cattle as well. There will be loud wailing throughout Egypt—worse than there has ever been or ever will be again. But among the Israelites not a dog will bark at any man or animal.' Then you will know that the LORD makes a distinction between Egypt and Israel. All these officials of yours will come to me, bowing down before me and saying, 'Go, you and all the people who follow you!' After that I will leave." Then Moses, hot with anger, left Pharaoh. The LORD had said to Moses, "Pharaoh will refuse to listen to you—so that my wonders may be multiplied in Egypt." Moses and Aaron performed all these wonders before Pharaoh, but the LORD hardened Pharaoh's heart, and he would not let the Israelites go out of his country.
Silence

Let my people go

Not without suffering
did we win our way though the deadly waters
to the shore of refuge and new life.
The oppressor's fury grows as his grip begins to weaken.
In his rage he pursues us even to his own destruction.
In his drowning

part of us is lost as well.
The remnant sings songs,
yet a sadness remains.

So many must die,
slave and master alike,
before a few can sing.
O God,
teach us to rejoice in freedom,
but not in its cost
for us and our enemies.
Let their come a day
when hate and greed shall be no more,
and we will be free
to rejoice without sadness,
to sing without tears.

THURSDAY

If only He had given us their wealth,
And not divided the sea for us!
It would have been enough!

If only He had divided the sea for us,
And not made our way through the midst of it on dry land!
It would have been enough!

If only He had made our passage on dry land,
And not drowned our oppressors in the depths of the sea!
It would have been enough!

Exodus 12:31-39, 42
During the night Pharaoh summoned Moses and Aaron and said,
"Up! Leave my people, you and the Israelites! Go, worship the LORD
as you have requested. Take your flocks and herds, as you have said,
and go. And also bless me." The Egyptians urged the people to hurry

and leave the country. "For otherwise," they said, "we will all die!" So the people took their dough before the yeast was added, and carried it on their shoulders in kneading troughs wrapped in clothing. The Israelites did as Moses instructed and asked the Egyptians for articles of silver and gold and for clothing. The LORD had made the Egyptians favourably disposed towards the people, and they gave them what they asked for; so they plundered the Egyptians. The Israelites journeyed from Rameses to Succoth. There were about six hundred thousand men on foot, besides women and children. Many other people went up with them, as well as large droves of livestock, both flocks and herds. With the dough they had brought from Egypt, they baked cakes of unleavened bread. The dough was without yeast because they had been driven out of Egypt and did not have time to prepare food for themselves. Because the LORD kept vigil that night to bring them out of Egypt, on this night all the Israelites are to keep vigil to honour the LORD for the generations to come.

Silence

Let my people go

The Song of Moses and Miriam
Exodus 15:1-9

1. I will sing to the Lord, who has triumphed gloriously;
the horse and rider have been thrown into the sea.
2. The Lord is my strength and my song
and has become my salvation.
3. This is my God whom I will praise
the God of my forebears whom I will exalt.
4. The Lord fights for his people,
the Lord is his name.
5. Your right hand, O Lord, is glorious in power:
your right hand, O Lord, shatters the enemy.
6. At the blast of your nostrils, the sea covered them;
they sank as lead in the mighty waters.
7. In your unfailing love, O Lord,
you lead the people whom you have redeemed,

8. And by your invincible strength
you will guide them to your holy dwelling.
9. You will bring them in and plant them, O Lord,
in the sanctuary which your hands have established. (RSV)

You have redeemed your people, O Lord

Remember us, Lord, as you have in ages past.
You made the world and our human race; you shaped its history,
correcting your people with judgement yet with love.
Your mercy endures for ever and we give you thanks
for you are good.
Blessed be God for ever!

FRIDAY

Before the Saviour's face
The ransomed nations bow,
O'erwhelmed at his almighty grace
For ever new;
He shows his prints of love-
They kindle to a flame,
And sound through all the worlds above
The slaughtered Lamb.

Revelation 5:6-13

Then I saw a Lamb, looking as if it had been slain, standing in the centre of the throne, encircled by the four living creatures and the elders. He had seven horns and seven eyes, which are the seven spirits of God sent out into all the earth. He came and took the scroll from the right hand of him who sat on the throne. And when he had taken it, the four living creatures and the twenty-four elders fell down before the Lamb. Each one had a harp and they were holding golden bowls full of incense, which are the prayers of the saints. And they sang a new song: "You are worthy to take the scroll and to open its seals, because you were slain, and with your blood you purchased for God members of every tribe and language and people and nation. You have made them to be a kingdom and priests to serve our God, and they will reign on the earth." Then I looked and heard the voice of many angels, numbering thousands upon thousands, and ten thousand times ten thousand. They encircled the throne and the living creatures and the elders. In a loud voice they sang: "Worthy is the Lamb, who was slain, to receive power and wealth and wisdom and strength and honour and glory and praise!" Then I heard every creature in heaven and on earth and under the earth and on the sea, and all that is in them, singing: "To him who sits on the throne and to the Lamb be praise and honour and glory and power, for ever and ever!"

Silence

To him who sits on the throne and to the Lamb be praise and honour and glory and power, for ever and ever!

Psalm 105:1-9

1. Give thanks to the Lord and call upon his name;
   make known his deeds among the peoples.
2. Sing to him, sing praises to him,
   and speak of his marvellous works.
3. Glory in his holy name;
   let the hearts of those who seek the Lord rejoice.
4. Search for the Lord and his strength;
   continually seek his face.
5. Remember the marvels he has done,
   his wonders and the judgements of his mouth.
6. O offspring of Abraham his servant,
   O children of Jacob he has chosen.
7. He is the Lord our God;
   his judgements prevail in all the world.
8. He has always been mindful of his covenant,
   the promise he made for a thousand generations.
9. The covenant he made with Abraham,
   the oath he swore to Isaac.

Give thanks to the Lord and call upon his name

Christians, to the Pascal Victim
Offer your thankful praises!
A Lamb the sheep redeemeth:
Christ, who only is sinless,
Reconcileth sinners to the Father.

SATURDAY

The whole triumphant host
Give thanks to God on high;
'Hail! Father, Son, and Holy Ghost,'
They ever cry;
Hail! Abraham's God and mine!
(I join the heavenly lays)
All might and majesty are thine,
And endless praise.

An Ancient Author
The spiritual Pasch

The Pasch which we have celebrated brings salvation to all men, beginning from the first, for he is given salvation and life when they are given to us all.

The imperfect events which took place in time are the images and symbols of what is perfect and eternal; they were devised to foreshadow the reality which is now dawning. In the presence of the reality, the symbol has no point, just as when the king comes on a visit, no one dares to ignore the king in person and pay homage to his statue.

We can see the extent to which the symbol is inferior to the reality from this: the symbol recalls the short life of the Jewish first-born, the reality recalls the eternal life of all men.

It is no great thing that one should escape death for a short time, if he will die soon afterwards; but it is certainly a great thing to escape death altogether. That is what happens to us, because Christ, our paschal lamb, has been sacrificed for us.

The very name of the feast points to the way in which it is surpassed, if it is correctly explained. The word 'Pasch' means 'passage', because when the angel of death was striking down the first-born, he passed over the houses of the Hebrews. But with us the passage of the angel of death is a reality, for it passes over us once for all, when Christ raises us up to eternal life.

Silence

Christ raises up to eternal life

The Easter Anthems

1. Christ our passover has been sacrificed for us,
   so let us celebrate the feast,
2. Not with the old leaven of corruption and wickedness
   but with the unleaved bread of sincerity and truth.
3. Christ once raised from the dead dies no more;
   death has no more dominion over him.
4. In dying, he died to sin once for all;
   in living, he lives to God.
5. See yourselves, therefore, as dead to sin
   and alive to God in Jesus Christ our Lord.
6. Christ has been raised from the dead;
   the first fruits of those who sleep.
7. For since by one man came death,
   by another has come also the resurrection of the dead,
8. For as in Adam all die,
   even so in Christ shall all be made alive. (RSV)

Christ our passover has been sacrificed for us

The Lamb's high banquet called to share,
Arrayed in garments white and fair,
The Red Sea past, we fain would sing
To Jesus our triumphant King.

YEAR 2

Byzantine Daily Worship
Stichera of the Resurrection

Let God arise and his enemies will scatter,
and those who hate Him will flee before Him.

Our Passover, Christ the Redeemer is revealed to us today as a noble Passover. It is a new and holy Passover, a mystical Passover, a blameless Passover, a glorious Passover, a Passover for the faithful, a Passover that opens for us the gates of paradise, a Passover that sanctifies all believers.

A glorious Passover has shone upon us, a Passover of the Lord, a Passover perfectly honourable: let us then embrace one another with joy. O what a Passover delivering from sorrow, for Christ coming out of the tomb as from a nuptial chamber fills the women with joy in telling them to bring the happy news to the disciples.

Behold today is the day of the resurrection: let us glory in the feast, let us embrace one another in joy and say: "O brothers and enemies too: we forgive everything on resurrection day. Let us sing together:

Christ is risen from the dead!

Silence

Christ is risen! He is truly risen!

WEEKDAY READINGS

**MONDAY: Exodus 5:1-9
Let my people go**

**TUESDAY: Exodus 10:1-20
How long will you refuse to humble yourself before me?**

**WEDNESDAY: Exodus 12:1-13
Is the Lord's PASSOVER**

**THURSDAY: Exodus 14:5-18
The Lord will fight for you**

**FRIDAY: 1 Peter 1:18-25
Christ, a lamb without blemish or defect**

SATURDAY

Melito of Sardis
On the Pasch

You must understand, dearly beloved, how the mystery of the Pasch is new and old, eternal and transient, corruptible and incorruptible, mortal and immortal.

... He was led as a sheep to the slaughter, but he was not a sheep; he was as a lamb without voice, but he was not a lamb. The figure has passed away, the reality has come: it is God who has come in place of the lamb, man in place of the sheep, and in the man is Christ, who contains all things.

So the immolation of the sheep, and the solemn rite of the Pasch, and the letter of the law have come to accomplishment in Christ Jesus. Everything in the old law, and more particularly everything in the new, was directed towards him.

For the law has become the Word and the old new (each coming from Sion and Jerusalem); the commandment has become grace, and the type reality, the lamb has become Son, the sheep a man, and man has become God.

' ... Come then, all you nations of men defiled by sin, receive the forgiveness of sin. For it is I who am your forgiveness, the pasch of your salvation, the lamb slain for you; it is I who am your ransom, your life, your resurrection, your light, your salvation, your king. I am bringing you to the heights of heaven, I will show you the Father who is from all eternity, I will raise you up with my right hand.

Silence

I will raise you up

YEAR 3

SUNDAY

Louis Bouyer
The Two Paschs

It is, however, no longer a matter of a simple *coup de théâtre* effected from the outside, like a supernatural charm paralyzing the enemy while the chosen people escape. No exterminating angel is going to descend from heaven striking the Egyptians in the silence of the night while Israel is hastening to consume the propitiatory victim. He who this time has set up the table where He will offer Himself is the very One who, acting in the name of the guests, will give battle to the enemy. And at a stroke the infamous power will not only be suspended: in those guests, it will be destroyed. The new Israel will not leave the land of slavery for another terrestrial city where demons, sooner or later, can rejoin it. The divine kingdom itself will await it, will call it. It will be translated into those heavenly places from which the devil was hurled headlong to earth and to which he will never again be able to ascend. Having instituted the Eucharist, Jesus will say to His followers: "In the world you shall have distress, but have confidence. I have overcome the world". The victory over the serpent and the reconciliation thereby effected make strangers and travellers of those whom that victory has redeemed from slavery and those whose gaze is no longer fixed upon the hills of Juda. Partaking in the sacrifice of the new and eternal Lamb has fortified them with an all-powerful viaticum for the passage from the kingdom of darkness to that of the Son of divine love, in order that, according to His words, where He is they also may be.

Silence

Then I saw a Lamb, looking as if it had been slain

WEEKDAY READINGS

MONDAY: Exodus 5:22-6:5
I have heard the groaning of my people

TUESDAY: Exodus 10:21-29
Let my people go

WEDNESDAY: Exodus 12:21-30
There was loud wailing in Egypt

THURSDAY: Exodus 14:19-31
The people feared the Lord and put their trust in him

FRIDAY: 1 Corinthians 5:6-8
Christ our Passover lamb, has been sacrificed

SATURDAY

Gregory Nazianzen
We shall share in the pasch

We shall share in the pasch, for the present certainly in what is still a figure, though a plainer one than the ancient pasch ... In a short time, however, our sharing will be more perfect and less obscure, when the Word will drink the pasch with us new in the kingdom of his Father, revealing and teaching what he has now shown in a limited way. For what is now being made known is ever new.

... Let us not sacrifice your calves or lambs with horns and hoofs, which are for the most part dead, insensate things. But let us offer a sacrifice of praise to God on the altar on high along with the choirs of heaven. Let us go through the first veil, let us come to the second, let us look into the holy of holies.

To say something greater still, let us sacrifice ourselves to God, further, let us go on every day offering ourselves and all our activities.

... If you are Simon of Cyrene, take up the cross and follow. If you are crucified with him as a robber, have the honesty to acknowledge God ... If you are Joseph of Arimathea, ask the executioner for the body: make your own expiation of the world.

If you are Nicodemus, the man who served God by night, prepare him for burial with perfumes.

I you are one or other Mary, or Salome or Joanna, shed tears early in the morning. Be the first to see the stone removed, and perhaps the angels too, and even Jesus himself.

Silence

We shall share in the pasch

PRAYER OF PENITENCE

O God,
you have made us for yourself,
and against your longing there is no defence.
Mark us with your love,
and release in us a passion for your justice
in our disfigured world;

that we may turn from our guilt and face you,
our heart's desire.

THE PRAYERS

If only He had left our oppressors in the depths of the sea,
And not taken good care of us for forty years!
It would have been enough!

If only He had watched over us for forty years,
and not fed us with manna!
It would have been enough!

If only He had fed us with manna,
And not given to us the Sabbath!
It would have been enough!

If only He had given us the Sabbath,
And not brought us before the face of Mount Sinai!
It would have been enough!

If only He had brought us before Mount Sinai,
And not given the Torah to us!
It would have been enough!

If only He had given us Torah,
and not brought us to the Land of Israel!
It would have been enough!

If only He had brought us into the Land of Israel,
And not built for us His Holy Temple!
It would have been enough!

If only he had redeemed us from our sins,
And not sacrificed His only Son for us!
It would have been enough!
For Christ our Passover lamb, has been sacrificed.
Let us keep the Festival!

Christ is risen!

MEDITATION

Desmond Tutu
Hope and Suffering

I need to point out that God was first experienced by the Israelites in the event of the Exodus. That was how they came into contact with God. They were at the time just a rabble of slaves. They did not encounter God in some religious event such as sacrifice or at worship. God was revealed in helping them to escape from bondage ... And when God redeemed us in our Lord and Saviour Jesus Christ, it was not through a religious event. No, it was through an act of execution, used against common criminals.

At the Lamb's high feast we sing
Praise to our victorious King:
Who hath washed us in the tide
Flowing from his pierced side;
Praise we him whose love divine
Gives the guests his blood for wine,
Gives his body for the feast,
Love the Victim, Love the Priest.

Where the Paschal blood is poured,
Death's dark angel sheathes his sword;
Israel's hosts triumphant go
Through the wave that drowns the foe.
Christ the Lamb whose blood was shed,
Paschal victim, Paschal bread!
With sincerity and love
Eat we manna from above

EASTER II:

THE
BREAD
OF
LIFE

SUNDAY

Lord, enthroned in heavenly splendour,
First-begotten from the dead,
Thou alone, our strong defender,
Liftest up thy people's head.
Alleluia!
Jesu, true and living Bread.

Edward Schillebeeckx
Our sharing of bread is not in vain

Celebrating the eucharist we confess that the everyday history of injustice and inequality does not have the last word. In the liturgy we confess that in the end the powerful do not have the last word. We may not trivialize the barren, barbarian everyday reality of injustice, poverty and world hunger when we celebrate the eucharist on Sunday in a happy and relaxed way. Nevertheless, in the liturgy we move away from everyday life, and we dwell in a world in which we confess our faith and celebrate our hope. We dwell in the world of the sacramental word and the sacramental sign. We confess and celebrate there the dimension of faith and immense hope for the future. There we celebrate a future which is still not there but which is opened to us through God in Jesus as a future which is also possible for us. *Why him and not us?* However, if we do not collaborate with God's grace, if we do not follow Jesus in actual love and dedication for men and women, then the coming of this better future is sheer ideology.

Silence

Why him and not us?

Psalm 116:1-8

1. I love the Lord,
because he has heard the voice of my supplication,
because he has inclined his ear to me
whenever I called upon him.
2. The chords of death entangled me;
the grip of the grave took hold of me;
I came to grief and sorrow.
3. The I called upon the name of the Lord:
'O Lord, I pray you, save my life.'
4. Gracious is the Lord and righteous;
our God is full of compassion.
5. The Lord watches over the innocent;
I was brought very low and he helped me.
6. Turn again to your rest, O my soul,
for the Lord has treated you well.
7. For you have rescued me from death,
my eyes from tears and my feet from stumbling.
8. I will walk in the presence of the Lord
in the land of the living.

I love the Lord

Lord you have put gladness in our hearts,
you have satisfied our hunger with good things.
In giving all, you have not withheld from us
your own dear Son, your very self:
How can we withhold anything from you,
our Lord and our God?
Renew us day by day with the gift of your Spirit,
that we may give ourselves completely to your service,
and walk with joy in the footsteps
of Jesus Christ our Lord.

MONDAY

Life-imparting heavenly Manna,
Stricken Rock with streaming side,
Heaven and earth with loud Hosanna
Worship thee, the Lamb who died,
Alleluia!
Risen, ascended, glorified!

Exodus 16:1-5

The whole Israelite community set out from Elim and came to the Desert of Sin, which is between Elim and Sinai, on the fifteenth day of the second month after they had come out of Egypt. In the desert the whole community grumbled against Moses and Aaron. The Israelites said to them, "If only we had died by the Lord's hand in Egypt! There we sat around pots of meat and ate all the food we wanted, but you have brought us out into this desert to starve this entire assembly to death." Then the LORD said to Moses, "I will rain down bread from heaven for you. The people are to go out each day and gather enough for that day. In this way I will test them and see whether they will follow my instructions. On the sixth day they are to prepare what they bring in, and that is to be twice as much as they gather on the other days."

Silence

I will test them

Psalm 105:1-5, 37-43

1. Give thanks to the Lord and call upon his name;
   make known his deeds among the peoples.
   2. Sing to him, sing praises to him,
   and speak of all his marvellous works.
   3. Glory in his holy name;
   let the hearts of those who seek the Lord rejoice.

4. Search for the Lord and his strength;
continually seek his face.

5. Remember the marvels he has done,
his wonders and the judgements of his mouth.

37. He led out his people with silver and gold;
in all their tribes there was not one that stumbled.

38. Egypt was glad of their going,
because they were afraid of them.

39. He spread out a cloud for a covering
and a fire to give light in the night season.

40. They asked and quails appeared,
and he satisfied them with bread from heaven.

41. He opened the rock and water flowed,
so the river ran in dry places.

42. For God remembered his holy word
and Abraham his servant.

43. So he led forth his people with gladness,
his chosen with shouts of joy.

Give thanks to the Lord and call upon his name

*Ever faithful God,
you gave manna from heaven
to your people in the desert.
Increase in us our desire
to receive the Bread of the new Alliance,
and grant that we may find in it
a life that is stronger than death
through Christ, our Lord.*
                              Amen.

TUESDAY

Bread of heaven, on thee we feed ,
for thy Flesh is meat indeed;
Ever may our souls be fed
With this true and living Bread;
Day by day with strength supplied
Through the life of him who died.

John 6:30-40

So they asked him, "What miraculous sign then will you give that we may see it and believe you? What will you do? Our ancestors ate the manna in the desert; as it is written: 'He gave them bread from heaven to eat.'" Jesus said to them, "I tell you the truth, it is not Moses who has given you the bread from heaven, but it is my Father who gives you the true bread from heaven. For the bread of God is he who comes down from heaven and gives life to the world." "Sir," they said, "from now on give us this bread." Then Jesus declared, "I am the bread of life. Whoever comes to me will never go hungry, and whoever believes in me will never be thirsty. But as I told you, you have seen me and still you do not believe. All that the Father gives me will come to me, and whoever comes to me I will never drive away. For I have come down from heaven not to do my will but to do the will of him who sent me. And this is the will of him who sent me, that I shall lose none of all that he has given me, but raise them up at the last day. For my Father's will is that all those who look to the Son and believe in him shall have eternal life, and I will raise them up at the last day."

Silence

It is my Father who gives you the true bread from heaven

Psalm 34:1-10

1. I will bless the Lord at all times;
 his praise shall be ever in my mouth.
 2. I will glory in the Lord;
 let the humble hear and rejoice.
3. Proclaim with me the greatness of the Lord;
 let us exalt his name together.
 4. I sought the Lord and he answered me
 and delivered me out of my terror.
 5. Look upon him and be radiant,
 and let not your faces be ashamed.
6. I called in my affliction and the Lord heard me
 and saved me from my troubles.
7. The angel of the Lord encompasses those who fear him,
 and he will deliver them.
 8. Taste and see that the Lord is good;
 happy are they who trust in him!
 9. Fear the Lord, you that are his saints,
 for those who fear him lack nothing.
10. The young lions lack and suffer hunger,
but those who seek the Lord lack nothing that is good.

I will bless the Lord at all times

Everloving God,
your Son Jesus Christ
gave himself as living bread
for the life of the world;
give us such a knowledge of his presence
that we may be strengthened
and sustained by his risen life
to serve you continually;
through Jesus Christ our Lord. Amen.

WEDNESDAY

This is the bread I give before I go,
bread milled and ground of pain,
my body's grief,
the pain of men, man's failure and defeat,
your groans and tears, your paid and all men's woe:
Take the bread, take the bread,
take the bread and eat.

1 Corinthians 11:17-26
In the following directives I have no praise for you, for your meetings do more harm than good. In the first place, I hear that when you come together as a church, there are divisions among you, and to some extent I believe it. No doubt there have to be differences among you to show which of you have God's approval. When you come together, it is not the Lord's Supper you eat, for as you eat, each of you goes ahead without waiting for anybody else. One remains hungry, another gets drunk. Don't you have homes to eat and drink in? Or do you despise the church of God and humiliate those who have nothing? What shall I say to you? Shall I praise you for this? Certainly not! For I received from the Lord what I also passed on to you: The Lord Jesus, on the night he was betrayed, took bread, and when he had given thanks, he broke it and said, "This is my body, which is for you; do this in remembrance of me." In the same way, after supper he took the cup, saying, "This cup is the new covenant in my blood; do this, whenever you drink it, in remembrance of me." For whenever you eat this bread and drink this cup, you proclaim the Lord's death until he comes.

Silence

Do this in remembrance of me

Psalm 111:1-9

1. Alleluia! I will give thanks to the Lord with my whole heart,
   in the assembly of the upright, in the congregation.
   2. Great are the deeds of the Lord!
   They are studied by all who delight in them.
   3. His work is full of majesty and splendour,
   and his righteousness endures for ever.
   4. He makes his marvellous works to be remembered;
   the Lord is gracious and full of compassion.
   5. He gives food to those who fear him;
   he is ever mindful of his covenant.
   6. He has shown his people the power of his works
   in giving them the lands of the nations.
   7. The works of his hands are faithfulness and justice;
   all his commandments are sure.
   8. They stand fast for ever and ever,
   because they are done in truth and equity.
   9. He sent redemption to his people;
   he commanded his covenant for ever;
   holy and awesome is his name.

Great are the deeds of the Lord!

We pray to God,
our merciful Father:
That we may break our bread with others
and share life with one another;
that we may do this
in order to remember him
who asked us to do
what he had done before.

THURSDAY

This is the cup that bought the world again,
red with the wine my hands have
blessed to blood,
poured out in streams more rich than
you can think,
my testament, the home, the hope of all men:
Take the cup, take the cup,
take the cup and drink

1 Corinthians 10:16-22

Is not the cup of thanksgiving for which we give thanks a participation in the blood of Christ? And is not the bread that we break a participation in the body of Christ? Because there is one loaf, we, who are many, are one body, for we all partake of the one loaf. Consider the people of Israel: Do not those who eat the sacrifices participate in the altar? Do I mean then that a sacrifice offered to an idol is anything, or that an idol is anything? No, but the sacrifices of pagans are offered to demons, not to God, and I do not want you to be participants with demons. You cannot drink the cup of the Lord and the cup of demons too; you cannot have a part in both the Lord's table and the table of demons. Are we trying to arouse the Lord's jealousy? Are we stronger than he?

Silence

We, who are many, are one body, for we all partake of the one loaf

Psalm 145:1-12

1. I will exalt you, O God my King,
and bless your name for ever and ever.
2. Every day I will bless you
and praise your name for ever and ever.
3. Great is the Lord and greatly to be praised;
there is no end to his greatness.

4. One generation shall praise your works to another
        and shall declare your power.
5. I will ponder the glorious splendour of your majesty
        and all your marvellous works.
6. They shall speak of the might of your wondrous acts,
        and I will tell of your greatness.
7. They shall publish the remembrance of your great goodness;
        they shall sing of your righteous deeds.
8. The Lord is gracious and full of compassion,
        slow to anger and of great kindness.
9. The Lord is loving to everyone
    and his compassion is over all his works.
10. All your works praise you, O Lord,
    and your faithful servants bless you.
11. They make known the glory of your kingdom
        and speak of your power;
12. That the peoples may know of your power
    and the glorious splendour of your kingdom.

Every day I will bless you and praise your name

Father of mercy,
keep us joyful in your salvation
and faithful to your covenant;
and, as we journey to your kingdom,
ever feed us with the bread of life,
your Son, our Saviour Jesus Christ.
                                        Amen.

FRIDAY

Look, Father, look on his anointed face,
And only look on us as found in him;
Look not on our misusings of thy grace,
Our prayer so languid and our faith so dim:
For lo, between our sins and their reward
We set the Passion of thy Son our Lord.

Matthew 26:20-25

When evening came, Jesus was reclining at the table with the Twelve. And while they were eating, he said, "I tell you the truth, one of you will betray me." They were very sad and began to say to him one after the other, "Surely not I, Lord?" Jesus replied, "The one who has dipped his hand into the bowl with me will betray me. The Son of Man will go just as it is written about him. But woe to that man who betrays the Son of Man! It would be better for him if he had not been born." Then Judas, the one who would betray him, said, "Surely not I, Rabbi?" Jesus answered, "You yourself have said it."

Silence

Is it I?

Psalm 41

1. Happy are they who consider the poor and needy!
   The Lord will deliver them in time of trouble.
2. The Lord preserves them and keeps them alive,
      so that they may be happy in the land;
he does not hand them over to the will of their enemies.
3. The Lord sustains them on their sick-bed
      and ministers to them in their illness.

4. I said, 'Lord be merciful to me;
   heal me, for I have sinned against you.'
5. My enemies are saying wicked things about me:
   'When will he die and his name perish?'
6. Even if they come to see me, they speak empty words;
      their heart collects false rumours;
      they go outside and spread them.
7. All my enemies whisper together about me
      and devise evil against me.

8. 'A deadly thing', they say, 'has fastened on him;
he has taken to his bed and will never get us again.'
9. Even my best friend whom I trusted,
who broke bread with me,
has lifted up his heel and turned against me.
10. But you, O Lord, be merciful to me and raise me up,
and I shall repay them.
11. By this I know that you are pleased with me,
that my enemy does not triumph over me.
12. In my integrity you hold me fast,
and shall set me before your face for ever.
13. Blessed be the Lord God of Israel,
from age to age. Amen. Amen.

Lord, be merciful to me

Heavenly Father,
whose Son suffered denial and betrayal of trust
from those who shared his bread:
raise us up, O Lord,
and prevent us in the time of trial
from falling away from you;
through Jesus Christ our Lord. Amen.

SATURDAY

This is the body raised to life and breath,
this is the blood that sings again like wine,
the scars that glow in sign of victory.
Rejoice with me, for I have conquered death;
live in me, live in me, live and love in me.

Madeleine L'Engle
At Communion

Whether I kneel or stand or sit in prayer,
I am not caught in time nor held in space,
but thrust beyond this posture I am where
time and eternity come face to face;
infinity and space meet in this place
where crossbar and high upright hold the one
in agony and in all Love's embrace.
The power in helplessness that was begun
when all the brilliance of the flaming sun
contained itself in the small confines of a child
now comes to me in strange action done
in mystery. Break me, break space, O wild
and lovely power. Break me: thus I am dead,
and resurrected now in wine and bread.

Silence

And resurrected now in wine and bread

Psalm 116:10-17

10. How shall I repay the Lord
for all the good things he has done for me?
11. I will lift up the cup of salvation
and call upon the name of the Lord.
12. I will fulfil my vows to the Lord
in the presence of his people.
13. Precious in the sight of the Lord
is the death of his servants.
14. O Lord, I am your servant;
I am your servant and the child of your handmaid;
you have freed me from my bonds
15. I will offer you the sacrifice of thanksgiving
and call upon the name of the Lord.

16. I will fulfil my vows to the Lord
in the presence of all his people.
17. In the courts of the Lord's house,
in the midst of you, O Jerusalem.
Alleluia!

How shall I repay the Lord
for all the good things he has done for me?

Father, your Son gave his disciples a sign
by which to remember him until he comes again;
as bread is broken and wine poured out
may our eyes be opened to know him, Jesus our Lord.
Alleluia! Bread of angels,
Thou on earth our food, our stay;
Alleluia! Here the sinful
Flee to thee from day to day:
Intercessor, Friend of sinners,
Earth's Redeemer, plead for me,
Where the songs of all the sinless
Sweep across the crystal sea.

YEAR 2

SUNDAY

Alexander Schmemann
The Eucharist

For more than thirty years I have served the Church as a priest and a
theologian, as a pastor and a teacher. Never in those thirty years have I
ceased to feel called to think about the eucharist and its place in the life of
the Church. Thoughts and questions on this subject, which go back to early
adolescence, have filled my whole life with joy. For the more real became
my experience of the eucharistic liturgy, the sacrament of Christ's victory
and of his glory, the stronger became my feeling that there is a eucharistic
crisis in the Church. In the tradition of the Church, nothing has changed.
What has changed is the perception of the eucharist, the perception of its
very essence. Essentially, this crisis consists in a lack of connection and

cohesion between what is accomplished in the eucharist and how it is perceived, understood and lived. To a certain degree this crisis has always existed in the Church. The life of the Church, or rather of the people of the Church, has never been perfect, ideal. With time, however, this crisis has become chronic. That schizophrenia that poisons the life of the Church and undermines its very foundations has come to be seen as its normal state.

Silence

What has changed is the perception of the eucharist, the perception of its very essence

WEEKDAY READINGS

MONDAY: Exodus 16:31-35
See the bread I gave you to eat

TUESDAY: John 6:41-51
But here is the bread that comes down from heaven, which people may eat and not die

WEDNESDAY: Luke 22:14-22
This is my body given for you

THURSDAY: 1 Corinthians 11:27-34
We ought to examine ourselves before we eat of the bread and drink of the cup

FRIDAY: Mark 14:17-21
Surely not I?

SATURDAY

Evelyn Underhill
Corpus Christi

I

Come, dear Heart!
The fields are white to harvest: come and see
As in a glass the timeless mystery
Of love, whereby we feed
On God, our bread indeed.
Torn by the sickles, see him share the smart

Of travailing Creation: maimed, despised,
Yet by his lovers the more dearly prized
Because for us he lays his beauty down–
Last toll paid by perfection for our loss!
Trace on these fields his everlasting Cross,
And o'er the stricken sheaves the Immortal Victim's crown

II

From far horizons came a Voice that said,
'Lo! From the hand of Death take thou thy daily bread.'
Then I, awakening, saw
A splendour burning in the heart of things:
The flame of living love which lights the law
Of mystic death that works the mystic birth.
I knew the patient passion of the earth,
Maternal, everlasting, whence there springs
The Bread of Angels and the life of man.

III

Now in each blade
I, blind no longer, see
The glory of God's growth: known it to be
An earnest of the Immemorial Plan.
Yea, I have understood
How all things are one great oblation made:
He on our altars, we on the world's rood.
Even as this corn,
Earth-born,
We are snatched from the sod;
Reaped, ground to grist,
Crushed and tormented in the Mills of God,
And offered at Life's hands, a living Eucharist.

Silence

A living Eucharist

SUNDAY

Aidan Kavanagh
The Shape of Baptism: The Rite of Christian Initiation

To know Christ sacramentally only in terms of bread and wine is to know him only partially, in the dining room as host and guest. It is a valid enough knowledge, but its ultimate weakness when isolated is that it is perhaps too civil ... However elegant the knowledge of the dining room may be, it begins in the soil, in the barnyard, in the slaughterhouse; amid the quiet violence of the garden, strangled cries, and fat spitting in the pan. Table manners depend on something's having been grabbed by the throat. A knowledge that ignores these dark and murderous human *gestes* is losing its grip on the human condition.

Silence

To know Christ sacramentally only in terms of bread and wine is to know him only partially

WEEKDAY READINGS

MONDAY: Exodus 16:11-18
It is the bread the Lord has given you

TUESDAY: John 6:52-66
This is a hard teaching

WEDNESDAY: Matthew 26:26-30
Jesus took bread, gave thanks, and broke it

THURSDAY: Acts 20:7-12
On the first day of the week we came together to break bread

FRIDAY: John 13:18-30
It is the one to whom I will give this piece of bread

SATURDAY

John Masefield
The Everlasting Mercy

Slow up the hill the plough team plod,
Old Callow at the task of God,
Helped by man's wit, helped by the brute
Turning a stubborn clay to fruit,
His eyes for ever on some sign
To help him plough a perfect line.
At top of rise the plough team stopped,
The fore-horse bent his head and cropped.
Then the chains chack, the brasses jingle,
The lean reins gather through the cringle,
The figures move against the sky,
The clay wave breaks as they go by.
I kneeled there in the muddy fallow,
I knew that Christ was there with Callow,
That Christ was standing there with me,
That Christ had taught me what to be,
That I should plough, and as I ploughed
My Saviour Christ would sing aloud,
And as I drove the clods apart
Christ would be ploughing in my heart,
Through rest-harrow and bitter roots,
Through all my bad life's rotten fruits.

O Christ who holds the open gate,
O Christ who drives the furrow straight,
O Christ the plough, O Christ, the laughter
Of holy white birds flying after,
Lo, all my heart's field red and torn,
And Thou wilt bring the young green corn
The young green corn divinely springing,
The young green corn for ever singing;
And when the field is fresh and fair
Thy blessèd feet shall glitter there.
And we will walk the weeded field,
And tell the golden harvest's yield,
The corn that makes the holy bread
By which the soul of man is fed,

The holy bread, the food unpriced,
Thy everlasting mercy, Christ.

Silence

The holy bread, the food unpriced

PRAYER OF PENITENCE

Lord, we heard that your were hungry
And we did not share our food.
Forgive us, Lord, forgive.

Lord, we heard that you were thirsty
And we kept our drink to ourselves.
Forgive us, Lord, forgive.

Lord, we saw you as a stranger
And we closed our door and our heart.
Forgive us, Lord, forgive.

Lord, we saw you go naked
And we fussed about our clothes.
Forgive us, Lord, forgive.

Lord, we discovered that you were sick
And we avoided contact with you.
Forgive us, Lord, forgive.
Lord, we heard that you were in prison
And we pretended we did not know you.
Forgive us, Lord forgive.

Lord, you came to us again and again
And we closed up in ourselves.
Forgive us, Lord, forgive.

THE PRAYERS

We know that we come together for the Lord's supper
in a world where one is hungry and another is drunk;
where we ourselves are well-fed, secure and articulate;
where success and wealth are worshipped, and the cross

of Christ is a folly and a scandal;
where there are divisions we recognize
and those we fail to see.

Let us wait for one another before we eat and drink,
and bring these divisions with us:
let us wait for the hungry and the dispossessed,
remembering those we have met, and in whom we have
seen the face of God;
let us wait for those who, in their struggle for justice,
have challenged us and changed us;
let us wait for those who, with nothing to give,
have treated us as guests
and shown us the generosity of God;
let us wait for those whom we oppose,
who actively undermine the poor,
or in their apathy support injustice.

Let us bring to this table those with whom we long to share,
and those we disapprove of;
and in our dividedness,
let us proclaim the Lord's death until he comes.

MEDITATION

Aidan Kavanagh
Elements of Rite

The eucharist is not a mnemonic tableau of an historical event. It is a sweeping thanksgiving for the whole of the Father's benevolence toward the world and his people in Christ and the Holy Spirit. It does no more than what Jesus did in all the meals he took with those he loved. What he did at those meals quite escaped the bounds of any one meal on any one occasion. What he did was to make human beings free and forgiven table partners with God.

EASTER III:

THE WATER OF LIFE

SUNDAY

Jesus, the gift divine I know,
The gift divine I ask of thee;
That living water now bestow—
The Spirit and thyself, on me;
Thou, Lord, of life the fountain art;
Now let me find thee in my heart.

Alexander Schmemann
Of Water and the Spirit

There can be no life without water, and because of this the "primitive" identifies water as the principle of life, sees in it the *prima essentia* of the world: "And the Spirit of God was moving on the face of the waters" (Genesis 1:2). But if water reflects and symbolizes the world as cosmos and life, it is also the symbol of destruction and death. It is the mysterious death which kills and annihilates, the dark habitation of the demonic powers, the very image of the irrational, uncontrollable, elemental in the world. The principle of life, a life-giving power, and the principle of death, the power of destruction: such is the essentially ambiguous intuition of water in our religious worldview. And finally, water is the principle of purification, of cleanliness, and therefore regeneration and renewal. It washes away stains, it recreates the pristine purity of the earth. It is the fundamental religious symbolism of water – symbolism rooted in the self-evident and natural attributes of water – that permeates the Bible and the whole biblical story of creation, fall and salvation.

Silence

There can be no life without water

Song: Isaiah 44:1-5

1. "But now listen, O Jacob,
my servant, Israel, whom I have chosen.
2. This is what the LORD says—
he who made you, who formed you in the womb,
and who will help you:
Do not be afraid,
O Jacob, my servant, Jeshurun, whom I have chosen.
3. For I will pour water on the thirsty land,
and streams on the dry ground;
I will pour out my Spirit on your offspring,
and my blessing on your descendants.
4. They will spring up like grass in a meadow,
like poplar trees by flowing streams.
5. Some will say, 'I belong to the LORD';
others will call themselves by the name of Jacob;
and still others will write on their hand, 'The LORD's,'
and will take the name Israel."

The Lord will pour out his Spirit upon us

Godhead!
Godhead!
Eternal Godhead!
I proclaim and do not deny it:
you are a peaceful sea
in which the soul feeds and is nourished
as she rests in you
in love's affection and union
by conforming her will with your high eternal will—
that will which wants nothing other
than that we be made holy.

Thee let me drink, and thirst no more
For drops of finite happiness;
Spring up, O well, in heavenly power,
In streams of pure perennial peace,
In joy that none can take away,
In life which shall for ever stay.

Genesis 7:11-16

In the six hundredth year of Noah's life, on the seventeenth day of the second month—on that day all the springs of the great deep burst forth, and the floodgates of the heavens were opened. And rain fell on the earth forty days and forty nights. On that very day Noah and his sons, Shem, Ham and Japheth, together with his wife and the wives of his three sons, entered the ark. They had with them every wild animal according to its kind, all livestock according to their kinds, every creature that moves along the ground according to its kind and every bird according to its kind, everything with wings. Pairs of all creatures that have the breath of life in them came to Noah and entered the ark. The animals going in were male and female of every living thing, as God had commanded Noah. Then the LORD shut him in.

And the floodgates of the heavens were opened

Psalm 69:1-7, 16-17

1. Save me, O God,
for the waters have risen up to my neck.
2. I am sinking in deep mire,
there is no firm ground for my feet.
3. I have come into deep waters,
and the torrent washes over me.

4. I have grown weary with my crying;
my throat is inflamed;
my eyes have failed from looking for my God.
5. Those who hate me without cause
are more than the hairs of my head;
my lying foes who would destroy me are mighty.
Must I give them back what I never stole?
6. O God, you know my foolishness,
and my faults are not hidden from you.
7. Let not those who hope in you
be put to shame through me,
Lord God of hosts;
Let not those who seek you
be disgraced because of me,
O God of Israel.

16. 'Save me from the mire; do not let me sink;
let me be rescued from those who hate me
and out of the deep waters.
17. 'Let not the torrent of waters wash over me,
neither let the deep swallow me up;
do not let the Pit shut its mouth upon me.

Save me, O God

O God,
our rainbow, our dove, our promised land:
in the resurrection of your Son
you have brought us into your ark.
Protect us from storm,
and ferry us to your welcoming shore
through Christ our Lord.
Amen.

TUESDAY

Father, on me the grace bestow,
Unblamable before thy sight,
Whence all the streams of mercy flow;
Mercy, thine own supreme delight,
To me, for Jesus' sake, impart,
And plant thy nature in my heart

Exodus 17:1-7

The whole Israelite community set out from the Desert of Sin, travelling from place to place as the LORD commanded. They camped at Rephidim, but there was no water for the people to drink. So they quarrelled with Moses and said, "Give us water to drink." Moses replied, "Why do you quarrel with me? Why do you put the LORD to the test?" But the people were thirsty for water there, and they grumbled against Moses. They said, "Why did you bring us up out of Egypt to make us and our children and livestock die of thirst?" Then Moses cried out to the LORD, "What am I to do with these people? They are almost ready to stone me." The LORD answered Moses, "Walk on ahead of the people. Take with you some of the elders of Israel and take in your hand the staff with which you struck the Nile, and go. I will stand there before you by the rock at Horeb. Strike the rock, and water will come out of it for the people to drink." So Moses did this in the sight of the elders of Israel. And he called the place Massah and Meribah because the Israelites quarrelled and because they tested the LORD saying, "Is the LORD among us or not?"

Silence

Give us water to drink

Psalm 63:1-8

1. O God, you are my God; eagerly I seek you;
     my soul thirsts for you, my flesh faints for you,
   as in a barren and dry land where there is no water.
2. Therefore I have gazed upon you in your holy place,
       that I might behold your power and your glory.
3. For your loving-kindness is better than life itself;
              my lips shall give you praise.
        4. So I will bless you as long as I live
           and lift up my hands to your name.
5. My soul is content, as with marrow and fatness,
      and my mouth praises you with joyful lips.
      6. When I remember you upon my bed,
     and meditate on you in the night watches.
        7. For you have been my helper,
   and under the shadow of your wings I will rejoice.
          8. My soul clings to you;
           your right hand holds me fast.

My soul thirsts for you

O Christ,
you take upon yourself all our burdens so that,
freed of all that weighs us down,
we can constantly begin anew to walk,
with lightened step,
from worry towards trusting,
from the shadows towards the clear flowing waters,
from our own will
towards the vision of the coming kingdom.
And then we know, though we hardly dared hope so,
that you offer to make every human being
a reflection of your face.

WEDNESDAY

Thy mind throughout my life be shown,
While, listening to the sufferer's cry,
The widow's and the orphan's groan,
On mercy's wings I swiftly fly,
The poor and helpless to relieve,
my life, my all, for them to live.

2 Kings 5:1-3, 9-14

Now Naaman was commander of the army of the king of Aram. He was a great man in the sight of his master and highly regarded, because through him the LORD had given victory to Aram. He was a valiant soldier, but he had leprosy. Now bands from Aram had gone out and had taken captive a young girl from Israel, and she served Naaman's wife. She said to her mistress, "If only my master would see the prophet who is in Samaria! He would cure him of his leprosy."

So Naaman went with his horses and chariots and stopped at the door of Elisha's house. Elisha sent a messenger to say to him, "Go, wash yourself seven times in the Jordan, and your flesh will be restored and you will be cleansed." But Naaman went away angry and said, "I thought that he would surely come out to me and stand and call on the name of the LORD his God, wave his hand over the spot and cure me of my leprosy. Are not Abana and Pharpar, the rivers of Damascus, better than any of the waters of Israel? Couldn't I wash in them and be cleansed?" So he turned and went off in a rage. Naaman's servants went to him and said, "My father, if the prophet had told you to do some great thing, would you not have done it? How much more, then, when he tells you, 'Wash and be cleansed'!" So he went down and dipped himself in the Jordan seven times, as the man of God had told him, and his flesh was restored and became clean like that of a young boy.

Silence

Wash and be cleansed

Psalm 46:1-8

1. God is our refuge and strength,
a very present help in time of trouble;
2. Therefore we will not fear, though the earth be moved,
and though the mountains be toppled
into the depths of the sea;
3. Though its waters rage and foam,
and though the mountains tremble at its tumult.
4. The Lord of hosts is with us;
the God of Jacob is our stronghold.
5. There is a river whose streams make glad the city of God,
the holy habitation of the Most High.
6. God is in the midst of her;
she shall not be overthrown;
God shall help her at break of day.
7. The nations make much ado and the kingdoms are shaken;
God has spoken and the earth shall melt away.
8. The Lord of Hosts is with us;
The God of Jacob is our stronghold.

God is our refuge and strength

Lord in your mercy give us living water,
always springing up as a fountain of healing:
free us, body, mind and spirit from every danger
and admit us to your presence in purity of heart.
Grant this through Christ our Lord. Amen.

THURSDAY

Thus may I show thy Spir't within,
Which purges me from every stain;
Unspotted from the world and sin,
My faith's integrity maintain;
The truth of my religion prove
By perfect purity and love.

Isaiah 43:16-21

This is what the LORD says—he who made a way through the sea, a path through the mighty waters, who drew out the chariots and horses, the army and reinforcements together, and they lay there, never to rise again, extinguished, snuffed out like a wick: "Forget the former things; do not dwell on the past. See, I am doing a new thing! Now it springs up; do you not perceive it? I am making a way in the desert and streams in the wasteland. The wild animals honour me, the jackals and the owls, because I provide water in the desert and streams in the wasteland, to give drink to my people, my chosen, the people I formed for myself that they may proclaim my praise.

Silence

See, I am doing a new thing!

Song: Jonah 2:1-7

1. From inside the fish Jonah prayed to the LORD his God.

2. He said: "In my distress I called to the LORD,
    and he answered me.
From the depths of the grave I called for help,
    and you listened to my cry.

3. You hurled me into the deep,
    into the very heart of the seas,
    and the currents swirled about me;
all your waves and breakers swept over me.

4. I said, 'I have been banished from your sight;
yet I will look again towards your holy temple.'

5. The engulfing waters threatened me,
    the deep surrounded me;
seaweed was wrapped around my head.

6. To the roots of the mountains I sank down;
    the earth beneath barred me in forever.
But you brought my life up from the pit, O LORD my God.

7. "When my life was ebbing away,
    I remembered you, LORD,
and my prayer rose to you, to your holy temple.

In my distress I called to the Lord

O God, you are the unsearcheable abyss of peace,
the ineffable sea of love,
and the fountain of blessings.
Water us with plenteous streams
from the riches of your grace;
and from the most sweet springs of your kindness,
make us children of quietness
and heirs of peace.
              Amen.

FRIDAY

I heard the voice of Jesus say,
'Behold, I freely give
The living water, thirsty one;
Stoop down, and drink and live:'
I came to Jesus, and I drank
Of that life-giving stream;
My thirst was quenched, my soul revived,
And now I live in him

John 7:37-43

On the last and greatest day of the Feast, Jesus stood and said in a loud voice, "Let anyone who is thirsty come to me and drink. Whoever believes in me, as the Scripture has said, will have streams of living water flowing from within." By this he meant the Spirit, whom those who believed in him were later to receive. Up to that time the Spirit had not been given, since Jesus had not yet been glorified. On hearing his words, some of the people said, "Surely this man is the Prophet." Others said, "He is the Christ." Still others asked, "How can the Christ come from Galilee? Does not the Scripture say that the Christ will come from David's family and from Bethlehem, the town where David lived?" Thus the people were divided because of Jesus.

Silence

Let anyone who is thirsty come to me and drink

Psalm 42:1-10

1. As the deer longs for the water-brooks,
so longs my soul for you, O God.
2. My soul is athirst for God, athirst for the living God;
when shall I come to appear before the presence of God?
3. My tears have been my food day and night,
while all day long they say to me,
'Where now is your God?'
4. I pour out my soul when I think on these things:
how I went with the multitude
and led them into the house of God,
5. With the voice of praise and thanksgiving,
among those who keep holy-day.
6. Why are you so full of heaviness, O my soul?
And why are you so disquieted within me?
7. Put your trust in God;
for I will yet give thanks to him,
who is the help of my countenance, and my God.

8. My soul is heavy within me;
therefore I will remember you from the land of Jordan,
and from the peak of Mizar among the heights of Hermon.
9. One deep calls to another in the noise of your cataracts;
all your rapids and floods have gone over me.
10. The Lord grants his loving-kindness in the daytime;
in the night season his song is with me,
a prayer to the God of my life.

My soul is athirst for God

Eternal Trinity,
you are a deep sea,
into which the more I enter the more I find,
and the more I find the more I seek.
The soul ever hungers in your abyss, Eternal Trinity,
longing to see you with the light of your light,
and as the deer yearns for the springs of water,
so my soul yearns to see you in truth.

SATURDAY

Come, let us drink of the New River,
Not from barren rock divinely poured,
But the fount of life that is for ever
From the sepulchre of Christ the Lord.

Hans Urs von Balthasar
Heart of the World

He would let the world do its will and thereby accomplish the will of
the Father; he would grant the world its will, thereby breaking the
world's will; he would allow his own vessel to be shattered, thereby
pouring himself out; but pouring out one single drop of the divine
Heart's blood he would sweeten the immense and bitter ocean. This
was intended to be the most incomprehensible of exchanges: from

the most extreme opposition would come the highest union, and the might of his supreme victory was to prove itself in his utter disgrace and defeat. For his weakness would already be the victory of his love for the Father, reconciliation in the eyes of the Father, and, as a deed of his supreme strength this weakness would be so great that it would far surpass and sustain in itself the world's pitiful feebleness. He alone would henceforth be the measure and thus also the meaning of all impotence. He wanted to sink so low that in the future all falling would be a falling into him, and every streamlet of bitterness and despair would henceforth run down into his lowermost abyss.

Silence

He would allow his own vessel to be shattered, thereby pouring himself out

Song: Isaiah 55:1-5

1. "Come, all you who are thirsty,
   come to the waters;
   and you who have no money,
   come, buy and eat!
Come, buy wine and milk without money and without cost.

2. Why spend money on what is not bread,
   and your labour on what does not satisfy?
   Listen, listen to me, and eat what is good,
   and your soul will delight in the richest of fare.

3. Give ear and come to me;
   hear me, that your soul may live.
I will make an everlasting covenant with you,
   my faithful love promised to David.

4. See, I have made him a witness to the peoples,
   a leader and commander of the peoples.

5. Surely you will summon nations you know not,
and nations that do not know you will hasten to you,
because of the LORD your God,
the Holy One of Israel,
for he has endowed you with splendour."

Come, all who are thirsty

Your love, Jesus,
is an ocean with no shore to bound it.
And if I plunge into it,
I carry all the possessions I have.
Your know, Lord, what these possessions are –
the souls you have seen fit to link with mine.

YEAR 2

John Chrysostom
Baptismal Instructions

The Jews saw miracles. Now you shall see greater and much more brilliant
ones than those seen when the Jews went forth from Egypt. You did not see
Pharaoh and his armies drowned, but you did see the drowning of the devil
and his armies. The Jews passed through the sea; you have passed through
the sea of death. They were delivered from the Egyptians; you are set free
from the demon. They put aside their servitude to barbarians; you have set
aside the far more hazardous servitude to sin.

Since, then, we have here such a fountain and our life here is such, since
our table groans under the weight of countless blessings and spiritual gifts
abound on every side, let us come forward with a sincere heart and with a
clean conscience, that we may receive his grace and mercy to help us in our
need, by the grace and kindness of the only-begotten Son, our Lord and
Saviour Jesus Christ, through whom and with whom be to the Father and the
life-giving Spirit glory, honour, power, now and forever, world without end.
Amen.

Silence

We have here such a fountain

SATURDAY

Columbanus
Let those who thirst come to me and drink

My dearest brethren, give ear to our words, as men about to hear something essential; slake the thirst of your mind from the streams of the divine fountain of which we now wish to speak, but do not quench it; drink, but be not sated; for now the living fountain, the fountain of life, calls us to himself, and says, 'Let him that is athirst come unto me and drink.' What you are to drink, take note. Let Jeremiah tell you, let the fountain himself tell you, 'They have forsaken me the fountain of living water, says the Lord.' Thus the Lord himself, our God Jesus Christ, is the fountain of life, and so he calls us to himself the fountain, that we may drink of him. He who loves drinks of him, he drinks who is satisfied by the word of God, who sufficiently adores, who longs sufficiently, he drinks who burns with the love of wisdom.

Observe whence the fountain flows; it flows from that place whence also the bread came down; since he is the same who is bread and fountain, the only Son, our God Christ the Lord, for whom we should ever hunger. Though we eat him in loving, though we feast on him in desiring, let us desire him as though hungering for him. Likewise as the fountain, let us ever drink of him with overflows of love, let us ever drink of him with fullness of longing, and let us be gladdened by some savour of his loveliness.

Silence

He calls us to himself the fountain, that we may drink of him

SUNDAY

Gertrude the Great
Of the pleasure which God took in making His abode in her soul

Whilst Thou didst act so lovingly towards me, and didst not cease to draw my soul from vanity to Thyself, it happened on a certain day, between the festival of the Resurrection and Ascension, that I went into the court before Prime, and seated myself near the fountain, – and I began to consider the beauty of the place, which charmed me on account of the clear and flowing stream, the verdure of the trees which surrounded it, and the flight of the birds, and particularly of the doves, – above all, the sweet calm, – apart from all, and considering within myself what would make this place most useful to me, I thought that it would be friendship of a wise and intimate companion, who would sweeten my solitude or render it useful to others, when Thou, my Lord and my God who are a torrent of inestimable pleasure, after having inspired me with the first impulse of this desire, Thou didst will to be also the end of it, inspiring me with the thought that if by continual gratitude I return Thy graces to Thee, as a stream returns to its source; if, increasing in the love of virtue, I put forth, like the trees, the flowers of good works; furthermore, if, despising the things of earth, I fly upwards, freely, like the birds, and thus free my senses from distraction of exterior things, – my soul would then be empty, and my heart would be an agreeable abode for Thee.

Silence

Thou, my Lord and my God who are a torrent of inestimable pleasure

WEEKDAY READINGS

MONDAY: Genesis 8:1-14
But God remembered Noah

TUESDAY: Isaiah 12:1-6
With joy you will draw water from the wells of salvation

WEDNESDAY: Ezekiel 47:1-12
Son of man, do you see this?

THURSDAY: Jeremiah 31:10-14
They will be like a well-watered garden

FRIDAY: John 4:11-26
Those who drink of the water I give them will never thirst

SATURDAY

Cyril of Jerusalem
The living water of the Holy Spirit

'The water that I shall give him will become in him a spring of water, welling up to eternal life'. This is a new kind of water, living, welling up, welling up for those who are worthy. Why did he call the grace of the Spirit water? Because all living things depend on water. Water produced herbs and living things. Water comes down from heaven as rain: water always comes down in the same form, yet its effects are manifold – thus it takes one form in the palm-tree and other in the vine; it is in all things and takes all forms, though it is uniform and always remains itself ... Similarly with the Holy Spirit. He is one and of one nature and indivisible, but he apportions his grace as he wills to each one ... His approach is gentle, his presence fragrant, his yoke very light; rays of light and knowledge shine forth before him as he comes. He comes with the heart of a true protector; he comes to save, to heal, to teach, to admonish, to strengthen, to console, to enlighten the mind, first of the man who receives him, then through him the minds of others also.

Silence

All things depend on water

PRAYER OF PENITENCE

By the water that flowed from the rock,
the thirst of the people was quenched.
In the fountain of Christ,
the thirst of the peoples is quenched.

The rod of Moses opened the rock,
and streams flowed forth;
and they were refreshed by its draught,
who had grown faint with thirst.

Form the side of Christ flowed the stream that bestows life.
The Gentiles drank that were weary,
and in it forgot their pains.
Sprinkle my vileness with your dew,
and my crimes shall be atoned!
And I shall be, O my Lord, at your right hand,
and with your saints I shall be joined!

THE PRAYERS

O my God, from you I proceed;
to you I belong;
you I adore.

You are the Fountain of my whole being
Fountain of a thousand springs
of mercy, pardon, and loving kindness;
Source of light, Well of grace;
you I adore.

Yours is the voice of many waters
now loud, now low, and lovely always,
calling me to your work and mine,
calling to faith, to hope, to resolve,
calling to love, the greatest of these;
you I adore.

Fountain of joy and melody in the heart,
Fountain of peace and quietness of soul,
Fountain of will to do thy will,
you I adore.

Spring and Fountain and River and Flood,
O God most holy,
from you I proceed,
to you I belong,
my Beginning, my Goal, my All,
you I adore.

MEDITATION

Henry Vaughan
From *The Waterfall*

O useful element and clear!
My sacred wash and cleanser here,
My first consigner unto those
Fountains of life, where the Lamb goes,
What sublime truths, and wholesome themes
Lodge in thy mystical, deep streams!
Such as dull man can never find,
Unless the Spirit lead his mind,
Which first upon thy face did move,
And hatched all with his quickening love.
As his loud brook's incessant fall
In streaming rings restagnates all,
Which reach by course the bank, and then
Are no more seen, just so pass men.
O my invisible estate,
My glorious liberty, still late!
Thou are the channel my soul seeks,
Not this with cataracts and creeks.

Christina Rossetti

I have no wit, no words, no tears;
My heart within me like a stone
Is numbed too much for hopes or fears;
Look right, look left, I dwell alone;
I lift mine eyes, but dimmed with grief
No everlasting hills I see;
My life is fading like a leaf
O Jesus, quicken me.

My life is like a faded leaf,
My harvest dwindled to a husk;
Truly my life is void and brief
And tedious in the barren dusk;
My life is like a frozen thing,

No bud or greenness can I see:
Yet rise it shall – the sap of Spring;
O Jesus, rise in me.

My life is like a broken bowl,
A broken bowl that cannot hold
One drop of water for my soul
Or cordial in the searching cold;
Cast in the fire the perished thing,
Melt and remould it, till it be
A royal cup for him my King:
O Jesus, drink of me.

EASTER IV:

FIRE
&
LIGHT

SUNDAY

O Worship the King all glorious above;
O gratefully sing his power and his love;
Our Shield and Defender, the Ancient of Days,
Pavilioned in splendour and girded with praise.

John of the Cross
O Living Flame

O living flame of love
That, burning, assails
My inmost soul with tenderness untold,
Since you freely move,
Consume the veil
Which sunders this sweet converse that we hold.

O burn that never sears!
O wound of deep delight!
O gentle hand! O touch of love supernal
That quickens life for ever, Puts all my woes to flight,
And, slaying, changes death to eternal life.

And O, lamps of fire,
In whose resplendent light
The deepest caverns where the senses meet,
Once steep'd in darkness dire,
Blaze with new glories bright
And to the loved one give both light and heat!

How tender is the love
You waken in my breast
When you, alone and secretly, are there!
Whispering of things above,
Most glorious and most blest,
How delicate the love you make be bear!

Silence

O living flame of love!

The Prayer of Azariah: vvs 42-51

42. Bless the Lord, all rain and dew;
sing praises to him and highly exalt him for ever.
43. Bless the Lord, all you winds;
sing praises to him and highly exalt him for ever.
44. Bless the Lord, fire and heat;
sing praises to him and highly exalt him for ever.
45. Bless the Lord, winter cold and summer heat;
sing praises to him and highly exalt him for ever.
46. Bless the Lord, dews and falling snow;
sing praises to him and highly exalt him for ever.
47. Bless the Lord, nights and days;
sing praises to him and highly exalt him for ever.
48. Bless the Lord, light and darkness;
sing praises to him and highly exalt him for ever.
49. Bless the Lord, ice and cold;
sing praises to him and highly exalt him for ever.
50. Bless the Lord, frosts and snows;
sing praises to him and highly exalt him for ever.
51. Bless the Lord, lightenings and clouds;
sing praises to him and highly exalt him for ever.

NRSV

Come, Lord, work upon us,
set us on fire and clasp us close,
be fragrant to us, draw us to your loveliness,
let us love, let us run to you.

MONDAY

The earth with its store of wonders untold,
Almighty, thy power hath founded of old;
Hath stablished it fast by a changeless decree,
And round it hath cast, like a mantle, the sea.

Exodus 3:1-6

Now Moses was tending the flock of Jethro his father-in-law, the priest of Midian, and he led the flock to the far side of the desert and came to Horeb, the mountain of God. There the angel of the LORD appeared to him in flames of fire from within a bush. Moses saw that though the bush was on fire it did not burn up. So Moses thought, "I will go over and see this strange sight—why the bush does not burn up." When the LORD saw that he had gone over to look, God called to him from within the bush, "Moses! Moses!" And Moses said, "Here I am." "Do not come any closer," God said. "Take off your sandals, for the place where you are standing is holy ground." Then he said, "I am the God of your father, the God of Abraham, the God of Isaac and the God of Jacob." At this, Moses hid his face, because he was afraid to look at God.

Silence

This is holy ground

Psalm 104:1-9

1. Bless the Lord, O my soul;
O Lord my God, how excellent is your greatness!
You are clothed with majesty and splendour.

2. You wrap yourself with light as with a cloak
and spread out the heavens like a curtain.

3. You lay the beams of your chambers in the waters above;
you make the clouds your chariot;
you ride on the wings of the wind.

4. You make the wind your messengers
and flames of fire your servants.

5. You have set the world upon its foundations,
so that it never shall move at any time.

6. You covered it with the deep as a mantle;
the waters stood higher than the mountains.

7. At your rebuke they fled;
at the voice of your thunder they hastened away.
8. They went down into the hills
and down to the valleys beneath,
to the places you had appointed for them.
9. You set the limits that they should not pass;
they shall not again cover the earth.

Bless the Lord, O my soul

Blessed are you, Sovereign God,
our light and our salvation;
to you be glory and praise for ever!
You led your people to freedom
by a pillar of cloud by day
and a pillar of fire by night.
May we who walk in the light of your presence
acclaim your Christ, rising victorious,
as he banishes all darkness from our hearts and minds,
and praise you,
Father, Son and Holy Spirit.
Blessed be God for ever!

TUESDAY

O tell of his might, O sing of his grace,
Whose robe is the light, whose canopy space;
His chariots of wrath the deep thunder clouds form,
And dark is his path on the wings of a storm.

1 Kings 18:30-39

Then Elijah said to all the people, "Come here to me." They came to him, and he repaired the altar of the LORD, which was in ruins. Elijah took twelve stones, one for each of the tribes descended from Jacob, to whom the word of the LORD had come, saying, "Your name shall be Israel." With the stones he built an altar in the name of the LORD, and he dug a trench around it large enough to hold two seahs of seed. He arranged the wood, cut the bull into pieces and laid it on the wood. Then he said to them, "Fill four large jars with water and pour it on the offering and on the wood." "Do it again," he said, and they did it again. "Do it a third time," he ordered, and they did it the third time. The water ran down around the altar and even filled the trench. At the time of sacrifice, the prophet Elijah stepped forward and prayed: "O LORD, God of Abraham, Isaac and Israel, let it be known today that you are God in Israel and that I am your servant and have done all these things at your command. Answer me, O LORD, answer me, so these people will know that you, O LORD, are God, and that you are turning their hearts back again." Then the fire of the LORD fell and burned up the sacrifice, the wood, the stones and the soil, and also licked up the water in the trench. When all the people saw this, they fell prostrate and cried, "The LORD—he is God! The LORD—he is God!"

Silence

The Lord—he is God!

Psalm 43

1. Give judgement for me, O God,
and defend my cause against an ungodly people;
deliver me from the deceitful and the wicked.
2. For you are the God of my strength;
why have you put me from you?
And why do I go so heavily while the enemy oppresses me?
3. Send out your light and your truth,
that they may lead me,
and bring me to your holy hill
and to your dwelling.
4. That I may go to the altar of God,
to the God of my joy and gladness;
and on the harp I will give thanks to you, O God my God.

5. Why are you so full of heaviness, O my soul?
And why are you so disquieted within me?
6. Put your trust in God;
for I will yet give thanks to him,
who is the help of my countenance, and my God.

You are the God of my strength, in you I trust

Stand, O strong and merciful God,
against all oppression
and with all who are oppressed;
against the triumph of evil
and against the complacency of your people;
establish in Jesus Christ
your new order of generosity and joy.
Amen.

WEDNESDAY

From the night of ages waking
morning comes to heart and mind,
day of grace in splendour breaking,
mists and shadows fall behind;
in the brightness of his glory
Christ the Light of life has shined.

Matthew 3:7-12

But when he saw many of the Pharisees and Sadducees coming to where he was baptising, he said to them: "You brood of vipers! Who warned you to flee from the coming wrath? Produce fruit in keeping with repentance. And do not think you can say to yourselves, 'We have Abraham as our father.' I tell you that out of these stones God can raise up children for Abraham. The axe is already at the root of the trees, and every tree that does not produce good fruit will be cut down and thrown into the fire. "I baptise you with water for repentance. But after me will come one who is more powerful than I, whose sandals I am not fit to carry. He will baptise you with the Holy Spirit and with fire. His winnowing fork is in his hand, and he will clear his threshing floor, gathering his wheat into the barn and burning up the chaff with unquenchable fire."

Silence

He will baptise you with the Holy Spirit and with fire

Song: Isaiah 45:5-8

5. "I am the LORD, and there is no other;
    apart from me there is no God.
    I will strengthen you,
    though you have not acknowledged me,
6. "so that from the rising of the sun
    to the place of its setting
    people may know
    there is none besides me.
    I am the LORD,
    and there is no other.

7. "I form the light and create darkness,
    I bring prosperity and create disaster;
    I, the LORD, do all these things.

8. "You heavens above,
    rain down righteousness;
    let the clouds shower it down.
    Let the earth open wide,
    let salvation spring up,
    let righteousness grow with it;
    I, the LORD, have created it."

I am the Lord, and there is no other

Holy Spirit, Your fiery love warms the whole earth.
Your Beauty blazes into sun and fire.
You radiate Glory within and without.
The flame of your womanly Wisdom
burns in the shrine of my soul.
The heat of Your Compassion melts my cold heart,
and penetrates my whole body's being.
I rest in your radiance, and respond to Your calling,
filled with the Light of Your Divine Presence.
                                                    Amen.

THURSDAY

Christ in light immortal dwelling,
Word by whom the worlds were made;
Light of lights, our dark dispelling,
Lord of lords in light arrayed;
in the brightness of his glory
see the Father's love displayed.

John 9:1-12

As he went along, he saw a man blind from birth. His disciples asked
him, "Rabbi, who sinned, this man or his parents, that he was born
blind?" "Neither this man nor his parents sinned," said Jesus, "but
this happened so that the work of God might be displayed in his life.
As long as it is day, we must do the work of him who sent me. Night
is coming, when no-one can work. While I am in the world, I am the
light of the world." Having said this, he spat on the ground, made
some mud with the saliva, and put it on the man's eyes. "Go," he
told him, "wash in the Pool of Siloam" (this word means Sent). So
the man went and washed, and came home seeing. His neighbours
and those who had formerly seen him begging asked, "Isn't this the
same man who used to sit and beg?" Some claimed that he was.
Others said, "No, he only looks like him." But he himself insisted, "I
am the man." "How then were your eyes opened?" they demanded.

He replied, "The man they call Jesus made some mud and put it on my eyes. He told me to go to Siloam and wash. So I went and washed, and then I could see." "Where is this man?" they asked him. "I don't know," he said.

Silence

I am the light of the world

Psalm 36:5-11

5. Your love, O Lord,
reaches to the heavens,
and your faithfulness to the clouds.
6. Your righteousness is like the strong mountains,
your justice like the great deep;
you save both human and beast, O Lord.
7. How priceless is your love, O God!
Your people take refuge in the shadow of your wings.
8. They feast upon the abundance of your house;
you give them drink
from the river of your delights.
9. For with you is the well of life,
and in your light we see light.
10. Continue your loving-kindness
to those who know you,
and your favour to those who are pure of heart.
11. Let not the foot of the proud come near me,
nor the hand of the wicked push me aside.

How priceless is your love, O God!

Eternal Godhead, O sea profound,
what more could you give me than yourself?
You are a fire that never burns out;
You consume in your heat all the soul's self love;
You are the flame that drives away the cold.

Give me your light that I may know all truth,
clothe me with yourself, eternal truth,
that I may live this mortal life with true obedience,
and in the light of your most holy faith.
Amen.

FRIDAY

Risen Lord in radiance splendid,
Christ has conquered Satan's sway;
sin and shame and sorrow ended,
powers of darkness flee away;
in the brightness of his glory
walk as children of the day.

2 Corinthians 4:1-6

Therefore, since through God's mercy we have this ministry, we do not lose heart. Rather, we have renounced secret and shameful ways; we do not use deception, nor do we distort the word of God. On the contrary, by setting forth the truth plainly we commend ourselves to everyone's conscience in the sight of God. And even if our gospel is veiled, it is veiled to those who are perishing. The god of this age has blinded the minds of unbelievers, so that they cannot see the light of the gospel of the glory of Christ, who is the image of God. For we do not preach ourselves, but Jesus Christ as Lord, and ourselves as your servants for Jesus' sake. For God, who said, "Let light shine out of darkness," made his light shine in our hearts to give us the light of the knowledge of the glory of God in the face of Christ.

Silence

God has made his light shine in our hearts

Psalm 19:7-14

7. The law of the Lord is perfect
and revives the soul;
the testimony of the Lord is sure
and gives wisdom to the innocent.

8. The statues of the Lord are just
and rejoice the heart;
the commandment of the Lord is clear
and gives light to the eyes.

9. The fear of the Lord is clean and endures for ever;
the judgements of the Lord are true and righteous together.

10. More to be desired are they than gold
much more fine than gold,
sweeter far than honey, than honey in the comb.

11. By them also is your servant enlightened,
and in keeping them is great reward.

12. Who can tell how often he offends?
Cleanse me from my secret faults.

13. Above all, keep your servant from presumptuous sins;
let them not get dominion over me;
then I shall be whole and sound,
and innocent of a great offence.

14. Let the words of my mouth and the meditation of my heart
be acceptable in your sight,
O Lord, my strength and my redeemer.

O Lord, my light, my strength, and my redeemer

Dear Jesus, help me to spread your fragrance wherever I go.
Flood my soul with your spirit and life.
Penetrate and possess my whole being so utterly
that my life may only be a radiance of yours.
Stay with me, and then I shall begin to shine as you shine,
so to shine as a light to others,
the light, O Jesus will be all from you, none of it will be mine:
it will be you shining on others through me.

Let me thus praise you in the way you love best,
by shining on those around me. Amen

SATURDAY

Light to lighten every nation,
shining forth from shore to shore,
Christ who won the world's salvation
now let all the earth adore;
in the brightness of his glory
Light of life for evermore.

Byzantine Daily Worship
Prayer for the new Light

Lord Jesus Christ, Our God, Source of Life, and Immortality, Eternal
Light born of Eternal Light, Immortal Light, invisible,
incomprehensible, unchanging and unchangeable. You are the True
Light who dwells in the Unapproachable Light and shines forth from
Him; You are the Light of the Father's glory and its radiance; You
are the Light of the heavenly hosts and of every man who comes into
this world. O Saviour, You established a law for the first man who
lived in the state of light, in order to guide him and lead him to the
new world of heaven and incite him to grow in the love of eternal
life. But he transgressed the law, and fell from great glory in which
You had established Him, and by his fall he dealt death to himself
and estranged himself from You, O Glorious Light! But You, O
Lord, the Lover of mankind, in your great bounty and infinite mercy,
submitted Yourself to death and condescended to share the lowliness
of us wretched sinners, in order to lead us back to that former glory
and light from which we had fallen away. For the sake of us
transgressors of your divine law, You accepted to be buried, to go
down to Hades, to the depths of the earth. Then, O Lord, You
destroyed the gates of death, delivering and raising up those who had
been chained in its darkness; You filled our human nature with the

light of your resurrection, bestowing on the world a new life and a new light brighter than the sun. Merciful as You are, You restored our human nature to its former beauty and to that glorious light from which we had been exiled.

Silence

You filled our human nature with the light of your resurrection

Psalm 33:1-8

1. Rejoice in the Lord, you righteous;
   it is good for the just to sing praises.
2. Praise the Lord with the harp;
   play to him upon the psaltery and lyre.
3. Sing for him a new song;
   sound a fanfare with all your skill upon the trumpet.
4. For the word of the Lord is right,
   and all his works are sure.
5. He loves righteousness and justice;
   the loving-kindness of the Lord fills the whole earth.
6. By the word of the Lord were the heavens made,
   by the breath of his mouth all the heavenly hosts.
7. He gathers up the waters of the ocean as in a water skin
   and stores up the depths of the sea.
8. Let all the earth fear the Lord;
   let all who dwell in the world stand in awe of him.

Rejoice in the Lord!

O Christ,
enlighten my soul and my heart with your never setting light;
guide me to the reverence of you, O Lord,
for your commandments are the light of my eyes.

YEAR 2

Gertrude the Great
Ardent Fire

O ardent fire of my God, which contains, produces, and imprints those living ardours which attract the humid waters of my soul, and dry up the torrents of earthly delights, and afterwards soften my hard self-opinionatedness, which time has hardened so exceedingly! O consuming fire, which even amid ardent flames imparts sweetness and peace to the soul! In Thee, and in none other, do we receive this grace of being reformed to the image and likeness in which we were created. O burning furnace, in which we enjoy the true vision of peace, which tries and purifies the gold of the elect, and leads the soul to seek eagerly for its highest good, even Thyself, in Thy eternal truth.

Silence

O ardent fire of my God

WEEKDAY READINGS

MONDAY: Exodus 13:17-22
Neither the pillar of cloud by day nor the pillar of fire by night left its place in front of the people

TUESDAY: Daniel 3:16-30
We will not serve your gods or worship the image of gold

WEDNESDAY: John 1:1-9
The light shines in the darkness, but the darkness has not understood it

THURSDAY: John 8:12-20
Whoever follows me will never walk in darkness

FRIDAY: 1 John 1:5-10
God is light

SATURDAY

Julian of Norwich
Christ our Light

Our faith is a light, coming to us naturally from him who is our everlasting Day, our Father, and our God. By this light Christ, our Mother, and the Holy Spirit, our good Lord, lead us through these passing years. The light is measured to our individual needs as we face our night. Because of the light we live: because of the night we suffer and grieve. Through this grief we can earn reward and thanks from God! With the help of mercy and grace, we know and trust our light quite deliberately, and with it we go forward intelligently and firmly. When we are done with grief our eyes will be suddenly enlightened, and in the shining brightness of the light we shall see perfectly. For our light is none other than our God and Maker, and the Holy Spirit, in our Saviour, Christ Jesus.

So did I see and understand that faith is our light in darkness, and our light is God, the everlasting Day.

Silence

Faith is our light in darkness

YEAR 3

SUNDAY

Catherine of Siena
The Fire of Love

Your light, dear God, surpasses all other light, because all light comes from you. Your fire surpasses all fire, because your fire burns without destroying. The flames of your fire reach into the soul, consuming the sin and selfishness that lie there. But far from damaging the soul, your fire sets it ablaze with love.

What moved you to enlighten me with your truth? The fire of your love was the reason. You loved me so much that you could not bear to see me confused and perplexed. Can I ever repay the burning love which you have given me? No, because I have nothing of my own to give. Yet you assure me that the love which you put into my soul is repayment enough. You desire only the joy of seeing me receiving your gift. What more perfect Father could their be!

Silence

Your fire sets the soul ablaze with its love

MONDAY: Numbers 9:15-23
They obeyed the Lord's order

TUESDAY: Wisdom of Solomon 16:15-23 (Apocrypha)
To escape from your hand is impossible *(NRSV)*

WEDNESDAY: Revelation 22:1-5
There will be no more night

THURSDAY: John 12:35-40
Put your trust in the light

FRIDAY: Ephesians 5:8-14
For you were once darkness, but now you are light in the Lord

SATURDAY

Bishop John of Naples
The Lord is my Light

The man who is enlightened neither stumbles nor strays from the path; and he knows how to stay the course. He who sees his native land from afar bears adversity; he is not cast down by the things of this world, but is strengthened in God; he humbles his heart and endures, and by his humility has patience. The true light which 'enlightens every man who comes into this world' gives himself to those who fear him, pours light on whom he wills, where he wills, reveals himself to whom the Son wills.

He who formerly sat in darkness and in the shadow of death, in the darkness of evil and the shadow of sin, is appalled when the light rises. Then he looks closely at himself; he comes to his senses, and overcome with shame, he repents and says: 'The Lord is my light and my salvation: whom shall I fear?' My brothers, this is indeed a great salvation. This salvations fears no sickness, dreads no fatigue, sees no pain. Therefore we must cry out, not only with our lips, but also with our hearts, with complete and perfect faith: 'The Lord is my light and my salvation: whom then shall I fear?' If it is the Lord who enlightens, the Lord who saves, whom then shall I fear? Though the mists of temptation rise up, the Lord is my light.

Silence

The Lord is my light!

PRAYER OF PENITENCE

O star-like sun,
O guiding light,
O home of planets,
O fiery-maned and marvellous one,
O fertile, undulating, fiery sea,
Forgive

O fiery glow,
O fiery flame of Judgement,
Forgive

O holy story-teller, holy scholar,
O full of holy grace, of holy strength,
O overflowing, loving, silent one,
O generous and thunderous giver of gifts,
Forgive

O rock-like warrior of a hundred hosts,
O fair crowned one, victorious, skilled in battle,
Forgive

THE PRAYERS

O Thou who camest from above
The pure celestial fire to impart,
Kindle a flame of sacred love
On the mean altar of my heart!

There let it for thy glory burn
With inextinguishable blaze,
And trembling to its source return,
In humble prayer and fervent praise.

Jesus, confirm my heart's desire
To work, and speak, and think for thee;
Still let me guard the holy fire
And stir up thy gift in me–

Ready for all thy perfect will,
My acts of faith and love repeat,
Till death thy endless mercies seal,
And make the sacrifice complete.

MEDITATION

Aidan Kavanagh
The Shape of Baptism

Christians are not born but made. They do not just wonder in off the streets either. They are honed down by the teaching and discipline of the catechumenate until their metal is tough, resilient, sharp and glowing. The "enlightenment" of baptism is not a flickering flame but a burst of God's glory in those whose capacities to receive it have been expanded to their utmost.

Heather Murray Elkins
Diamonds Are Forever

I know the socks were new
but the dress was borrowed, just like the pool.
Everybody else got sprinkled,
but we had baptist blood on our mother's side.
So, there we stood, big girls in borrowed white like brides.
I kept my eyes on the buttons,
rhinestones like a river   .
running down banks of new breasts.
Sister went first;
water won't wash the birth order out.
I counted the times she drowned.
One for the Father. One for the Son.
    One for the Holy Ghost.
He was a Trinity man.
Twice he had to call my name across the water.
I counted my diamonds, descended the steps.
One. Two. Three. Four for the four-square gospel.
What I dreaded didn't happen.
My skirt bloomed like a rose, then folded,
weighted with old mother wisdom
and washers sewn in the hem.

Tall for a new-turned woman,
the old preacher measured just shoulder high.
Even tough as Moses,
It would take a miracle
to part the sea three times with me.

His hankie and hand covered my breath.
I clung to a button for life.
I was down to be buried in diamond-bright water,
baptized like Jesus in Jordan's deep grave.
The hard gospel sparkle strengthened its grip:
"Don't be afraid. God will lift too."

It's true.
I still have the button; came off in my hand.
I've never heard it explained,
the "how" of this part of the creed:
    "resurrection of the body."
But I need to believe;
the older I get, the younger I dream.
Leaning to swim in born-again skin,
we'll wear nothing but diamonds, forever.

for Inez Irons

EASTER V:

RISEN!
ASCENDED!
GLORIFIED!

SUNDAY

Rejoice! The Lord is King!
Your Lord and King adore;
Mortals, give thanks and sing,
And triumph evermore:
Lift up your heart, lift up your voice;
Rejoice, again I say, rejoice.

Karl Rahner
Prayer for Hope

You have loved the world so much that men take offence at your love and call the affirmation of the incarnation of your Son folly and madness. But we believe in the incomprehensibility, the overwhelming audacity of your love. And because we believe, we can exult in blessed hope: Christ in us is the hope of glory. For if you give us your Son, what can there be you have held back, what can there be which you have refused us? If we possess your son to whom you have given everything, your own substance, what could still be lacking to us? And he is truly ours. For he is the Son of Mary, who is our sister in Adam, he is a child of Adam's family, of the same race as we are, one in substance ad origin with man. And if we human beings in your plans and according to your will as creator are all to form a great community of descent and destiny, and if your Son is to belong to this one great community, then we, precisely we poor children of Eve, share the race and the lot of your own Son. We are brothers of the only-begotten, the brethren of your Son, co-heirs of his glory. We share in his grace, in his Spirit, in his life, in his destiny through the Cross and glorification, in his eternal glory. It is no longer *we* who live our life but Christ our brother lives his life in us and through us.

Silence

It is no longer *we* who live our life but Christ our brother lives his life in us and through us

Psalm 21:1-7

1. The king rejoices in your strength, O Lord;
    how greatly he exults in your victory!
2. You have given him his heart's desire;
    you have not denied him the request of his lips.
3. For you meet him with blessings of prosperity,
    and set a crown of fine gold upon his head.
4. He asked for life and you gave it to him;
    length of days, for ever and ever.
5. His honour is great, because of your victory;
    splendour and majesty have you bestowed upon him.
6. For you will give him everlasting felicity
    and will make him glad with the joy of your presence.
7. For the king puts his trust in the Lord;
    because of the loving-kindness of the Most High,
    he will not fall.

You have given him his heart's desire

God of majesty,
you led the Messiah through suffering into risen life,
and took him up into the glory of heaven:
clothe us with the power promised from on high,
and send us forth to the ends of the earth
as heralds of repentance and witnesses of Jesus Christ,
the firstborn from the dead,
who lives with you now and always
in the unity of the Holy Spirit, God for ever and ever. Amen.

MONDAY

Jesus, the Saviour, reigns,
The God of truth and love;
When he had purged our stains,
He took his seat above:
Lift up your heart, lift up your voice;
Rejoice, again I say, rejoice.

Daniel 7:9-10, 13-14

"As I looked, thrones were set in place, and the Ancient of Days took his seat. His clothing was as white as snow; the hair of his head was white like wool. His throne was flaming with fire, and its wheels were all ablaze. A river of fire was flowing, coming out from before him. Thousands upon thousands attended him; ten thousand times ten thousand stood before him. The court was seated, and the books were opened.

"In my vision at night I looked, and there before me was one like a son of man, coming with the clouds of heaven. He approached the Ancient of Days and was led into his presence. He was given authority, glory and sovereign power; all peoples, nations and men of every language worshipped him. His dominion is an everlasting dominion that will not pass away, and his kingdom is one that will never be destroyed."

Silence

He was given authority, glory and sovereign power

Psalm 24

1. The earth is the Lord's and all that is in it,
   the world and all who dwell therein.
2. For it is he who founded it upon the seas
   and made it firm upon the rivers of the deep.
3. 'Who can ascend the hill of the Lord?
   And who can stand in his holy place?'
4. 'Those who have clean hands and a pure heart,
   who have not pledged themselves to a falsehood,
   not sworn by what is a fraud.

5. 'They shall receive a blessing from the Lord
and a just reward from the God of their salvation.'
6. Such is the generation of those who seek him,
of those who seek your face, O God of Jacob.
7. Lift up your heads, O gates;
lift them high, O everlasting doors;
and the King of glory shall come in.
8. 'Who is the king of glory?'
'The Lord, strong and mighty,
the Lord, mighty in battle.'
9. Lift up your heads, O gates;
lift them high, O everlasting doors
and the King of glory shall come in.
10. 'Who is he, this King of glory:'
'The Lord of hosts,
he is the King of glory.'

Praise to the Lord of hosts, the King of glory!

Lord Jesus,
Alpha and Omega,
radiant Star of Morning,
you are raised to the glory of the Father.
But we know that you will come.
Yes. Come, Lord Jesus,
You who are the Living One,
for ever and ever. Amen.

TUESDAY

His kingdom cannot fail;
He rules o'er earth and heaven;
The keys of death and hell
Are to our Jesus given:
Lift up your heart, lift up your voice;
Rejoice, again I say, rejoice.

2 Samuel 23:1-5

These are the last words of David: "The oracle of David son of Jesse, the oracle of the man exalted by the Most High, the man anointed by the God of Jacob, Israel's singer of songs:

"The Spirit of the LORD spoke through me; his word was on my tongue. The God of Israel spoke, the Rock of Israel said to me: 'When one rules over men in righteousness, when he rules in the fear of God, he is like the light of morning at sunrise on a cloudless morning, like the brightness after rain that brings the grass from the earth.'

"Is not my house right with God? Has he not made with me an everlasting covenant, arranged and secured in every part? Will he not bring to fruition my salvation and grant me my every desire?

Silence

He is like the light of morning at sunrise

Psalm 97

1. The Lord is king; let the earth rejoice;
    let the multitude of the aisles be glad.
2. Clouds and darkness are around him,
    righteousness and justice
    are the foundations of his throne.
3. A fire goes up before him
    and burns up his enemies on every side.
4. His lightnings light up the world;
    the earth sees it and is afraid.
5. The mountains melt like wax at the presence of the Lord,
    at the presence of the Lord of the whole earth.
6. The heavens declare his righteousness,
    and all the peoples see his glory.
7. Confounded be all who worship carved images
    and delight in false gods!
    Bow down before him, all you gods.

8. Zion hears and is glad and the cities of Judah rejoice,
   because of your judgements, O Lord.
9. For you are the Lord: most high over all the earth;
   you are exalted far above all gods.
10. The Lord loves those who hate evil;
    he preserves the lives of his saints
and delivers them from the hand of the wicked.
11. Light has sprung up for the righteous,
and joyful gladness for those who are true-hearted.
12. Rejoice in the Lord, you righteous,
    and give thanks to his holy name.

Let us rejoice in the Lord!

Christ our lover
to whom we try to cling:
as you have reached into our depths
and draw us to love you,
so make us open, freely to let you go;
that you may return in unexpected power
to change the world through us,
in your name, Amen.

WEDNESDAY

He sits at God's right hand
Till all his foes submit,
And bow to his command,
And fall beneath his feet:
Lift up your heart, lift up your voice;
Rejoice, again I say, rejoice.

John 16:17-24

Some of his disciples said to one another, "What does he mean by saying, 'In a little while you will see me no more, and then after a little while you will see me,' and' Because I am going to the

Father'?" They kept asking, "What does he mean by 'a little while'? We don't understand what he is saying." Jesus saw that they wanted to ask him about this, so he said to them, "Are you asking one another what I meant when I said, 'In a little while you will see me no more, and then after a little while you will see me'? I tell you the truth, you will weep and mourn while the world rejoices. You will grieve, but your grief will turn to joy. A woman giving birth to a child has pain because her time has come; but when her baby is born she forgets the anguish because of her joy that a child is born into the world. So with you: Now is your time of grief, but I will see you again and you will rejoice, and no-one will take away your joy. In that day you will no longer ask me anything. I tell you the truth, my Father will give you whatever you ask in my name. Until now you have not asked for anything in my name. Ask and you will receive, and your joy will be complete.

Silence

You will grieve, but your grief will turn to joy

Psalm 67

1. May God be merciful to us and bless us,
   show us the light of his countenance
      and come to us.
   2. Let your ways be known upon earth,
      your saving health among all nations.
      3. Let the peoples praise you, O God;
         let all the peoples praise you.
4. Let the nations be glad and sing for joy,
   for your judge the peoples with equity
      and guide all the nations upon earth.
      5. Let the peoples praise you, O God;
         let all the peoples praise you.

6. The earth has brought forth her increase;
   may God, our own God,
   give us his blessing.
7. May God give us his blessing,
and may all the ends of the earth stand in awe of him.

May God be merciful to us and bless us

God of Light,
you sent your Son
into the darkness of our night,
and raised him to your glory;
not to abandon us to grief,
but to teach us to prepare in joy for his return.
We pray for all who have no hope,
that they may find it in the light of your Spirit,
according to the promise of Jesus, our Lord.
Amen.

ASCENSION DAY

Hail the day that sees him rise, Alleluia!
To his throne above the skies; Alleluia!
Christ, the Lamb for sinners given, Alleluia!
Enters now the highest heaven, Alleluia!

Acts 1:1-11

In my former book, Theophilus, I wrote about all that Jesus began to do and to teach until the day he was taken up to heaven, after giving instructions through the Holy Spirit to the apostles he had chosen. After his suffering, he showed himself to them and gave many convincing proofs that he was alive. He appeared to them over a period of forty days and spoke about the kingdom of God. On one occasion, while he was eating with them, he gave them this command: "Do not leave Jerusalem, but wait for the gift my Father promised, which you have heard me speak about. For John baptised with water, but in a few days you will be baptised with the Holy

Spirit." So when they met together, they asked him, "Lord, are you at this time going to restore the kingdom to Israel?" He said to them: "It is not for you to know the times or dates the Father has set by his own authority. But you will receive power when the Holy Spirit comes on you; and you will be my witnesses in Jerusalem, and in all Judea and Samaria, and to the ends of the earth." After he said this, he was taken up before their very eyes, and a cloud hid him from their sight. They were looking intently up into the sky as he was going, when suddenly two men dressed in white stood beside them. "You Galileans," they said, "why do you stand here looking into the sky? This same Jesus, who has been taken from you into heaven, will come back in the same way you have seen him go into heaven."

Silence

Why do you stand looking into the sky?

Psalm 47

1. Clap your hands, all you peoples;
   shout to God with a cry of joy.
2. For the Lord Most High is to be feared;
   he is the great king over all the earth.
3. He subdues the peoples under us,
   and the nations under our feet.
4. He chooses our inheritance for us,
   the pride of Jacob whom he loves.
5. God has gone up with a shout,
   the Lord with the sound of the ram's-horn.
6. Sing praises to God, sing praises;
   sing praises to our king, sing praises.
7. For God is king of all the earth;
   sing praises with all your skill.
8. God reigns over the nations;
   God sits upon his holy throne.
9. The nobles of the peoples have gathered together
   with the people of the God of Abraham.

10. The rulers of the earth belong to God,
   and he is highly exalted.

God has gone up with a shout!

O God,
you withdraw from our sight
that you may be known by our love:
help us to enter the cloud
where you are hidden,
and surrender all our certainty
to the darkness of faith in Jesus Christ, Amen.

FRIDAY

He has raised our human nature
On the clouds to God's right hand;
There we sit in heavenly places,
There with him in glory stand:
Jesus reigns, adored by angels;
Man with God is on the throne;
Mighty Lord, in thine Ascension
We by faith behold our own.

Ephesians 4:1-13
As a prisoner for the Lord, then, I urge you to live a life worthy of the calling you have received. Be completely humble and gentle; be patient, bearing with one another in love. Make every effort to keep the unity of the Spirit through the bond of peace. There is one body and one Spirit—just as you were called to one hope when you were called—one Lord, one faith, one baptism; one God and Father of all, who is over all and through all and in all. But to each one of us grace has been given as Christ apportioned it. This is why it says: "When he ascended on high, he led captives in his train and gave gifts to people." (What does "he ascended" mean except that he also

descended to the lower, earthly regions ? He who descended is the very one who ascended higher than all the heavens, in order to fill the whole universe.) It was he who gave some to be apostles, some to be prophets, some to be evangelists, and some to be pastors and teachers, to prepare God's people for works of service, so that the body of Christ may be built up until we all reach unity in the faith and in the knowledge of the Son of God and become mature, attaining to the whole measure of the fullness of Christ.

Silence

He who descended is the very one who ascended higher than all the heavens

Psalm 96:1-8

1. Sing to the Lord a new song;
   sing to the Lord, all the whole earth.
2. Sing to the Lord and bless his name;
proclaim the good news of his salvation from day to day.
3. Declare his glory among the nations
   and his wonders among all peoples.
4. For great is the Lord and greatly to be praised;
   he is more to be feared than all gods.
5. As for all the gods of the nations, they are but idols;
   but it is the Lord who made the heavens.
6. O the majesty and magnificence of his presence!
   O the power and splendour of his sanctuary!
7. Ascribe to the Lord, you families of the peoples;
   ascribe to the Lord honour and power.
8. Ascribe to the Lord the honour due to his name;
   bring offerings and come into his courts.

Sing to the Lord and bless his name

Risen Christ, glorious you now ascend into heaven,
there to take your seat and be acclaimed by angels.
In vain we seek to imagine the heights to which you aspire.

Higher than high, further than our most perceptive thoughts,
closer to God than our best imagining,
you reign, celestial, and supreme.
Yet here on earth, your footprints are still seen,
and your words are still warm.
Hallowed be your name in heaven
and followed be your name on earth.

SATURDAY

See him who is gone before us
Heavenly mansions to prepare,
See him who is ever pleading
For us with prevailing prayer,
See him who with sound of trumpet
And with his angelic train,
Summoning the world to judgement,
On the clouds will come again.

St. Augustine
The Ascension

Christ is now raised above the heavens; but he still experiences on earth whatever sufferings we his members feel. He showed that this is true when he called out from heaven: 'Saul, Saul, why do you persecute me?' And: 'I was thirsty and you gave me drink.'

Why then do we not exert ourselves on earth so as to be happy with him already in heaven through the faith, hope and charity which unite us with him? Christ, while in heaven is also with us; and we, while on earth, are also with him. He is with us in his godhead and his power and his love; and we, though we cannot be with him in godhead as he is with us, can be with him in our love, our love for him.

He did not leave heaven when he came down to us from heaven; he did not leave us when he ascended to heaven again. His own words show that he was heaven while he was here: 'No one has ascended into heaven but he descended from heaven, the Son of man who is in heaven.'

He said this because of the unity between us and himself, for he is our head and we are his body. The words 'no one but he' are true, since we are Christ, in the sense that he is the Son of man because of us, and we are the children of God because of him.

Silence

Christ, while in heaven is also with us; and we, while on earth, are also with him

Psalm 96:9-13

9. Worship the Lord in the beauty of holiness;
    let the whole earth tremble before him.
10. Tell it out among the nations: 'The Lord is king!
he has made the world so firm that it cannot be moved;
    he will judge the peoples with equity.'
11. Let the heavens rejoice and let the earth be glad;
    let the sea thunder and all that is in it;
    let the field be joyful and all that is therein.
12. Then shall all the trees of the wood shout for joy
    before the Lord when he comes,
    when he comes to judge the earth.
13. He will judge the world with righteousness
    and the peoples with his truth.

Let the heavens rejoice and let the earth be glad

God of glory,
you have put all things into the hands of your Son Jesus,
and have made him pass from this world to you.
Keep our faith unshaken,
for he has promised to be with us all our days,
and to receive us into glory
where he lives and reigns for ever and ever. Amen.

SUNDAY

John Donne
Ascension

Salute the last and everlasting day,
Joy at the uprising of this Sun, and Son,
Ye whose just tears, or tribulation
Have purely washed, or burnt your drossie clay;
Behold the Highest, parting hence away,
Lightens the dark clouds, which he treads upon,
Nor doth he by ascending, show alone,
But first he, and he first enters the way.
O strong Ram, which hast batter'd heaven for me,
Mild Lamb, which with thy blood, hast mark'd the path;
Bright Torch, which shinest, that I the way may see
Oh, with thy own blood quench thy own just wrath,
And if thy holy Spirit, my Muse did raise,
Deign at my hands this crown of prayer and praise.

Silence

Salute the last and everlasting day

WEEKDAY READINGS

MONDAY: Ezekiel 43:1-5
And I saw the glory of the God of Israel

TUESDAY: Jeremiah 10:1-10
No-one is like you, O Lord

WEDNESDAY: John 16:25-37
Take heart! I have overcome the world

THURSDAY: as for Year 1

FRIDAY: Ephesians 1:15-end
May the eyes of our heart be enlightened that we may know the hope to which God has called us

Byzantine Daily Worship
Of the Ascension

The Lord ascended into heaven so that He could send the Comforter into this world. The heavens prepared his throne, and the angels marvelled at the sight of a human being more exalted and more glorious than themselves. Today the Father receives again into his bosom the One who was in Him from all eternity, and the Holy Spirit gives command to all the angels: "lift up your gates, O you Princes." – O you nations on earth, clap your hands, for Christ has gone up to the place where He has been from all eternity."

O Christ, splendour and glory of the Father, when we behold your ascension on the Holy Mountain, we sing a hymn of praise to the beauty of your countenance: we bow down to your passion, venerate your resurrection and glorify your noble ascension. Have mercy on us!

O Lord, live-giving Christ, when the apostles saw You ascending upon the clouds, a great sadness filled them: they shed burning tears and exclaimed: "O Master, do not leave us as orphans: we are your servants whom You loved so tenderly. Since you are most merciful, send down to us your All-Holy Spirit to enlighten our souls, according to your promise."

Silence

Send down to us your All-Holy Spirit to enlighten our souls!

YEAR 3

SUNDAY

John Brooks Wheelwright
From *Forty Days*

   – The fortieth day was spent.
He took a wild black iris between his toes
plucked it and let it fall.
(I thought even him reluctant to give up
friendships he had found sweetly
bedded in life's bitterness.)
– 'I go!
Going I precede you.
I come
and coming, judge you by those things

in which I proceed you.
Nor shall I come again till two be one:
till top be bottom; left be right;
all that which is without, within;
male with the female, each both male and female:
future forward, past and left behind.'
And speaking, grew less tangible
than to the three on the transfigured mount.
'I have shown you my glory.
As a bee leaves the flower
I go,
but cleave a seed – I am there;
split the rock, you shall find me,
and where the lonely ones
gather together, there I am.'

I saw him stretch his arms,
I thought him tired and yawning,
but with a shock of shame, I knew
the benediction in the attitude.
(I had not seen him die.)
We saw his wounds glow red,
the body fulminate
and Him of Fire,
mounting on subservient Seraphim
whirl, twist away.

Silence

**We stared not only in wonder, not with loneliness,
feeling him with us, permanent ...**

WEEKDAY READINGS

**MONDAY: Jeremiah 23:5-8
I will raise up to David a righteous Branch, a King who will reign wisely**

**TUESDAY: Acts 7:52-60
I see heaven open and the Son of Man standing at the right hand of God**

**WEDNESDAY: John 6:62-end
What if you see the Son of man ascend to where he was before?**

THURSDAY: as for Year 1

FRIDAY: Philippians 2:6-11
Therefore God exalted him to the highest place

SATURDAY

Hans Kung
The New Life

Assumption into ultimate reality. If we are not to talk in metaphors, raising (resurrection) and exaltation (taking up, ascension, glorification) must be seen as one identical, single happening. And indeed as a happening in connection with death in the impenetrable hiddeness of God. The Easter message in all its different variations means simply one thing: Jesus did not die into nothingness. In death from death he *died into* and was *taken up* by that *incomprehensible and comprehensive ultimate reality* which we designate by the name of God. When man reaches his escaton, the absolute final point in his life, what awaits him? Not nothing, as even believers in nirvana would say. But that All which for Jews, Christians and Muslims is God. Death is transition to God, is retreat into God's hiddeness, is assumption into his glory. Strictly speaking, only an atheist can say that death is the *end of everything*.

... Jesus died into God, he has reached God: he is assumed into that domain which surpasses all imagination, which no human eye has ever seen, eluding our grasp, comprehension, reflection or fantasy. The believer knows that what awaits him is not nothing, but his Father.

Silence

Jesus did not die into nothingness

PRAYER OF PENITENCE

Forgive us, Father,
when we are rooted to the earth,
unable to see beyond the present,
blind to the glory of your presence.
We become engrossed in what is happening now
and forget all that you have yet in store for us.
We are so concerned with what is immediate,
temporary, and short-lived that we leave ourselves no time

for the things that are eternal and full of your love.
Lift up our heads, Father,
that we may see Christ in all his glory
and all things in their true perspective.
We ask this with the forgiveness of our sins,
in your name. Amen.

THE PRAYERS

Father, we are in your Spirit and we hear your voice:
'I am the first and the last, who is, who was, and who is to come.'
Before the worlds were made, Christ was alive.
Through him you created everything in heaven and on earth,
the seen and the unseen, spiritual powers, lords and authorities,
the whole universe created through him and for him.
Lord of glory
we worship and adore you.

You sent him, the visible likeness
of the invisible God,
to reflect the brightness of your glory,
to sustain the universe with his word of power,
to achieve forgiveness for the sins of all.
Lord of glory
we worship and adore you.

And now he rules in heaven, mighty risen Lord,
his hair as white as snow, his eyes like fire,
his feet like polished brass, his hands full of stars,
his face bright as the noonday sun,
his voice like a roaring waterfall:
'I am the living one!
I was dead but now I am alive for ever and ever.'
Lord of glory
we worship and adore you.

MEDITATION

Matthew 28:20

And surely I am with you always, to the very end of the age.

Eric Milner-White
Ascension

O risen Saviour, bid me rise with you
and seek those things which are above;
not only seek, but set my whole heart upon them.

You are in heaven, ever raising lives to yourself;
O, by your grave, may mine be making that ascent
not in dream, but in truth,
now, tomorrow, always.

Daily in spirit, in your Holy Spirit,
let me behold you on the throne of God,
O King reigning in holiness,
O Conqueror of all evil,
O Majesty of Love,

very God and very Man,
of glory unimaginable and eternal,
in whom all hope is sure.

So, longing for your courts,
let me rise, ascend, seek;
finding in the nearer light of your countenance
higher and yet higher things
to love, to do, to attain.

EASTER VI:

PILGRIMAGE

SUNDAY

Guide me, O thou great Redeemer,
Pilgrim through this barren land;
I am weak, but thou art mighty;
Hold me with thy powerful hand:
Bread of heaven,
Feed me now and evermore.

Etty Hillesum
An Interrupted Life

I often walk with a spring in my step along the barbed wire and then time and again it soars straight from my heart – I can't help it, that's just the way it is, like some elementary force – the feeling that life is glorious and magnificent, and that one day we shall be building a whole new world. Against every new outrage and every fresh horror we shall put up one more piece of love and goodness, drawing strength from within ourselves. We may suffer, but we must not succumb.

In the past I, too, used to be one of those who occasionally exclaimed, 'I really am religious, you know'. Or something like that. But now I sometimes actually drop to my knees beside my bed, even on a cold winter night. And I listen in to myself, allow myself to be led, not by anything on the outside, but by what wells up from deep within. It's still no more than a beginning, it has already taken root.

For once you have begun to walk with God, you need only keep on walking with Him and all of life becomes one long stroll.

Silence

You need only keep on walking with Him

St. Augustine

O thou full of compassion,
I commit and commend myself unto thee,
in whom I am, and live, and know.

Be thou the goal of my pilgrimage,
and my rest by the way.

Let my soul take refuge
from the crowding turmoil of worldly thoughts
beneath the shadow of thy wings;
let my heart, this sea of restless waves,
find peace in thee, O God.

Thou bounteous giver of all good gifts,
give to him who is weary refreshing food,
gather our distracted thoughts and powers into harmony again;
and set the prisoner free.

See, he stands at the door and knocks;
be it opened to him, that he may enter with a free step,
and be quickened by thee.

For thou art the well-spring of life,
the light of eternal brightness,
wherein the just live who love thee.

Be it unto me according to thy word.

As we plan and make decisions
God be our way.
As we learn and ask questions
God be our truth
As we grow and as we change
God be our life.

MONDAY

Open now the crystal fountain
Whence the healing stream doth flow;
Let the fiery cloudy pillar
Lead me all my journey through:
Strong deliverer,
Be thou still my strength and shield.

Genesis 12:1-9

The LORD had said to Abram, "Leave your country, your people and
your father's household and go to the land I will show you. I will
make you into a great nation and I will bless you; I will make your
name great, and you will be a blessing. I will bless those who bless
you, and whoever curses you I will curse; and all peoples on earth
will be blessed through you." So Abram left, as the LORD had told
him; and Lot went with him. Abram was seventy-five years old when
he set out from Haran. He took his wife Sarai, his nephew Lot, all
the possessions they had accumulated and the people they had
acquired in Haran, and they set out for the land of Canaan, and they
arrived there. Abram travelled through the land as far as the site of
the great tree of Moreh at Shechem. At that time the Canaanites were
in the land. The LORD appeared to Abram and said, "To your
offspring I will give this land." So he built an altar there to the LORD,
who had appeared to him. From there he went on toward the hills
east of Bethel and pitched his tent, with Bethel on the west and Ai on
the east. There he built an altar to the LORD and called on the name
of the LORD. Then Abram set out and continued towards the Negev.

Silence

**Leave your country, your people and your father's household
and go to the land I will show you.**

Psalm 121

1. I lift up my eyes to the hills;
from where is my help to come?
2. My help comes from the Lord,
the maker of heaven and earth.
3. He will not let your foot be moved
and he who watches over you will not fall asleep.
4. Behold, he who keeps watch over Israel
shall neither slumber nor sleep;
5. The Lord himself watches over you;
the Lord is your shade at your right hand,
6. so that the sun shall not strike you by day,
nor the moon by night.
7. The Lord shall preserve you from all evil;
it is he who shall keep you safe.
8. The Lord shall watch over your going out
and your coming in,
from this time forth for evermore.

My help comes from the Lord

O Lord God,
who called your servants
to ventures of which we cannot see the ending,
by paths as yet untrodden, through perils unknown:
Give us faith to go out with good courage,
not knowing where we are going,
but only that your hand is leading us,
and your love supporting us;
to the glory of your name. Amen

TUESDAY

When I tread the verge of Jordan,
Bid my anxious fears subside;
Death of death, and hell's destruction,
Land me safe on Canaan's side:
Songs and praises
I will ever give to thee.

Psalm 84

How lovely is your dwelling place, O LORD Almighty! My soul yearns, even faints, for the courts of the LORD; my heart and my flesh cry out for the living God. Even the sparrow has found a home, and the swallow a nest for herself, where she may have her young— a place near your altar, O LORD Almighty, my King and my God. Blessed are those who dwell in your house; they are ever praising you. Blessed are those whose strength is in you, who have set their hearts on pilgrimage. As they pass through the Valley of Baca, they make it a place of springs; the autumn rains also cover it with pools. They go from strength to strength, till each appears before God in Zion. Hear my prayer, O LORD God Almighty; listen to me, O God of Jacob. Look upon our shield, O God; look with favour on your anointed one. Better is one day in your courts than a thousand elsewhere; I would rather be a doorkeeper in the house of my God than dwell in the tents of the wicked. For the LORD God is a sun and shield; the LORD bestows favour and honour; no good thing does he withhold from those whose walk is blameless. O LORD Almighty, blessed are those who trust in you.

Silence

Blessed are those whose strength is in you, who have set their hearts on pilgrimage

Song: Deuteronomy 32:10-14

10. In a desert land he found him,
in a barren and howling waste.
He shielded him and cared for him;
he guarded him as the apple of his eye,

11. like an eagle that stirs up its nest and hovers over its young,
that spreads its wings to catch them
and carries them on its pinions.

12. The LORD alone led him;
no foreign god was with him.

13. He made him ride on the heights of the land
and fed him with the fruit of the fields.
He nourished him with honey from the rock,
and with oil from the flinty crag,

14. with curds and milk from herd and flock
and with fattened lambs and goats,
with choice rams of Bashan and the finest kernels of wheat.
You drank the foaming blood of the grape.

The Lord will guard us as the apple of his eye

*Heavenly Father, protector of all who trust in you,
you led your people through the desert
and brought them to a land of plenty.
Guide me as I begin my journey today.
Fill me with your spirit of love.
Preserve me from all harm
and bring me safely to my destination.
I ask this through Christ our Lord. Amen.*

WEDNESDAY

Through the night of doubt and sorrow
Onward goes the pilgrim band,
Singing songs of expectation,
Marching to the Promised Land,
Clear before us through the darkness
Gleams and burns the guiding light;
Brother clasps the hand of brother,
Stepping fearless through the night.

Nehemiah 1:1-9

The words of Nehemiah son of Hacaliah: In the month of Kislev in the twentieth year, while I was in the citadel of Susa, Hanani, one of my brothers, came from Judah with some other men, and I questioned them about the Jewish remnant that survived the exile, and also about Jerusalem. They said to me, "Those who survived the exile and are back in the province are in great trouble and disgrace. The wall of Jerusalem is broken down, and its gates have been burned with fire." When I heard these things, I sat down and wept. For some days I mourned and fasted and prayed before the God of heaven. Then I said: "O LORD, God of heaven, the great and awesome God, who keeps his covenant of love with those who love him and obey his commands, let your ear be attentive and your eyes open to hear the prayer your servant is praying before you day and night for your servants, the people of Israel. I confess the sins we Israelites, including myself and my father's house, have committed against you. We have acted very wickedly toward you. We have not obeyed the commands, decrees and laws you gave your servant Moses. "Remember the instruction you gave your servant Moses, saying, 'If you are unfaithful, I will scatter you among the nations, but if you return to me and obey my commands, then even if your exiled people are at the farthest horizon, I will gather them from there and bring them to the place I have chosen as a dwelling for my Name.'"

I will gather them and bring them to the place I have chosen

Psalm 126

1. When the Lord restored the fortunes of Zion,
   then were we like those who dream.
2. Then was our mouth filled with laughter,
   and our tongue with shouts of joy.
3. Then they said among the nations,
   'The Lord has done great things for them.'
4. The Lord has done great things for us,
   and we are glad indeed.
5. Restore our fortunes, O Lord,
   like the watercourses of the Negev.
6. Those who sow with tears
   will reap with songs of joy.
7. Those who go out weeping, carrying the seed,
   will come again with joy, shouldering their sheaves.

The Lord has done great things for us

If we have forgotten those who bear the marks
of exile, desert, home, upon their hands and feet
and suffer them to go on bleeding
if we have dismembered the body of God
Have mercy on us, God who brings us down to earth,
ground us in justice, root us in right relationship,
give flesh to our words and our worship
with the breath and peace of your Spirit
until joy and our only holy, common ground.
                                         Amen

THURSDAY

One the light of God's own presence
O'er his ransomed people shed,
Chasing far the gloom and terror,

> *Brightening all the path we tread:*
> *One the object of our journey,*
> *One the faith which never tires,*
> *One the earnest looking forward,*
> *One the hope our God inspires.*

Deuteronomy 30:11-20

Now what I am commanding you today is not too difficult for you or beyond your reach. It is not up in heaven, so that you have to ask, "Who will ascend into heaven to get it and proclaim it to us so we may obey it?" Nor is it beyond the sea, so that you have to ask, "Who will cross the sea to get it and proclaim it to us so we may obey it?" No, the word is very near you; it is in your mouth and in your heart so you may obey it. See, I set before you today life and prosperity, death and destruction. For I command you today to love the LORD your God, to walk in his ways, and to keep his commands, decrees and laws; then you will live and increase, and the LORD your God will bless you in the land you are entering to possess. But if your heart turns away and you are not obedient, and if you are drawn away to bow down to other gods and worship them, I declare to you this day that you will certainly be destroyed. You will not live long in the land you are crossing the Jordan to enter and possess. This day I call heaven and earth as witnesses against you that I have set before you life and death, blessings and curses. Now choose life, so that you and your children may live and that you may love the LORD your God, listen to his voice, and hold fast to him. For the LORD is your life, and he will give you many years in the land he swore to give to your fathers, Abraham, Isaac and Jacob.

Silence

Now choose life

Psalm 108:1-8

1. My heart is firmly fixed, O God, my heart is fixed;
    I will sing and make melody.

2. Wake up, my spirit; awake, lute and harp;
I myself will waken the dawn.
3. I will confess you among the peoples, O Lord;
I will sing praises to you among the nations.
4. For your loving-kindness is greater than the heavens,
and your faithfulness reaches to the clouds.
5. Exalt yourself above the heavens, O God,
and your glory over all the earth.
6. So that those who are dear to you may be delivered,
save with your right hand and answer me.
7. God spoke from his holy place and said,
'I will exult and parcel out Shechem;
I will divide the valley of Succoth.
8. Gilead is mine and Manasseh is mine;
Ephraim is my helmet and Judah my sceptre.'

My heart is firmly fixed, O God, my heart is fixed

Cleanse the eye of our perception,
O God,
and purify our hearts,
that we may will one thing,
that your way indeed be followed through and through
and beyond the complexities
we cannot escape.

FRIDAY

One the strain that lips of thousands
Lift as from the heart of one:
One the conflict, one the peril,
One the march in God begun:
One the gladness of rejoicing
On the far eternal shore,
Where the one almighty Father
Reigns in love for evermore.

John 14:1-9

"Do not let your hearts be troubled. Trust in God; trust also in me. In my Father's house are many rooms; if it were not so, I would have told you. I am going there to prepare a place for you. And if I go and prepare a place for you, I will come back and take you to be with me that you also may be where I am. You know the way to the place where I am going." Thomas said to him, "Lord, we don't know where you are going, so how can we know the way?" Jesus answered, "I am the way and the truth and the life. No-one comes to the Father except through me. If you really knew me, you would know my Father as well. From now on, you do know him and have seen him." Philip said, "Lord, show us the Father and that will be enough for us." Jesus answered: "Don't you know me, Philip, even after I have been among you such a long time? Anyone who has seen me has seen the Father. How can you say, 'Show us the Father'?"

Silence

You know the way to the place where I am going

Psalm 37:24-33

24. Our steps are directed by the Lord;
   he strengthens those in whose way he delights.
25. If they stumble, they shall not fall headlong,
   for the Lord holds them by the hand.
26. I have been young and now I am old,
   but never have I seen the righteous forsaken,
   or their children begging bread.
27. The righteous are always generous in their lending,
   and their children shall be a blessing.
28. Turn from evil and do good,
   and dwell in the land for ever.
29. For the Lord loves justice;
   he does not forsake his faithful ones.
30. They shall be kept safe for ever,
   but the offspring of the wicked shall be destroyed.

31. The righteous shall possess the land
and dwell in it for ever.
32. The mouth of the righteous utters wisdom,
and their tongue speaks what is right.
33. The law of their God is in their heart,
and their footsteps shall not falter.

Our steps are directed by the Lord

We give you thanks, God our Father,
for Jesus Christ, your Son;
He has gone to prepare a place for us in your house,
and we wait for him to come and take us to be with him.
Do not forget any of those you have given him,
but lead all to the joy of your dwelling place,
where they will bless you
for ever and ever. Amen

SATURDAY

Onward, therefore, pilgrim brothers,
Onward with the Cross our aid;
Bear its shame, and fight its battle,
Till we rest beneath its shade.
Soon shall come the great awakening,
Soon the rending of the tomb;
Then the scattering of all shadows,
And the end of toil and gloom.

John Bunyan
Pilgrim's Progress

Then they addressed themselves to the water, and entering, Christian
began to sink; and, crying out to his good friend Hopeful, he said, 'I
sink in deep waters; the billows go over my head; all the waves go
over me.'

... Hopeful, therefore, here had much ado to keep his brother's head above water; yea, sometimes he would be quite gone down, and then, ere a while, he would rise up again half dead. Hopeful also would endeavour to comfort him, saying Brother, I see the gate, and men standing by to receive us; but Christian would answer, 'Tis you, 'tis you they wait for; you have been hopeful ever since I knew you. And so have you said he to Christian. Ah, brother, said he, surely if I were right he would now arise to help me: but for my sins he hath brought me into his snare, and hath left me. Then said Hopeful, These troubles and distresses that you go through are no sign that God hath forsaken you; but are sent to try you, whether you will call to mind that which heretofore you have received of his goodness, and live upon him in your distresses.

Then I saw in my dream that Christian was in a muse a while, but soon brake out with a loud voice, Oh, I see him again! And he tells me. 'When thou passest through the waters, I will be with thee.' Then they both took courage, and the enemy was after that as still as stone until they were gone over.

Silence

When you pass through the waters I will be with you

Psalm 139:1-6

1. Lord, you have searched me out and know me;
   you know my sitting down and my rising up;
       you discern my thoughts from afar.
2. You trace my journeys and my resting-places
       and are acquainted with all my ways.
3. Indeed, there is not a word on my lips,
       but you, O Lord, know it altogether.
4. You press upon me behind and before
       and lay your hand upon me.
5. Such knowledge is too wonderful for me;
       it is so high that I cannot attain to it.
6. Where can I go to flee from your Spirit?
       where can I flee from your presence?

Lord, you have searched me out

O Father, give my spirit power to climb
To the fountain of all light, and be purified.
Break through the mists of earth, the weight of clay,
Shine forth in splendour, you who are calm weather,
And quiet resting-place for faithful souls.
You carry us, and you go before;
You are the journey, and the journey's end

YEAR 2

SUNDAY

K. George
The Silent Roots

In the history of the Church, radical Christians burning with prophetic zeal for the kingdom of God have often deplored the failure of institutional Christianity to recall that Jesus lived the life of a wanderer and a pilgrim. Born in a manger, rejected by the social structures of security and comfort, Jesus' ministry pervaded throughout by the sense of homelessness ... He gathered his disciples, not into a secure and stable home, but to share in his work of an itinerant preacher of the kingdom to come and a wandering healer of all kinds of sickness ...

The self-emptying of God incarnate in the incarnate Christ was God's act of self-exile, the undertaking of a new pilgrimage to the heart of created reality. Christ the new Adam, the stranger to the scheme of this world, became co-traveller with Adam, the outcast wandering on the rugged earth and with Cain the murderer, the condemned and solitary wonderer.

Silence

God's self-exile – a new pilgrimage

WEEKDAY READINGS

MONDAY: Genesis 28:10-22
I am with you and will watch over you wherever you go

TUESDAY: Exodus 19:1-8
I carried you on eagles' wings and brought you to myself

WEDNESDAY: Isaiah 49:8-13
He who has compassion on them will guide them

THURSDAY: Jeremiah 6:16-21
Ask where the good way is, and walk in it

FRIDAY: Philippians 3:12-21
I press on towards the goal

SATURDAY

St Augustine
The Rough Journey

If we long ardently to arrive at that great good, we need have no fear of the rough journey. He who has promised is faithful, and in promising he cannot deceive us. Let us say to him then in all honesty, 'Because of your word I kept my feet firmly in your paths; there was no faltering in my steps'. Why are you afraid of those paths through suffering and tribulation? He has trodden them himself. 'But after all, he was Christ!' you may say. Well, the apostles went that way too. And still you argue, 'But they were the apostles!' All right then, but answer me: did not many other men tread the same path after them? And did not women tread it too?

Have you come to it well on in years? Then you should not be afraid of losing your life, for you are close to death in any case. Or have you come as a youth? Many young people, people who had life and its promises before them have travelled along this way ... How can the track be so rough, when such crowds have worn it smooth with their feet?

Silence

Because of your word I kept my feet firmly in your paths

SUNDAY

Sir Walter Raleigh
The Passionate Man's Pilgrimage

Give me my scallop-shell of quiet,
My staff of faith to walk upon,
My scrip of joy, immortal diet,
My bottle of salvation,
My gown's glory, hope's true gage,
And thus I'll take my pilgrimage.

Blood must be my body's balmer,
No other balm will there be given,
While my soul like a white palmer
Travels to the land of heaven,
Over the silver mountains,
Where spring the nectar fountains;
And there I'll kiss,
The bowl of bliss,
And drink my eternal fill
On every milken hill.
My soul will be a-dry before,
But after it will ne'er thirst more.

And by that happy blissful way
More peaceful pilgrims I shall see,
That have shook off their gowns of clay
And go apparelled fresh like me.
I'll bring them first
To slake their thirst,
And then to taste those nectar suckets
At the clear wells
Where sweetness dwells,
Drawn up by saints in crystal buckets . . .

And this is my eternal plea
To him that made heaven, earth and sea:
Seeing my flesh must die so soon,
And want a head to dine next noon,
Just at the stroke when my veins start and spread,

Set on my soul an everlasting head.
Then I am ready, like a palmer fit,
To tread those blest paths which before I writ.

Silence

Give me my staff of faith to walk upon

WEEKDAY READINGS

MONDAY: Genesis 46:1-7; 28-30
Do not be afraid

TUESDAY: Exodus 33:1-6
Leave this place

WEDNESDAY: Amos 9:11-15
I will bring back my exiled people

THURSDAY: Proverbs 4:10-27
I will guide you in the way of wisdom and lead you along straight paths

FRIDAY: Hebrews 11:11-16
They were longing for a better country

SATURDAY

Basil Hume
To Be A Pilgrim

So there is meaning in our journey. We in search of God, and God in search of us. God, in Jesus Christ, spoke indeed of things I could not see or touch, and with words which dispelled the darkness of my mind and brought warmth to the coldness of my heart. I saw clearly that the Stranger who had become my friend was himself God who had become man. The Son of God had become the Son of man. My mind could hardly receive the truth, so great and so wondrous was it. In his presence I was overcome. I knelt and could but say: 'Depart from me for I am a sinful man'. What once did seem absurd to me now dawned upon my mind as real and true. I knew, but my senses had not told me. Other voices spoke, but they were speaking and commanding in ways that were strange and unknown. It was the voice of him who knows and loves, and came in search of us. It was a light that pierced the darkness of my mind and gave me strength to see.

We in search of God, and God in search of us

PRAYER OF PENITENCE

God of strangeness and desire
we bless you for enticing us
to the last place we wanted to be
the place where we can hide no longer
where we must face our emptiness
and see our false gods fall.
We bless you for the immeasurable relief
of self-exposure
for the miracle of survival
and for coming to us in unexpected guises
Blessed are you
God of strangeness and desire

But if we have turned in upon our emptiness
refused the risks you have required of us
idolised our self-sufficiency
and clung to our captivity
Have mercy on us,
God who wrestles and embraces us,
shatter our illusions,
refuse your comfort of angels,
Feed our hope and our hunger
with the adventurous faith
of your Spirit
until grace is our only sufficiency. Amen.

THE PRAYERS

Our brother Jesus, you set feet upon the way
and sometimes where you lead we do not like or understand.

Bless us with courage
where the way is fraught with dread or danger;
Bless us with graceful meetings where the way is lonely;
Bless us with good companions
where the way demands a common cause;

Bless us with night vision where we travel in the dark,
keen hearing where we have not sight,
to hear the reassuring sounds of fellow travellers;
Bless us with humour–
we cannot travel lightly weighed down with gravity;
Bless us with humility to learn from those around us;
Bless us with decisiveness where we must move with speed;
Bless us with lazy moments, to stretch and rest and savour;
Bless us with love, given and received.
And bless us with your presence,
even when we know it in your absence.
Lead us into exile,
until we find that on the road is where you are,
and where you are is going home.
Bless us, lead us, love us, bring us home
bearing the gospel of life.

Amen.

MEDITATION

The Christian journey through life is rather like pole-vaulting – blindfold. *First* they blindfold you, *then* you are allowed to select a pole. Armed with what you consider is a strong and suitable implement, you set off running in what you hope is the right direction. Sometimes you are aware that you are running with others, and you are carried along by their shouts and encouragement. Often you feel as though you are running alone. When you think about the leap you will eventually have to make doubts and questions come into your mind. Will you be able to reach the bar? Has *someone* moved it!? Or will there be a bar at all? Will there be a soft landing? - Which is, I suppose, where faith comes in.

Anonymous
From *The Wanderer*

Often the wanderer pleads for pity
and mercy from the Lord; but for a long time,
sad in mind, he must dip his oars
into icy waters, the lanes of the sea;
he must follow the paths of exile: fate is inflexible . . .

A wise man must fathom how eerie it will be
when all the riches of the world stand waste,
as now in diverse places in this middle earth
walls stand, tugged at by winds
and hung with hoar-frost, buildings in decay.
The wine-halls crumble, lords lie dead . . .
'Here possessions are fleeting, here friends are fleeting,
here man is fleeting, here kinsman is fleeting,
the whole world becomes a wilderness.'
So spoke the wise man in his heart as he sat apart in thought.
Brave is the man who holds to his beliefs; nor shall he ever
show the sorrow in his heart before he knows how he
can hope to heal it. It is best for a man to seek
mercy and comfort from the Father in heaven where
security stands for us all.

PENTECOST

PENTECOST

The fiftieth day is come, the Feast of the Spirit. This day is sometimes called the 'birthday' of the Church. But is this true? The Holy Spirit did not come to found an institution, but to inspire and empower Jesus' followers with the spiritual gifts that would be needed to carry the gospel message out into the world.

This community was already established, with its roots in the call of Abraham, who in obedience to God left all that was familiar to journey into the unknown.

This community was waiting – waiting for another Counsellor, the Holy Paraclete, to ignite the fire of faith that would sweep across the land and not be quenched.

The Holy Spirit, the rushing, the burning, the sevenfold gifting! As yesterday, so today – if we allow it.

Come, Holy Spirit,
our souls inspire.

Be the Power of All Things Within Us

O God the Holy Ghost who art Light unto thine elect,
    Evermore enlighten us.
Thou who art Fire of love,
    Evermore enkindle us.
Thou who art Lord and Giver of Life,
    Evermore live in us.
Thou who bestowest sevenfold grace,
    Evermore replenish us.
As the wind is thy symbol,
    So forward our goings.
As the dove,
    So launch us heavenwards.
As water,
    So purify our spirits.
As a cloud,
    So abate our temptations.
As dew,
    So revive our languor.
As fire,
    So purge our dross.

[1]Christina Rossetti

---

[1] *The Lion Christian Poetry Collection*, compiled by Mary Batchelor, Oxford, 1995, p. 323.

SUNDAY

Come down, O Love divine,
Seek thou this soul of mine,
And visit it with thine own ardour glowing;
O Comforter draw near,
within my heart appear,
And kindle it, thy holy flame bestowing.

Richard Challoner
The Holy Spirit

Consider, secondly, that the Holy Ghost came down upon the Apostles, in the shape of *tongues*, to signify that he came to make them fit preachers of his word; and to endow them with the gift of *tongues*, accompanied with heavenly wisdom, and understanding of the mysteries of God, and all the gospel truths; to the end that they might be enable to teach and publish, throughout the whole world, the faith and law of Christ. And these *tongues* were *of fire*, to signify how this divine Spirit sets those souls on fire, in which he abides; enflaming them with divine love; consuming the dross of their earthly affections; putting them in a continual motion of earnest desires and endeavours, to go forward from virtue to virtue, as fire is always in motion; and carrying them upwards towards the God of gods in his heavenly Son; as the flame is always ascending upwards towards its element. O blessed fire, when shall I partake of thy sacred flames? O come and take possession of my heart; consume all these bonds that tie it to the earth; and carry it up with thee, towards the heavenly furnace, from whence thou comest. Sweet Jesus, thou hast said (Luke 12:49): *I am come to cast fire on earth; and what will I but that it be kindled?* O cast this fire into my soul, that it may be kindled there!

Silence

O blessed fire, when shall I partake of thy sacred flames?

Psalm 29

1. Ascribe to the Lord, you gods,
ascribe to the Lord glory and strength.
2. Ascribe to the Lord the glory due to his name;
worship the Lord in the beauty of holiness.
3. The voice of the Lord is upon the waters;
the God of glory thunders; the Lord is upon the mighty waters.
4. The voice of the Lord is a powerful voice;
the voice of the Lord is a voice of splendour.
5. The voice of the Lord breaks the cedar trees;
the Lord breaks the cedars of Lebanon;
6. He makes Lebanon skip like a calf,
and Mount Hebron like a young wild ox.
7. The voice of the Lord splits the flames of fire;
the voice of the Lord shakes the wilderness;
the Lord shakes the wilderness of Kadesh.
8. The voice of the Lord makes the oak trees writhe
and strips the forest bare.
And in the temple of the lord all are crying, 'Glory!'
9. The Lord sits enthroned above the flood;
the Lord sits enthroned as king for evermore.
10. The Lord shall give strength to his people;
the Lord shall give his people the blessing of peace.

The Lord shall give strength to his people

*Living God, eternal Holy Spirit,
let your bright intoxicating energy
which fired those first disciples
fall on us to turn the world again.*

MONDAY

O let it freely burn,
Till earthly passions turn
To dust and ashes in its heat consuming;
And let thy glorious light
Shine ever on my sight,
And clothe me round, the while my path illuming.

Joel 2:23-29

Be glad, O people of Zion, rejoice in the LORD your God, for he has given you the autumn rains in righteousness. He sends you abundant showers, both autumn and spring rains, as before. The threshing floors will be filled with grain; the vats will overflow with new wine and oil. 'I will repay you for the years the locusts have eaten—the great locust and the young locust, the other locusts and the locust swarm—my great army that I sent among you. You will have plenty to eat, until you are full, and you will praise the name of the LORD your God, who has worked wonders for you; never again will my people be shamed. Then you will know that I am in Israel, that I am the LORD your God, and that there is no other; never again will my people be shamed. 'And afterward, I will pour out my Spirit on all people. Your sons and daughters will prophesy, your old men will dream dreams, your young men will see visions. Even on my servants, both men and women, I will pour out my Spirit in those days.

Silence

I will pour out my Spirit on all people

Psalm 48:7-13

7. As we have heard, so we have seen,
in the city of the LORD of hosts, in the city of our God;
God has established her for ever.
8. We have waited in silence on your loving-kindness, O God,
in the midst of your temple.

9. Your praise, like your name, O God,
      reaches to the world's end;
      your right hand is full of justice.
10. Let mount Zion be glad
      and the cities of Judah rejoice,
      because of your judgements.
11. Make the circuit of Zion; walk round about her;
      count the numbers of her towers.
12. Consider well her bulwarks; examine her strongholds;
      that you may tell those who come after.
13. This God is our God for ever and ever;
      he shall be our guide for evermore.

As we have heard, so we have seen

Spirit calls to spirit–
Know me as I know you;
Seek me a I seek you;
Claim me as I claim you;
Learn my love that you may love;
Choose my will that you may live,
And take my life to do it.
And Spirit answers spirit–
O Lord I am a child that has no knowledge, so teach me:
And blind and see not the way, so lead me:
And weak, most weak, to choose aright, so supply your power:
And love myself too well,
So show me, give me, love,
true love, yourself.

TUESDAY

Let holy charity
Mine outward vesture be,
And lowliness become mine inner clothing:
True lowliness of heart,
Which takes the humbler part,
And o'er its own shortcomings weeps with loathing.

John 14:15-26

"If you love me, you will obey what I command. And I will ask the Father, and he will give you another Counsellor to be with you forever—the Spirit of truth. The world cannot accept him, because it neither sees him nor knows him. But you know him, for he lives with you and will be in you. I will not leave you as orphans; I will come to you. Before long, the world will not see me anymore, but you will see me. Because I live, you also will live. On that day you will realise that I am in my Father, and you are in me, and I am in you. Whoever has my commands and obeys them, he is the one who loves me. He who loves me will be loved by my Father, and I too will love him and show myself to him."

Then Judas (not Judas Iscariot) said, "But, Lord, why do you intend to show yourself to us and not to the world?" Jesus replied, "Those who love me will obey my teaching. My Father will love them, and we will come to them and make our home with them. Anyone who does not love me will not obey my teaching. These words you hear are not my own; they belong to the Father who sent me. All this I have spoken while still with you. But the Counsellor, the Holy Spirit, whom the Father will send in my name, will teach you all things and will remind you of everything I have said to you."

Silence

He will give you another Counsellor to be with you for ever

Psalm 36:5-10

5. Your love, O Lord,
reaches to the heavens, and your faithfulness to the clouds.
6. Your righteousness is like the strong mountains,
your justice like the great deep;
you save both human and beast, O Lord.
7. How priceless is your love, O God!
Your people take refuge under the shadow of your wings.

8. They feast upon the abundance of your house;
you give them drink from the river of your delights.
9. For with you is the well of life.
And in your light we see light.
Continue your loving-kindness to those who know you,
and your favour to those who are true of heart.

For with you is the well of life

Loving God,
Open our hearts,
so that we may feel the breath and play of your Spirit.
Unclench our hands
so that we may reach out to one another,
and touch and be healed.
Open our lips
that we may drink in the delight and wonder of life.
Unclog our ears
to hear your agony in our inhumanity.
Open our eyes,
so that we may see Christ in friend and stranger.
Breathe your Spirit into us,
and touch our lives with the life of Christ. Amen.

WEDNESDAY

And so the yearning strong,
With which the soul will long,
Shall far outpass the power of human telling;
For none can guess its grace,
Till he becomes the place
Wherein the Holy Spirit makes his dwelling.

Acts 2:1-12
When the day of Pentecost came, they were all together in one place.
Suddenly a sound like the blowing of a violent wind came from
heaven and filled the whole house where they were sitting. They saw

what seemed to be tongues of fire that separated and came to rest on each of them. All of them were filled with the Holy Spirit and began to speak in other tongues as the Spirit enabled them. Now there were staying in Jerusalem God-fearing Jews from every nation under heaven. When they heard this sound, a crowd came together in bewilderment, because each one heard them speaking in his own language. Utterly amazed, they asked: "Are not all these who are speaking Galileans? Then how is it that each of us hears them in his own native language? Parthians, Medes and Elamites; residents of Mesopotamia, Judea and Cappadocia, Pontus and Asia, Phrygia and Pamphylia, Egypt and the parts of Libya near Cyrene; visitors from Rome (both Jews and converts to Judaism); Cretans and Arabs—we hear them declaring the wonders of God in our own tongues!" Amazed and perplexed, they asked one another, "What does this mean?"

Silence

What does this mean?

Pentecost

O Eternal Wisdom,
we praise you and give you thanks,
for, as you revealed yourself of old
in fire and storm and precious law,
so you did not leave you followers comfortless,
but came upon them on this day
in thunder, wind and flame,
filling them with clarity and power,
and making them drunk with longing
to utter your uncontainable word.
And now you have poured out your spirit
upon all flesh,
that your sons and daughters may prophesy,
that old and young may share a vision,
and even the slaves find a voice.

Come now, spirit of integrity,
of tenderness, judgement and dance;
touch our speechlessness,
kindle our longing,
reach into our silence,
and fire our words with your truth;
that each may hear in their own language
the mighty works of God.

By your Spirit of freedom, Lord our God,
you transformed the Apostles.
From being afraid,
they boldly preached the kingdom;
from being imprisoned, they joyfully went out.
Pour out this same Spirit on your Church at prayer.
Grant that this may be today a sign of new freedom,
for all the world, in Jesus, the Christ, our Lord.
Amen.

THURSDAY

Come, Holy Ghost, our souls inspire,
And lighten with celestial fire;
Thou the anointing Spirit art,
Who dost thy sevenfold gifts impart.

1 Corinthians 3:10-23
By the grace God has given me, I laid a foundation as an expert builder, and someone else is building on it. But each one should build with care. For no-one can lay any foundation other than the one already laid, which is Jesus Christ. If any-one builds on this foundation using gold, silver, costly stones, wood, hay or straw, his work will be shown for what it is, because the Day will bring it to light. It will be revealed with fire, and the fire will test the quality of

everyone's work. If the building survives, the builder will receive a reward. If it is burned up, the builder will suffer loss; the builder, however, will be saved, but only as one escaping through the flames. Don't you know that you yourselves are God's temple and that God's Spirit lives in you? If anyone destroys God's temple, God will destroy him; for God's temple is sacred, and you are that temple. Do not deceive yourselves. If any of you think you are wise by the standards of this age, you should become as "fools" so that you may become wise. For the wisdom of this world is foolishness in God's sight. As it is written: "He catches the wise in their craftiness"; and again, "The Lord knows that the thoughts of the wise are futile." So then, no more boasting about human leaders! All things are yours, whether Paul or Apollos or Cephas or the world or life or death or the present or the future—all are yours, and you are of Christ, and Christ is of God.

Silence

The fire will test the quality of everyone's work

Psalm 139:7-12

7. If I climb up to heaven, you are there;
if I make the grave my bed, you are there also.
8. If I take the wings of the morning
and dwell in the uttermost parts of the sea,
9. Even there your hand will lead me
and your right hand hold me fast.
10. If I say, 'Surely the darkness will cover me,
and the light around me turn to night',
11. Darkness is not dark to you;
the night is as bright as the day;
darkness and light to you are both alike.
12. For you yourself created my innermost parts;
you knit me together in my mother's womb.

Where can I go from your Spirit?

Come, O Spirit of God,
with God the Father's love; by Christ's Body and Blood;
in the new birth of my own breath.
Come to cover my littlenesses and consume my sins,
to direct all my desires and doings;
come with counsel on my perplexities,
with light from your everlasting scriptures;
come to reveal the deep things of God,
and what he prepares for those who love him;
come with your prayer into mine.
O most Holy Spirit, possess me by your peace,
illuminate me by the truth, fire me by your flame,
enable me by thy power, be made visible in me by your fruits,
lift me by grace upon grace from glory to glory,
O Spirit of the Lord;
one with the Father and the Son one God,
world without end. Amen.

FRIDAY

Thy blessed unction from above
Is comfort, life, and fire of love;
Enable with perpetual light
The dullness of our blinded sight.

2 Timothy 1:6-14
For this reason I remind you to fan into flame the gift of God, which is in you through the laying on of my hands. For God did not give us a spirit of timidity, but a spirit of power, of love and of self-discipline. So do not be ashamed to testify about our Lord, or ashamed of me his prisoner. But join with me in suffering for the gospel, by the power of God, who has saved us and called us to a holy life—not because of anything we have done but because of his own purpose and grace. This grace was given us in Christ Jesus

before the beginning of time, but it has now been revealed through the appearing of our Saviour, Christ Jesus, who has destroyed death and has brought life and immortality to light through the gospel. And of this gospel I was appointed a herald and an apostle and a teacher. That is why I am suffering as I am. Yet I am not ashamed, because I know whom I have believed, and am convinced that he is able to guard what I have entrusted to him for that day. What you heard from me, keep as the pattern of sound teaching, with faith and love in Christ Jesus. Guard the good deposit that was entrusted to you—guard it with the help of the Holy Spirit who lives in us.

Silence

Fan into flame the gift of God

A SONG OF GOD'S CHILDREN

1. In Christ Jesus, the life-giving law of the Spirit
    has set us free from the law of sin and death.
2. All who are led by the Spirit of God are children of God;
    it is the Spirit that enables us to cry, 'Abba!' Father.
3. The Spirit itself bears witness
    that we are God's children;
    and if God's children, then heirs of God.
4. We are heirs of God and fellow-heirs with Christ;
    if we share his sufferings now
    we shall be glorified with him hereafter.
5. These sufferings that we now endure
    are not worth comparing
    with the glory that shall be revealed.
6. For the creation waits with eager longing
    for the revealing of the children of God. (RSV)

It is the Spirit that enables us to cry, 'Abba!' Father

Hail, O power of the Son!
Hail, O beauty of the Father!
Hail, O Spirit most pure,
Bond of the Son and the Father!
O Christ, send down on me
This Spirit with the Father,
That he may sprinkle my soul with his dew
and fill it with royal gifts.

O living flame of love
that wounds my soul so tenderly in its deepest centre;
since, by your grace, I can endure your touch,
perfect your work in me
according to your will. Amen

SATURDAY

Anoint and cheer our soiled face
With the abundance of thy grace:
Keep far our foes, give peace at home;
Where thou art guide no ill can come.

Edward Schillebeeckx
The feast of the giving of the Spirit

In ancient writings and liturgical texts Christians have tried to give the Spirit a name, many names: not abstract titles but words of flesh and blood. Wind, breath of life, comforter, helper, father of the poor, the one who dries tears, the feminine face of God. Spirit is a heartfelt desire, a passion: spiritual passion. A medieval mystic called it 'the mystical laugh'; he is the Spirit, the pushing power, of God, a squall and breath of life. Sometimes the pictures suddenly change: 'spirit' then becomes unquenchable fire, warmth, fiery tongues; spiritual anointing; a power which prompts people to unheard-of deeds, getting them going, keeping them going, making space in chaos. It is a Spirit which breaks with the law, with a letter that kills; a spirit of space which God gives to men and women in Jesus. We can speak of the spirit only in images, in many languages and tongues. Spirit brings repose to the startled, warms those who are petrified with cold and heals those who are wounded. And new liturgical songs describe the Spirit in the same way: 'The spirit of God is like a fire, like fierce flames, consuming any injustice, a glow of compassion ... The Spirit of God works in the stillness, drives on with gentle power, a wise mother who holds us, a source of good powers. It gives us courage to endure, helps people to understand one another again, surrounds us like a cloak' (M. Koyck). Finally the Spirit is God's *'cri de coeur'*. 'Spirit of God' is an incalculable, astonishing risk taken by God!

Silence

The mystical laugh

O Great Spirit

O Great Spirit
whose voice I hear in the winds,
and whose breath gives life to the world, hear me.
I come to you as one of your many children.
I am small and weak.
I need your strength and your wisdom.
May I walk in beauty.
Make my eyes ever behold the red and purple sunset.
Make my hands respect the things you have made,
and my ears sharp to hear your voice.
Make me wise so that I may know
the things you have taught your children,
the lesson you have hidden in every leaf and rock.
Make me strong
so that I may not be superior to other people
but able to fight my greatest enemy, which is myself.
Make me ever ready to come to you with straight eyes
so that, when life fades as the fading sunset,
my spirit may come to you without shame.

I need your strength and wisdom

Spirit of truth whom the world can never grasp,
touch our hearts with the shock of your coming;
fill us with desire for your disturbing peace
and fire us with longing to speak your uncontainable word
through Jesus Christ. Amen.

YEAR 2

SUNDAY

James K. Baxter
Song to the Holy Spirit

Lord, Holy Spirit,
You blow like the wind in a thousand paddocks,
Inside and outside the fences,
You blow where you wish to blow.

Lord, Holy Spirit,
You are the sun who shines on the little plant,
You warm him gently, you give him life,
You raise him up to become a tree with many leaves.

Lord, Holy Spirit,
You are as the mother eagle with her young,
Holding them in peace under your feathers.
On the highest mountain you have built your nest,
Above the valley, above the storms of the world,
Where no hunter ever comes.

Lord, Holy Spirit,
You are the kind fire who does not cease to burn,
Consuming us with flames of love and peace,
Driving us out like sparks to set the world on fire.

Lord, Holy Spirit,
In the love of friends you are building a new house,
Heaven is with us when you are with us.
You are singing your song in the hearts of the poor.
Guild us, wound us, heal us. Bring us to the Father.

Silence

Bring us to the Father

MONDAY: Ezekiel 36:23-28
And I will put my Spirit in you

TUESDAY: John 20:19-23
Receive the Holy Spirit

WEDNESDAY: as for Year 1

THURSDAY: John 3:1-14
Flesh gives birth to flesh, but the Spirit gives birth to spirit

FRIDAY: 1 Corinthians 12:3-13
There are different kinds of gifts, but the same Spirit

SATURDAY

Hans Kung
Unholy and holy Spirit

When holders of high office in the Church did not know how to justify their own claim to infallibility, they pointed to the Holy Spirit. When theologians did not know how to justify a particular doctrine, a dogma or a biblical term, they appealed to the Holy Spirit. When mild or wild fanatics did not know how to justify their subjectivist whims, they invoked the Holy Spirit. The Holy Spirit was called in to justify absolute power of teaching or ruling, to justify statements of faith without convincing content, to justify pious fanaticism and false security in faith. The Holy Spirit was made a substitute for cogency, authorization, plausibility, intrinsic credibility, objective discussion. It was not so in the early Church or even in the medieval. This simplification of the role of the Holy Spirit is a typically modern development, emerging on the one hand from Reformation fanaticism and on the other hand from the defensive attitude of the great Churches, seeking to immunize themselves from rational criticism.

But we may look at the matter in another way. In primitive Christendom how was the fact to be expressed that God, that Jesus Christ, is truly close to the believer, to the community of faith: wholly real, present, effective? To this the writings of the New Testament give a unanimous response, but without regard to power claims for Church, theology and piety: God, Jesus Christ are close in the Spirit to the believer, to the community of faith; present in the Spirit and indeed as Spirit. It is not then through our memory, but through the spiritual reality, presence, efficacy of God, of Jesus Christ himself. What is the meaning of "Spirit" here?

Perceptible and yet not perceptible, invisible and yet powerful, real like the energy-charged air, the wind, the storm, as important for life as the air we breathe: this is how people in ancient times frequently imagined the "Spirit" and God's invisible working.

Silence

God, Jesus Christ are close in the Spirit to the believer, to the community of faith

YEAR 3

SUNDAY

Kahlil Gibran
The Prophet

And it is with this belief and this knowledge that I say,
> You are not enclosed within your bodies, nor confined to
houses or fields
> That which is you dwells above the mountains and roves with
the wind.
> It is not a thing that crawls into the sun for warmth or digs
holes into darkness for safety.
> But a free thing, a spirit envelops the earth and moves in the ether . . .
> But you do not see, nor do you hear, and it is well.
> The veil that clouds your eyes shall be lifted by the hands that wove it,
> And the clay that fills your ears shall be pierced by those fingers that
kneaded it.
> And you shall see,
> And you shall hear.
> Yet you shall not deplore having known blindness, nor regret having
been deaf.
> For in that day you shall know the hidden purposes in all things,
> And you shall bless the darkness as you would bless the light.

Silence

And you shall see, And you shall hear.

MONDAY: Genesis 11:1-9
There the LORD confused the language of the whole world

TUESDAY: John 15:26-16:11
Unless I go away, the Counsellor will not come to you

WEDNESDAY: as for Year 1

THURSDAY: 1 Corinthians 2:6-16
The Spirit searches all things, even the deep things of God

FRIDAY: Galations 5:16-26
So I say, live by the Spirit

SATURDAY

William Temple
Readings in St. John's Gospel

When we pray "Come, Holy Ghost, our souls inspire", we had better know what we are about. He will not carry us to easy triumphs and gratifying successes; more probably He will set us to some task for God in the full intention that we shall fail, so that others, learning wisdom by our failure, may carry the good cause forward. He may take us through loneliness, desertion by friends, apparent desertion even by God; that was the way Christ went to the Father. He may drive us into the wilderness to be tempted of the devil. He may lead us from the Mount of Transfiguration (if He ever lets us climb it) to the hill that is called the Place of the Skull. For if we invoke Him, it must be to help us in doing God's will, not ours. We cannot call upon the

> Creator Spirit, by whose aid
> The world's foundations first were laid

in order to use omnipotence for the supply of our futile pleasures of the success of our futile plans. If we invoke Him, we must be ready for the glorious pain of being caught by His power out of our petty orbit into the eternal purposes of the Almighty, in whose onward sweep our lives are as a speck of dust. The soul that is filled with the Spirit must have become purged of all pride or love of ease, all self-complacence and self-reliance;

but that soul has found the only real dignity, the only lasting joy. Come, then, Great Spirit, come, Convict the world; and convict my timid soul.

Silence

Convict my timid soul

PRAYER OF PENITENCE

Spirit of God,
you are the breath of creation,
the wind of change that blows through our lives,
opening us up to new dreams, and new hopes,
new life in Jesus Christ.
Forgive us our closed minds
which barricade themselves against new ideas,
preferring the past to what you might want to do
through us tomorrow.
Forgive us our closed eyes
which fail to see the needs of your world,
blind to opportunities of service and love.
Forgive us our closed hands
which clutch our gifts and our wealth for our own use alone.
Forgive us our closed hearts
which limit our affections to ourselves and our own.

Spirit of new life,
forgive us and break down the prison walls of our selfishness,
that we might be open to your love
and open for the service of your world;
through Jesus Christ our Lord. Amen.

THE PRAYERS

Exuberant Spirit of God,
bursting with the brightness of flame,
into the coldness of our lives
to warm us with a passion for justice and beauty
we praise you.

Exuberant Spirit of God,
sweeping us out of the dusty corners of our apathy
to breathe vitality into our struggles for change,
we praise you.

Exuberant Spirit of God,
speaking words that leap over barriers of mistrust
to convey messages of truth and new understanding,
we praise you.

Exuberant spirit of God,
flame
wind
speech,
burn, breathe, speak in us;
fill your world with justice and with joy.

MEDITATION

Mechtild of Magdeburg

Do you wish to know my meaning?
Then lie down in the Fire.
See and taste the flowing Godhead
through your being.
Feel the Holy Spirit moving and
compelling
you within the flowing Fire and
Light of God.

PENITENTIAL
RITE

NOTE

In the Christian tradition attitudes towards acts of penance have varied throughout the centuries, and within the Churches. The order provided here is intended for use by the individual on a regular basis, and includes an examination of conscience. The rite is placed within the context of the themes of Lent and Holy Week.

RESPONSARY

[1]Blessed are those
whose sin the LORD does not count against them
and in whose spirit is no deceit.
Blessed are those whose transgressions are forgiven.

When I kept silent, my bones wasted away
through my groaning all day long.
Blessed are those whose transgressions are forgiven.

For day and night your hand was heavy upon me;
my strength was sapped as in the heat of summer.
Blessed are those whose transgressions are forgiven.

Then I acknowledged my sin to you
and did not cover up my iniquity.
I said, "I will confess my transgressions to the LORD"
and you forgave the guilt of my sin.
Blessed are those whose transgressions are forgiven.

Silence

[2] Let us discover the power of the mystery;
for the Father, good beyond measure,
goes to meet his dissolute son,
who runs back from sin to his father's house,
and puts his arms around him and kisses him.
He gives him again the marks of the family glory,
and mystically perfects the celebration on high,
sacrificing the fatted calf,
so that we may lead lives appropriate
to the one who sacrifices,
the Father who loves humankind,
and to him who is gloriously sacrificed,
the Saviour of our souls.

AN EXAMINATION OF CONSCIENCE

ON THE LOVE OF GOD

[3]*Do I love Christ with a love that passes all love?*

Have I in my heart, in imagination or in truth, another God than he?

Is Christ truly living for me, at my side, and in my mind?

Do I set aside a daily regular period of time for private prayer and converse with Christ?

Do I truly keep holy one day in the week, in more fervent prayer to God, and a deeper knowledge of the life of the Holy Spirit within me, in true rest which makes me desire the return of Christ and eternal life with him?

Do I make an effort to appreciate the community life and worship of my parish and the preaching of my pastor, not indulging constantly in carping criticism, but rather making the best contribution I can to the renewal of the Church?

Am I too sectarian or partisan in my attachment to a particular Christian tradition, despising those who do not believe or worship exactly as I do?

ON THE LOVE OF THE NEIGHBOUR

Do I love my neighbour irrespective of the sort of person he/she is or his/her position in life? Do I act as a brother/sister towards them?

Am I able to forgive quickly and forget a wrong done to me?

Am I too ready to think evil of my neighbour or my brother or sister, instead of excusing all things, believing all things, hoping all things, enduring all things? (1 Cor. 13:5-7)

Am I sufficiently open-hearted, ready to help anyone, to give myself generously, to give all my time to the lowliest person who needs my help?

Do I act lovingly, justly and reasonably towards my children, or towards those placed under my authority?

Have I a real concern for social justice? Am I doing my utmost to put an end to inequalities which are an offence in Christ's eyes?

Do I truly love and respect my parents?

Do I lack humility?

Have I a thoughtless – possibly unconscious – love of authority, power, or domination?

Am I selfishly unresponsive, enigmatic, taciturn towards others?

Do I find it hard to give of myself, my time, my labour, my goods?

Do I fully realise that my body is a temple of the Holy Spirit, and that I no longer belong to myself?

Do I allow myself to be a cause of temptation because of my failure to maintain a high standard of behaviour?

Have I an inordinate desire for that which it has not yet been given to me to possess, or which I will never have?

Do I at once wish to be forgiven by one to whom I have spoken harshly, or in anger?

[4]Good Father, I have gone far from you.
But do not abandon me,
nor deprive me of your kingdom.
The most wicked enemy has stripped me
and taken away my wealth.
I have squandered dissolutely
all the spiritual gifts you gave me.
But now I have got up and come back to you,
and I cry out:
Treat me like one of your hired hands.
For my sake on the cross
you opened wide your sinless hands,
rescue me from the terrible wild beast
and reclothe me as I was before.
For mercy is with you alone. Amen.

Silence

Lent & Holy Week
[5]Jesus, Son of God, our true and only Saviour:
you died on the cross, a criminal under a curse;
you are a God who forgives.
You died helpless, a failure and in pain.

You are a God with whom there is hope;
you showed us the greatest love there is;
for you died for us with the passover lambs.

Help us to forgive as you have forgiven us.
Help us to trust you, even when hope is failing.
Help us, if we are called to suffer,
to take up our cross
and to follow you in your redeeming work.

Easter

[6] Now the green blade riseth from the buried grain,
Wheat that in dark earth many days has lain;
Love lives again, that with the dead has been:
Love is come again, like wheat that springeth green.

In the grave they laid him, Love whom men had slain,
Thinking that never he would wake again,
Laid in the earth like grain that sleeps unseen:
Love is come again, like wheat that springeth green.

Forth he came at Easter, like the risen grain,
He that for three days in the grave had lain,
Quick from the dead, my risen Lord is seen,
Love is come again, like wheat that springeth green.

When our hearts are wintry, grieving or in pain,
Thy touch can call us back to life again,
Fields of our hearts, that dead and bare have been:
Love is come again, like wheat that springeth green.

Pentecost

[7] Breathe on me, Breath of God,
Fill me with life anew,
That I may love what thou dost love,
And do what thou wouldst do.

Breathe on me, Breath of God,
Until my heart is pure;
Until with thee I will one will,
To do and to endure.

Breathe on me, Breath of God,
Till I am wholly thine;
Until this earthly part of me
Glows with thy fire divine.

Breathe on me, Breath of God:
So shall I never die,
But live with thee the perfect life
Of thine eternity.

[1] Psalm 32:2-5.

[2] *Orthodox Lent, Holy Week and Easter: Liturgical Texts with Commentary*, SPCK, London, 1995, p.24

[3] Max Thurian, *Studies in Ministry and Worship: Confession*, SCM Press, London, 1958, Delachaux and Niestlé, Switzerland, 1953, pp.130-137, adapted.

[4] *Orthodox Lent, Holy Week and Easter: Liturgical Texts with Commentary*, pp. 25-26.

[5] *A New Zealand Prayer Book,* The Church of the Province of New Zealand, 1989, p. 535.

[6] J.M.C. Crum, copyright Oxford University Press, appearing in *The New English Hymnal,* No. 115.

[7] Edwin Hatch, *Hymns Ancient & Modern Revised*, Hymns Ancient & Modern Ltd., Norwich, 1950, No. 236.

MORNING
&
EVENING
PRAYER

NOTE

In common with Volume I of the Hallowing of Time, the intention of this book of prayer is to provide an act of worship for each day, constructed around a weekly theme. These short "liturgies" have their own integrity, and do not require any further resources to be used effectively. However, it is recognised that some individuals, and small groups, may wish to use the daily material within the context of a more formal "office type" style of worship. Therefore, forms of Morning and Evening Prayer are provided for each of the seasons of Lent and Easter (including Ascension and Pentecost), and for Holy Week, into which the daily material can be incorporated easily.

A second reading and psalm are provided for those who wish to say both Morning and Evening Prayer. The lections, in chapter and verse form only, are printed in the "Lectionary for a Second Reading" to be found at the back of the book (pp. 399 – 402).

It is assumed that these forms will be used primarily by individuals. Consequently, those parts of the service which may be termed "responsorial", for corporate use, appear in italics rather than the familiar bold typeface. This is to avoid over-emphasising the communal aspect of the service for the individual worshipper.

MORNING PRAYER
for the season of
LENT

¹ *If we claim to be without sin, we deceive ourselves and the truth is not in us*

THE HYMN VERSE (or this may be said):

²*Take up thy cross, the Saviour said,*
If thou wouldst my disciple be;
Deny thyself, the world forsake,
And humbly follow after me.

³ Your grace, Lord, has shone out,
the light of our souls has shone out.
See, now is the acceptable time;
See, now is the time of repentance.
Let us put off the works of darkness
and put on the armour of light;
that we may cross the fast's great ocean
and come to the Resurrection on the third day
of our Lord and Saviour Jesus Christ,
who saves us.

Silence

A PRAYER OF PENITENCE
of the week or this:

O Lord God,
Father most loving,
we would not, even if we could,
conceal anything from you,
but rejoice rather that you know us as we are
and see every desire and every motive of our hearts.

⁴*Help us, Lord,*
to strip off every mask and veil when we come into your presence,
and to spread before you

every thought and secret of our being,
that they may be forgiven, purified, amended, and blessed by you,
through Jesus Christ our Lord. Amen.

THE PSALM *for the day*

THE READING *for the day*

Silence

This **RESPONSARY** *may be said:*

[5]*Incline your ear to me;*
When I call, make haste to answer me.

Lord, hear my prayer, and let my cry come before you.
When I call, make haste to answer me.

Hide not your face from me in the day of my trouble.
When I call, make haste to answer me.

You, O Lord, endure for ever, and your name from age to age.
When I call, make haste to answer me.

You will arise and have compassion on Zion,
for it is time to have pity on her.
When I call, make haste to answer me.

One of the following **CANTICLES** *may be said:*

1.   *I WAS FORGETFUL OF YOU*[6]

What was I thinking about, my God,
when not of you?
What was I remembering
when I was forgetful of you?
Where was my heart when not set on you?
Truth should have been my food
and yet I gorged myself on vanity,
a slave to my own desires.
My God and my Saviour,
from now on I will think only of you;
No more will I think of things which displease you.

My memories will always be of your greatness
and of your mercy which you have so tenderly exercised on me.
My heart shall find its joy in you,
and you shall be the object of its love.
From now on I will detest the vain follies
which have occupied my days
and all the vain objects of my love.
Accept, O God,
these desires and aspirations, and give me your blessing,
that I may put them into practice through the grace of your Son,
who shed his blood for me on the cross.

Where was my heart when not set on you?

2. *LILIES AND ROSES*[7]

Dear God,
I want you to plant every virtue in my heart,
as if you were planting roses and lilies of every colour in a field.
And I want you to water those flowers with your Holy Spirit.
If any thorns or thistles of vice sprout amongst the flowers,
I want you to root our those weeds.
And I want you to prune and cut back those flowers,
regardless of the pain I will suffer,
that they may grow more strongly.
Finally I want seeds from those flowers to blow into other souls,
that they too may share the beauty which you alone can give.

Dear God, I want you to plant every virtue in my heart

3. *PLUNGING INTO GOD'S LOVE*[8]

As yet my love is weak, my heart imperfect,
and so I have great need of your strength and comfort.
Visit me often, I pray, and instruct me in the ways of your laws.
Set me free from all evil passions,
and heal my heart from all immoral desires.
And thus, healed and cleansed in spirit,
May I learn how blissful it is
to plunge into the depths of your love.
Let your love dissolve my hard heart.
Let your love raise me above myself.

Let your love reveal to me joy beyond imagination.
Let my soul exhaust itself in singing the praises of your love.
Let me love you more than I love myself,
and let me love myself only for your sake.
And let me see your love shining in the hearts of all people,
that I may love them as I love you.

Let your love dissolve my hard heart

4. *HAVE MERCY, LORD* [9]

Establish, Lord,
on the rock of your commandments my unstable heart:
for your only are holy
and Lord.
I have gained
as the source of life you, death's destroyer.
Before the end I call out to you from my heart:
I have sinned,
have mercy on me and save me.
Have mercy, Lord, I cry to you for mercy,
when you come with your angels
to pay back everyone for what they have done.
The prayer of those who praise you,
Lord, do not reject, but be merciful,
for you love humankind,
and forgive those who pray to you in faith

O Lord, be merciful to me, a sinner

5. *O DISCIPLE!* [10]

Come, you who are angry,
and make peace with your enemies.
Bow your head before them and embrace them.
Engrave in yourself the sign of the son of God
as he humbles himself before others,
so humble yourself!

O disciple who shows anger toward your neighbour,
look for another Lord than the crucified One.
Those who show anger, not love, toward the neighbour
are against the Lord.

O disciple who seeks to imitate the Lord,
come and see how Christ humbles himself
and, like him, seek humility.
He gave you the command of pardon
and gave the keys of pardon
to the head of the disciples.

O merciful One, you destroyed anger;
Through your blood you established peace
between the inhabitants of heaven and earth.
By your good news, you made all people brothers and sisters.
Glory and praise to the Trinity

O disciple seek to imitate the Lord

6. *A SONG OF CHRIST'S GOODNESS* [11]

1. Jesus, as a mother you gather your people to you;
   you are gentle with us as a mother with her children.
2. Often you weep over our sins and our pride,
   tenderly you draw us from hatred and judgement.
3. You comfort us in sorrow and bind up our wounds,
   in sickness you nurse us
   and with pure milk you feed us.
4. Jesus by your dying, we are born to new life;
   by your anguish and labour we come forth with joy.
5. Despair turns to hope through your sweet goodness;
   through your gentleness, we find comfort in fear.
6. Your warmth gives life to the dead,
   your touch makes sinners righteous.
7. Lord Jesus, in your mercy, heal us;
   in your love and tenderness, remake us.
8. In your compassion, bring grace and forgiveness,
   for the beauty of heaven, may your love prepare us.

Gather your little ones to you, O God,
as a hen gathers her brood to protect them.

7. *GREATER LOVE* [12]

You taught us, Lord,
that the greatest love a man can show
is to lay down his life for his friends.

But your love was greater still,
because you laid down your life for your enemies.
It was while we were still enemies that you reconciled us
to yourself by your death.
What other love has ever been,
or ever could be, like yours?
You suffered unjustly for the sake of the unjust.
You died at the hands of sinners for the sake of the sinful.
You became a slave to tyrants,
to set the oppressed free.

Was there ever such love as yours?

MEDITATION

THE PRAYERS
for the week, free prayer, or one of the following:

Lord, bless to me this Lent.

[13] Lord, let me fast most truly and profitably,
by feeding in prayer on your Spirit:
reveal me to myself in the light of your holiness.
Suffer me never to think
that I have knowledge enough to need no teaching,
wisdom enough to need no correction,
talents enough to need no grace,
goodness enough to need no progress,
humility enough to need no repentance,
devotion enough to need no quickening,
strength sufficient without your Spirit;
lest, standing still, I fall back for evermore.

Show me the desires that should be disciplined,
and sloths to be slain,
Show me the omissions to be made up
and habits to be mended.
And behind these, weaken, humble, and annihilate in me
self-will, self righteousness, self satisfaction,
self-sufficiency, self-assertion, vainglory.

May my whole effort be to return to you;
O make it serious and sincere

persevering and fruitful in result,
by the help of your Holy Spirit
and to your glory, my Lord and my God. Amen

Or
THANKSGIVING

[14] Blessed are you, O Lord our God,
the shepherd of Israel,
their pillar of cloud by day,
their pillar of fire by night.
In these forty days you lead us
into the desert of repentance
that in this pilgrimage of prayer
we might learn to be your people once more.
In fasting and service
you bring us back to your heart.
You open our eyes to your presence in the world
and you free our hands to lead others
to the radiant splendour of your mercy.
Be with us in these journey days
for without you we are lost and will perish.
To you alone be dominion and glory,
for ever and ever. Amen

THE LORD'S PRAYER

THE PRAYER OF THE DAY
or this:

[15] The kind of fast that pleases you, God of love,
is to free the oppressed,
and to share our bread with the hungry.
We offer you our fast;
may it help us be one with those who are hungry
not from choice but from necessity.
Hear us, through Jesus, the Christ, our Lord. Amen

[16] *Praise and glory to you, Jesus Christ our Saviour,*
for you do not call the righteous
but sinners to repentance.

You draw us away from the easy road
that would lead to our destruction.
You call us instead to seek God's kingdom,
to strive for what is right,
and to lay up our treasure in heaven.
Praise and glory to you, Jesus Christ our Saviour!

EVENING PRAYER
for the season of
LENT

[17]*And now I bend the knee of my heart, imploring you for your kindness*

THE HYMN VERSE *or this may be said:*

[18]*Take up thy cross! Let not its weight*
Fill thy weak spirit with alarm:
His strength shall bear thy spirit up,
And brace thy heart, and nerve thine arm.

[19] If we look for spiritual recompense,
let us perform our good deeds in secret;
let us not proclaim them in the streets,
but keep them hidden in our hearts.
Then the one who sees the secrets of all will reward us
for our abstinence.
Let us complete the Fast,
not with a sad countenance,
but praying in the inner chamber of our souls;
and without ceasing, let us cry:
Our Father in heaven,
lead us not into temptation, we pray,
but deliver us from the evil one.

Silence

A PRAYER OF PENITENCE
of the week or this:

[20]*I have gone astray, I have failed you.*
My heart shrinks with shame
when I hear your sweet, forgiving words.
When your clear, pure eyes look at me,
I turn my face away.
There was never a soul so hard, a heart so cold as mine.
And yet I can feel your soft love

causing my soul to crumble and my heart to melt.
Dear Lord, I have pursued false desires,
I have put my trust in worldly wisdom.
I have been besotted with the shallow pleasures.
I have been a faithless lover.
I cannot understand why you do not punish me,
beating me until my flesh is raw and bloody.
Instead you forgive me, beckoning me back to your side.
Yes, I will come.
I will always be true.
I will always trust your wisdom.
I will find pleasure only in your grace.

THE PSALM *for the day*

THE READING *for the day*

Silence

*This **RESPONSARY** may be said:*

[21]O Lord, do not forsake me;
be not far from me, O God.
O Lord, do not forsake me; be not far from me, O my God.

Make haste to help me,
O God of my salvation,
Be not far from me, O my God.

Glory to the Father, and to the Son,
and to the Holy Spirit.
O Lord, do not forsake me; be not far from me, O my God.

*One of the following **CANTICLES** may be said:*

1. *WHO WILL HELP ME?* [22]

Where am I?
How did I get here?
Whom can I ask to comfort me?
How will I break these chains of sin that enslave me?
Whose eye can bear to look

at these ugly spiritual wounds that disfigure me?
Whose hands will anoint me
with oil that I may be healed?
Who will help me unless it is you, O God?
Whenever I think of the glorious freedom which you promise,
my slavery to sin seems even more oppressive.
Whenever I think of the beauty of your Son,
my spiritual ugliness seems even more terrible.
Whenever I think of the joyful music of your love,
my soul sinks into despair.
Dear God, what will become of me?

Who will help me unless it is you, O God?

2. *HASTEN TO ME* [23]

Dear Christ, hasten to me.
Release me from my sins.
Free my arms from the chains of evil,
that I may embrace you.
Lift the scales of ignorance from my eyes,
that I may see you.
Why do you delay?
What are you waiting for?
You are my God and my Lord,
you are my refuge and my strength,
you are my glory and my hope.
In you I put my trust.
Dear Christ hasten to me.

You are my glory and my hope

3. *MAY YOU BE BLESSED FOREVER* [24]

May you be blessed forever, Lord,
for not abandoning me when I abandoned you.
May you be blessed forever, Lord,
for offering your hand of love in my darkest, most lonely moment.
May you be blessed forever, Lord,
for putting up with such a stubborn soul as mine.
May you be blessed forever, Lord,
for loving me more than I love myself.

May you be blessed forever, Lord,
for continuing to pour out your blessings upon me,
even though I respond so poorly.
May you be blessed forever, Lord,
for drawing our the goodness in all people, even including me.
May you be blessed forever, Lord,
for repaying our sin with love.
May you be blessed forever, Lord,
for being constant and unchanging,
amidst all the changes of the world
May you be blessed forever, Lord,
for your countless blessings on me and on all your creatures.

4. *MERCY GROWS TALL*[25]

Out of what door that came ajar in heaven
drifted this starry manna down to me,
to the dilated mouth both hunger given
and all satiety?

Who bore at midnight to my very dwelling
the gift of this imperishable food?
My famished spirit with its fragrance filling,
its savour certitude.

The mind and heart ask, and the soul replies
what store is heaped on these bare shelves of mine?
The crumbs of the immortal delicacies
fall with precise design.
Mercy grows tall with the least heart enlightened,
and I, so long a fosterling of this night,
here feast upon immeasurably sweetened
wafers of light.

5. *WORD OF THE FATHER*[26]

Word of the Father, Son of God Most high,
Reigning in power before the earth was made,
Speaking God's sacred word through fire and flame,
Bringing God's holiness, our souls to save:

Teach us to seek, beyond this world of time,
The prize of life, the splendour of your face;

Fed by your word, a lamp to guide our feet,
Strong in your steadfast love, O God of grace.

Saviour most holy, still, small voice of love,
Lead us by desert paths of purity;
Speak to our hearts, your will for our peace;
Bring us to love the truth that sets us free.

6.   THE COST[27]

O Son of man, Son of God,
in the Garden, at the Pillar, on the Cross
you take away the sin of the world,
and its darkness and its death;
yourself bearing the cost
in your own body and mind and soul,
all human, all divine.

Yet we sleep. Come, Lord, and wake us
from the absorptions and stupor of self-will.
Grant us to heed the tender warning,
Why do you sleep? Rise and pray,
lest you enter into temptation.
And still you speak to each one,
From all eternity I have loved you;
to all eternity I will love you;
can you not spare me one hour?

7.   LAMENT[28]

O LORD, you deceived me, and I was deceived ;
you overpowered me and prevailed.
I am ridiculed all day long; everyone mocks me.

Whenever I speak, I cry out proclaiming violence and destruction.
So the word of the LORD
has brought me insult and reproach all day long.

But if I say, "I will not mention him
or speak any more in his name,"
his word is in my heart like a fire, a fire shut up in my bones.
I am weary of holding it in; indeed, I cannot.

I hear many whispering,
"Terror on every side! Report him! Let's report him!"
All my friends are waiting for me to slip, saying,
"Perhaps he will be deceived;
then we will prevail over him and take our revenge on him."

But the LORD is with me like a mighty warrior;
so my persecutors will stumble and not prevail.

Sing to the LORD!
Give praise to the LORD!
He rescues the life of the needy
from the hands of the wicked.

MEDITATION

THE PRAYERS
for the week, free prayer, or one of the following:

[29]Jesus, Saviour,
Man of sorrows and acquainted with grief,
We come to you
for you alone can make us whole.

Jesus, Saviour,
Wounded for our transgressions,
Bruised for our iniquities,
We come to you
for you alone can make us whole.

Jesus, Saviour,
We come as a church broken by factions,
Weak in our mission,
Wavering in our faith.
We come to you
for you alone can make us whole.

Jesus, Saviour,
We come as people of the world,
Torn by war, ruined by greed, spoilt by selfishness.
We come to you
for you alone can make us whole.

Jesus, Saviour,
We come as members of a family,
Insensitive to each other,
Blind to tears and deaf to cries.
We come to you
for you alone can make us whole.

Jesus, Saviour,
We come with the sick at heart,
We come with the ill in mind,
We come with the diseased in body.
We come to you
for you alone can make us whole.

Or
THANKSGIVING

[30] God, we praise you for your love in Christ,
challenging all our definitions,
overturning all our stereotypes.

Wondering, amazed, in Christ we see you:
the king of the universe, washing dirty feet;
the creator of heaven and earth, hungry, cold and tired;
the saviour and healer, wounded with the pain of the world,
the almighty lord, found with the weak and the vulnerable.

God, help us to be strong in the love and liberty of Christ
so that we can follow the same pattern of service:
with the inner security that frees us
from the drive to seek reward or recognition;
with the confidence to give those whom we serve
the dignity of voicing their own needs;
with the patience
that does not try to impose your will or our own,
but works and waits for your justice.
In the name of Christ,
Amen.

THE LORD'S PRAYER

THE PRAYER OF THE DAY
or this:

[31]God of all seasons,
in your pattern of things,
there is a time for keeping and a time for losing,
a time for building up and a time for pulling down.
In this holy season of Lent,
as we journey with our Lord to the cross,
help us to discern in our lives
what we must lay down and what we must take up;
what we must end and what we must begin.
Give us grace to lead a disciplined life,
in glad obedience and with joy
which comes from a closer walk with Christ. Amen.

[32]*Jesus, raised up from the earth*
to draw all people to yourself,
let your face shine upon us,
and with your outstretched arms,
gather for the Father all his scattered children.

---

[1] 1 John 1:8 (NIV)

[2] C. W. Everest, *Hymns Ancient & Modern Revised*, N. 333, London, 1950.

[3] From Vespers on Sunday of the First Week of Lent, *Orthodox Lent, Holy Week and Easter: Liturgical Texts with Commentary*, Hugh Wybrew, SPCK, London, 1995, p. 43.

[4] Charles Vaughan, *The Book of a Thousand Prayers*, compiled by Angela Ashwin, HarperCollins, London, 1996, p. 121.

[5] Francis of Sales, 'The Love of God', trans., V. Ken, appearing in The *Fount Book of Prayer*, ed. Robert van der Weyer, HarperCollins, London, 1993, pp. 151-152.

[6] From Psalm 102.

[7] Hildegard of Bingen, *The Fount Book of Prayer*, pp. 195-196.

[8] Thomas à Kempis, The *Fount Book of Prayer*, p. 359.

[9] From the Great Canon of St. Andrew of Crete, Canticle Three, *Orthodox Lent, Holy Week and Easter: Liturgical Texts with Commentary*, p. 47, adapted.

[10] *Qurbono: The Book of Offering, Season of Great Lent and Passion Week*, copyright St. Maron Publications, 1994.

[11] Anselm of Canterbury, trans. Michael Vasey, *Celebrating Common Prayer*, copyright The European Province of the Society of St. Francis, 1992, p. 232.

[12] *The Fount Book of Prayer,* p. 65.

[13] Eric Milner-White, *My God, My Glory,* copyright SPCK, London, 1994, p. 29, The Friends of York Minster, adapted.

[14] From *Praise God in Song*, G.I.A. publications, Inc., Chicago, Illinois, copyright 1979.

[15] *Proclaiming All Your Wonders*, Dominican Publications, Dublin, 1991, Bayard Press International S.A., Paris, 1983, p. 45.

[16] *A New Zealand Prayer Book*, Collins Liturgical Publications, copyright the Church of the Province of New Zealand, London, 1989, p. 532.

[17] The Prayer of Manasseh vs. 11, *The Apocrypha - New Revised Standard Version.*

[18] C. W. Everest, *Hymns Ancient & Modern Revised*, No. 333.

[19] Byzantine Vespers, *A Lent Sourcebook: the Forty Days – Book One*, p. 79.

[20] *The Fount Book of Prayer,* p. 335.

[21] *Celebrating Common Prayer*, p. 150. (RSV)

[22] Hildegard of Bingen, *The Fount Book of Prayer,* p. 194.

[23] Aelred of Rievaulx, *The Fount Book of Prayer,* p. 21.

[24] Theresa of Avila, *The Fount Book of Prayer,* p. 349.

[25] Jessica Powers, *Selected Poetry of Jessica Powers,* eds. Regina Siegfried, and Robert F. Morneau, Sheed and Ward, Kansas City, 1989.

[26] Jennifer Moorcroft, copyright The Carmelite Monastery, Ware, Herts.

[27] Eric Milner-White, *My God, My Glory,* p. 62, adapted.

[28] Jeremiah 20:7-11,13, NIV.

[29] David Adam, *The Open Gate – Celtic prayer for growing spirituality*, SPCK, London, 1994, pp. 64-65.

[30] Jan Berry, Sheffield 1990, *Bread of Tomorrow,* ed., Janet Morley, SPCK and Christian Aid, London, 1992, pp. 80-81.

[31] *Book of Common Order of the Church of Scotland*, Saint Andrew Press, Edinburgh, 1994, pp. 431-432.

[32] *Proclaiming All Your Wonders*, p. 42.

MORNING PRAYER
for
HOLY WEEK

[1]*"Is it nothing to you, all you who pass by?*

THE HYMN VERSE *or this may be said:*

[2]*Dost thou truly seek renown*
Christ his glory sharing?
Wouldst thou win the heavenly crown
Victor's garland bearing?
Tread the path the Saviour trod,
Looking upon the crown of God,
See what he is wearing.

Silence

[3] Look! The bridegroom comes at midnight.
Blessed the servant he finds watching;
but worthless the one he finds idling.
Take care, then, my soul:
let not sleep overcome you,
lest you be handed over to death
and shut out the kingdom.
But be sober again and cry out:
Holy, holy are you, O God:
have mercy on us.

Silence

A PRAYER OF PENITENCE
of the week or this:

[4]*Almighty God,*
you loved the world so much
that you sent your Son
not to condemn the world
but that through him the world might be saved.
We who are quicker to judge than to bless
fall silent at the extravagance of your grace.

As we are confronted again
with the depths of human wickedness
and the greater depth of your divine compassion,
may we not remain unmoved.
As Christ's arms are stretched out and his body lifted up,
may we confess our part in the sin of the world,
repent of it,
know the reality of your forgiveness,
and be transformed. Amen.

THE PSALM *for the day*

THE READING *for the day*

Silence

*This **RESPONSARY** may be said:*

The preaching of the cross is folly to those who are perishing,
But to those who are being saved, it is the power of God.

To those who are called,
Christ is the power of God and the wisdom of God.

For the folly of God is wiser than human wisdom,
And the weakness of God is stronger than human strength.

We adore you, O Christ, and we bless you;
Because by your holy cross, you have redeemed the world.

*One of the following **CANTICLES** may be said:*

SUNDAY[5]

Carrying spiritual branches,
and with souls made clean,
let us joyfully cry out
with faith to Christ,
like the children,
loudly praising the Lord:
Blessed are you, Saviour!
You have come into the world
to save Adam from the primal curse.

Loving humankind, you were well pleased
to become spiritually the new Adam.
Glory to you, O Word,
for you have done all things for good.

MONDAY [6]

A spendthrift lover is the Lord
Who never counts the cost
Or asks if heaven can afford
To woo a world that's lost.
Our lover tosses coins of gold
Across the midnight skies
And stokes the sun against the cold
To warm us when we rise.

Still more is spent in blood and tears
To win the human heart,
To overcome the violent fears
That drive the world apart.
Behold the bruised and thorn-crowned face
Of one who bears our scars
And empties out the wealth of grace
That's hinted by the stars.

How shall we love this heart-strong God
Who gives us ev'rything,
Whose ways to us are strange and odd,
What can we give or bring?
Acceptance of the matchless gift
Is gift enough to give.
The very act will shake and shift
The way we love and live.

TUESDAY [7]

Ah, holy Jesu, how hast thou offended,
That man to judge thee hath in hate presented?
By foes derided, by thine own rejected,
O most afflicted.

Who was the guilty? Who brought this upon thee?
'Twas I, Lord Jesu, I it was denied thee:
I crucified thee.'

Lo, the good Shepherd for the sheep is offered;
The slave hath sinned, and the son hath suffered;
For man's atonement, while he nothing heedeth,
God intercedeth.

For me, kind Jesu, was thy incarnation,
Thy mortal sorrow and thy life's oblation;
Thy death of anguish and thy bitter passion,
For my salvation.

Therefore, kind Jesu, since I cannot pay thee,
I do adore thee, and will ever pray thee,
Think on thy pity and thy love unswerving,
Not my deserving.

WEDNESDAY[8]

I was desolate, and she came to me;
when there was neither hope nor help for pain
she was at my side;
in the shadow of the grave she has restored me.

My cup was spilling with betrayal,
but she has filled it with wine;
my face was wet with fear,
but she has anointed me with oil,
and my hair is damp with myrrh.
The scent of her love surrounds me;
it is more than I can bear.

She has touched me with authority;
in her hands I find strength.
For she acts on behalf of the broken,
and her silence is the voice of the unheard.
Though many may murmur against her, I will praise her;
and in the name of the unremembered,
I will remember her.

THURSDAY[9]

O Jesus, my feet are dirty.
Come even as a slave to me,
pour water into your bowl,

come and wash my feet.
I asking such a thing I know I am overbold,
but I dread what was threatened when you said to me,
"If I do not wash your feet I have no fellowship with you."
Wash my feet then,
because I long for your companionship.
And yet, what am I asking?
It was well for Peter to ask you to wash his feet,
for him that was all that was needed to be clean in every part.
With me it is different,
though you wash me now
I shall still stand in need of that other washing,
the cleansing you promised when you said,
"There is a baptism I must needs be baptised with".

FRIDAY [10]

Alone to sacrifice Thou goest, Lord,
Giving thyself to death whom thou wilt slay.
For us thy wretched folk is any word,
Whose sins have brought Thee to this agony?
Why must Thou suffer torture for our sin?
For they are ours, Lord, our deeds, our deeds.
Let our hearts suffer for Thy passion, Lord,
That very suffering may Thy mercy win.
This is the night of tears, the three days' space,
Sorrow abiding of the eventide,
Until the daybreak with the risen Christ,
And hearts that sorrowed shall be satisfied.
So may our hearts share in Thine anguish, Lord,
That there may shares of Thy glory be:
Heavy with weeping may the three days pass,
To win the laughter of Thine Easter Day.

SATURDAY [11]

I will get up now and go about the city,
through its streets and squares;
I will search for the one my heart loves.
So I looked for him but did not find him.

The watchmen found me as they made their rounds in the city. "Have you seen the one my heart loves?"
Scarcely had I passed them
when I found the one my heart loves.
I held him and would not let him go.

Place me like a seal over your heart,
like a seal on your arm;
for love is as strong as death,
its jealousy unyielding as the grave.
It burns like blazing fire,
like a mighty flame.

MEDITATION

THE PRAYERS
for the week, free prayer, or one of the following:

[12]Because for our sake you tasted gall,
may the Enemy's bitterness be killed in us.

Because for our sake you drank sour wine,
may what is weak in us be strengthened.

Because for our sake you were spat upon,
may we be bathed in the dew of immortality.

Because for our sake you were struck with a rod,
may we receive shelter at the last.

Because for our sake you accepted a crown of thorns,
may we that love you be crowned with garlands
that can never fade.

Because for our sake you were wrapped in a shroud,
may we be clothed in your all-enfolding strength.

Because you were laid in the new grave and the tomb,
may we receive renewal of soul and body.

Because you rose and returned to new life,
may we be brought to life again.

Or
THANKSGIVING

[13]O holy wisdom of God,
eternally offensive to our wisdom,
and compassionate towards our weakness,
we praise you and give you thanks,
because you emptied yourself of power
and entered our struggle,
taking upon you our unprotected flesh.
You opened wide your arms for us upon the cross,
becoming scandal for our sake,
that you might sanctify even the grave
to be a bed of hope for your people.
Therefore, with those who are detained without justice,
abandoned or betrayed by friends,
whose bodies are violated or in pain;
with those who have died alone
without dignity, comfort, or hope;
and with all the company of saints
who have carried you in their wounds
that they may be bodied forth with life
we praise you, saying:

Blessed is the one
who comes in the name of God;
hosanna in the highest.

THE LORD'S PRAYER

THE PRAYER OF THE DAY
or this:

[14] Merciful God,
creator of all the peoples of the earth
and lover of every soul;
have compassion on all those who do not know you,
let your gospel be preached with grace and power

to those who have not heard it,
turn the hearts of those who oppose it,
and bring home to your fold
all who have gone astray;
through Jesus Christ our Lord. Amen.

[15]*Father, the hour has come when your Son glorifies you.*
Do not allow darkness to cover the earth again.
Tear the veil and open the doors of your sanctuary,
so that all people may one day contemplate the glory
which you have given him,
for ever and ever.

EVENING PRAYER
for
HOLY WEEK

¹⁶But he was pierced for our transgressions, he was crushed for our iniquities; the punishment that brought us peace was upon him, and by his wounds we are healed.

THE HYMN VERSE (*or this may be said*):

¹⁷In thy most bitter passion
My heart to share doth cry,
With thee for my salvation
Upon the Cross to die.
Ah, keep my heart thus moved
To stand thy Cross beneath,
To mourn the, well-beloved,
Yet thank thee for thy death.

Silence

¹⁸He whom Isaiah proclaimed lamb
goes to the slaughter of his own free will.
He gives his back to flogging
and his cheeks to striking.
He does not turn his face away
from the shame of their pitting.
He is condemned to a shameful death.
All this he accepts willingly,
though he is without sin,
so that to all he may give
resurrection from the dead.

Silence

A PRAYER OF PENITENCE
of the week or this:

¹⁹*O Jesus, blessed Jesus, I gaze upon your Cross,*
O Saviour suffering to draw my love;

was ever love like yours, or thanks so poor as mine?
Your hands are outstretched for the love of me and all mankind,
and with my sin I have pierced you and keep on wounding you;
Bitterly I sorrow, and deepen my penitence.
Give me tears, that I may weep,
Give me strength that I may amend.
Take me to yourself,
keep me in your wounds, ever mindful of your presence,
ever to love you, in pain and in bliss,
on earth and in heaven,
with you for ever. Amen.

THE PSALM *for the day*

THE READING *for the day*

Silence

*This **RESPONSARY** may be said:*

[20] To this you were called, because Christ suffered for you,
leaving you an example, that you should follow in his steps.
He committed no sin,
and no deceit was found in his mouth

He himself bore our sins in his body on the tree,
so that we might die to sins and live for righteousness;
by his wounds you have been healed.
He committed no sin,
and no deceit was found in his mouth

For you were like sheep going astray,
but now you have returned
to the Shepherd and Overseer of your souls.
He committed no sin,
and no deceit was found in his mouth

*One of the following **CANTICLES** may be said:*

SUNDAY[21]

Fair and eloquent flowers
have the children strewn before the King:
the donkey was garlanded with them,
the path was filled with them;
they scattered praises like flowers,
their songs of joy like lilies.
Now too at this festival
does the crown of children scatter for you, Lord,
praises like blossoms.
Blessed is he who was acclaimed by young children.

It is as though our hearing embraced
an armful of children's voices,
while chaste songs, Lord, filled the bosoms of our ears.
Let each of us gather us a posy of such flowers,
and with these let all intersperse
blossoms of their own piece of land,
so that, for this great feast,
we may plait a garland.
Blessed is he who invited us to plait it!

Let the chief pastor weave together
his homilies like flowers,
let the priests make a garland of their ministry,
the deacons of their reading,
strong young men of their jubilant shouts,
children of their psalms,
young women of their songs,
chief citizens of their benefactions,
ordinary folk of their manner of life.
Blessed is he who gave us so many opportunities for good!

MONDAY[22]

1. Jesus, Saviour of the world,
come to us in your mercy:
we look to you to save and help us.
2. By your cross and your life laid down,
you set your people free:
we look to you to save and help us.

3.   When we were ready to perish,
you saved your disciples:
we look to you to save and help us.
4.   In the greatness of your mercy,
loose us from our chains:
we look to you to save and help us.
5.   Make yourself known
as our saviour and mighty deliverer;
save and help us that we may praise you.
6.   Come now and dwell with us, Lord Christ Jesus;
hear our prayer and be with us always.
7.   And when you come in your glory,
make us to be one with you
and to share the life of your kingdom.
we look to you to save and help us.

TUESDAY[23]

He is the Passover of our salvation.
He was present in many so as to endure many things.
In Abel he was slain; in Isaac bound;
in Jacob a stranger; in Joseph sold;
in Moses exposed; in David persecuted;
in the prophets dishonoured.
Not a bone of his was broken on the tree.
He was buried in the earth, but rose from the dead,
and was lifted up to the heights of heaven.
He is the silent lamb,
the slain lamb, born of Mary the fair ewe.
He was seized from the flock and dragged away to slaughter.
Towards evening he was sacrificed,
and at night he was buried.
But he who had no bone broken on the cross,
was not corrupted in the earth,
for he rose from the dead
and raised us up from the depths of the grave.

He is the Passover of our salvation.

WEDNESDAY[24]

Dear Lord Jesus,
the fragrance of your love draws me towards you,

like the perfume of the beloved attracts the lover.
I shall follow you, Lord,
walking over the beautiful hills
covered with sweet-smelling flowers.
And I will not desert you when you walk to Calvary.
I shall stay beside you,
and follow your body when it is taken to the tomb.
Let my flesh be buried with you in that tomb.
Because I no longer wish to live for myself,
but to rise with you into the fullness of life.

THURSDAY [25]

I am asleep in idleness of soul,
O Christ the bridegroom,
I have no lamps burning with virtue.
Like the foolish bridesmaids
I wander off when the time comes for action.
Do not harden your heart of mercy against me, Lord,
but drive from me dark sleep
and wake me up.
Lead me with the wise bridesmaids
into the marriage hall,
where resounds in purity
the voice of those who feast,
and never cease to sing:
'O Lord, glory to you.'

FRIDAY [26]

Before the world ever saw you,
it was I who carried you,
growing like a secret seed,
dancing in the darkness of the womb.
It was I who sang to you,
telling out the greatness of God,
though people scorned my singleness
in the littleness of their lives.
Because I said yes to God,
I had to be strong for my child:
you were the burden that I bore with love.

In my body, God's word
was transformed into flesh.
So, as you turned water into wine,
and fed the crowds with bread,
I had courage to bear your hard words
Because I too had a part in God's work
and could bear to witness to hope.
But what transformation can happen now?
We are both trapped
in what happens daily to ordinary people
who see no end to their suffering–
while God weeps.
We are both being torn apart
because, in the weight of that cross,
you are bearing the sins of the whole world.

I want to hide my eyes.
But I step forward from the crowd,
and reach out my hand
to offer my love, my strength, my pain.
God knows how I can bear it.

SATURDAY[27]

O God hear my cry,
for my loss is more than I can bear;
I am surrounded by darkness,
and I do not know myself.

In the hours before dawn I will arise,
while it I still dark.
Through the streets of the city, in the cold garden,
among those who have disappeared,
at the site of sudden death,
at the place of my abandonment,
and deep in my heart's anger, I will search you out.

In the speechless places of my soul,
and in that which I most fear, I will seek you;
through the strange landscape of my grief
I will return to the darkness as to my mother's womb.

I shall not fear wounding,
Nor shall I be appalled by violent men;
for the grave is naked before God,
and the pain of death has no covering.

I sought you early, my beloved,
but you had turned and gone.
I came while is was still dark;
I put my hand to the rock.
I looked for touch, and behold, terror;
for grief, and behold, annihilation.

Horror engulfed me,
and I did not hear your voice;
I was clothed with my tears,
your face hidden from me.
Then I was compelled by your presence,
and my heart turned within me.

MEDITATION

THE PRAYERS
for the week, free prayer, or one of the following:

[28] Lord Jesus, you have shaped our faith,
by making us believe you shared our mortal nature.
In Gethsemane real drops of sweat fell from your body.
Lord Jesus, you have given us hope,
because you endured all the spiritual and physical hardships
which mortal nature can suffer.
In Gethsemane your soul was in torment,
and your heart shook at the prospect of physical pain to come.
Your showed us the natural weakness of our flesh,
that we might know that you have truly borne our sorrows.

Sweet Jesus,
what soul can be so hardened as not to cry out at your plight?
Sweet Jesus,
what heart can be so hardened
as not to groan with compassion for you?
Sweet Jesus,
my ears can hardly bear to hear those horrible shouts:
"Away with him. Away with him. Crucify him."

Let my heart crack and crumble at the sight of him.
Let my soul break apart with compassion for his suffering.
Let it be shattered with grief
at my sins for which he dies.
Let it be softened with devoted love for him.

O Jesus, I am in every way unworthy of you.
Yet, like Joseph of Arimathea, I want to offer a space for you.
He offered his own tomb, I offer my heart.
Enter the darkness of my heart,
as your body entered the darkness of Joseph's tomb.
And make me worthy to receive you,
driving out all sin
that I may be filled with your spiritual light.

Or
THANKSGIVING

[29] By the death on Calvary's hill of him the first-born,
Who bears the wood and the flame of his own pyre:
Jesus Christ, we thank and bless you!
By the death, amid the thorns, of God's own shepherd,
The paschal lamb who was pierced by our despair:
Jesus Christ, we glorify you!
By the death of God's beloved outside his vineyard,
That we might change from murderer into heir:
Conquering God, we your people proclaim you.

By the wood which sings a song of nuptial gladness,
Of God who takes for his bride our human race:
Jesus Christ, we thank and bless you!
By the wood which raises up in his full vigour
The Son of Man who draws us all by his grace:
Jesus Christ, we glorify you!
By the wood where he perfects his royal priesthood
In one high priest who for sin is sacrifice:
Conquering God, we your people proclaim you!

Holy tree which reaches up from earth to heaven
That all the world may exult in Jacob's God:
Jesus Christ, we thank and bless you!

Mighty ship which snatches us from God's deep anger,
Saves us, with Noah, from drowning in the flood:
Jesus Christ we glorify you!
Tender wood which gives to brackish water sweetness,
And from rock shall strike fountains for our good:
Conquering God, we your people proclaim you.

THE LORD'S PRAYER

THE PRAYER OF THE DAY
or this:

[30]O Christ the Master Carpenter,
who at the last, through wood and nails,
purchased our whole salvation,
wield well your tools
in the workshop of your world,
so that we who come rough-hewn to your bench
may here be fashioned
to a truer beauty of your hand.
We ask it for your own name's sake. Amen.

[31]*In taking the road to Jerusalem,*
there to die, Lord Jesus,
you reveal to your Church
the true meaning of human suffering.
Grant us the grace to walk after you
towards the light of life
where you dwell for ever and ever.

---

[1] Lamentations 1:12, NIV.
[2] 13th century Latin, trans. Athelstan Riley, appearing in *The New English Hymnal*,
N. 81, v.1, copyright Oxford University Press.
[3] Hugh Wybrew, *Orthodox Lent, Holy Week and Easter: Liturgical Texts with
Commentary*, SPCK, London, 1995, p. 93, adapted.
[4] *Book of Common Order of the Church of Scotland*, St. Andrew Press, Edinburgh,
1994, pp. 437-438.
[5] *Orthodox Lent, Holy Week and Easter: Liturgical Texts with Commentary*, p. 89.
[6] Thomas H. Troeger and Carol Doran, *New Hymns for the Lectionary: To Glorify the
Maker's Name*, Oxford University Press, Oxford.

[7] Robert Bridges from J Heerman, based on an 11th century Latin meditation, *The New English Hymnal*, No. 62, Canterbury Press, Norwich, 1986.

[8] Janet Morley, *All Desires Known*, expanded edition, SPCK, London, and Morehouse Publishing, Harrisburg, Penn., 1992, p. 100.

[9] Origen, *A Reconciliation Sourcebook*, eds. Kathleen Hughes and Joseph A. Favazza, Liturgy Training Publications, copyright the Archdiocese of Chicago, Chicago, 1997, p. 158.

[10] Peter Abelard, *Medieval Latin Lyrics*, trans. Helen Waddell, Victor Gollancz Ltd., (Cassell Plc).

[11] Song of Songs 3:2-4, 8:6, NIV.

[12] Communion hymn, fifth century, *Early Christian Prayers*, ed. A. Hamman, trans. Walter Mitchell, Longmans, Green & Co., London, 1961.

[13] Janet Morley, *All Desires Known*, p. 52, adapted.

[14] *A New Zealand Prayer Book*, copyright the Church of the Province of New Zealand, 1989, p. 588.

[15] *Proclaiming All Your Wonders*, Dominican Publications, Dublin, 1991, Bayard Presse International S.A., Paris, 1983, p. 53.

[16] Isaiah 53:5, NIV.

[17] Paul Gerhardt from a 14th century Latin hymn, trans., Robert Bridges, *The new English Hymnal*, No. 90, v.4.

[18] *Orthodox Lent, Holy Week and Easter: Liturgical Texts with Commentary*, pp. 1-6-107.

[19] *A Pilgrim's Book of Prayers*, A. R. Mowbray & Co., Ltd. (Cassell Plc), London, 1960.

[20] 1 Peter 2:21, 22, 24, 25 NIV.

[21] Ephraim, fourth century, *Harp of the Spirit: eighteen poems of St Ephraim the Syrian*, trans. Sebastian Grock, Fellowship of St. Alban & St. Sergius, Oxford, by kind permission of the author and the Fellowship of St. Alban & St. Sergius.

[22] Henry Allon, A Song of Salvation, *Celebrating Common Prayer*, copyright The European Province of the Society of St. Francis, 1992, p. 237.

[23] Melito of Sardis, *The Divine Office*, Collins Liturgical Publications, London, 1974.

[24] Aelred of Rievaulx, *The Fount Book of Prayer*, ed. Robert van de Weyer, HarperCollins, London, 1993, p. 21.

[25] *Orthodox Lent, Holy Week and Easter: Liturgical Texts with Commentary*, p. 98.

[26] Jan Sutch Pickard, *Celebrating Women*, eds., Hannah Ward, Jennifer Wild, Janet Morley, SPCK, 1995, pp. 55-57, adapted.

[27] Janet Morley, *All Desires Known*, p. 101.

[28] Bonaventura, *The Fount Book of Prayer*, pp. 69-70.

[29] Didier Rimaud, 'Images of the Cross', trans. Fred Pratt Green, *The Hymns and Ballads of Fred Pratt Green*, copyright Hope Publishing Co., Carol Stream, IL., 1974.

[30] *Book of Common Order of the Church of Scotland*, p. 567.

[31] *Proclaiming All Your Wonders*, p. 38.

MORNING PRAYER
for the season of
EASTER

[1]*Why do you look for the living among the dead?* (Easter)

[2] *God has ascended amid shouts of joy.* (Ascension)

[3]*Suddenly a sound like the blowing of a violent wind came from heaven.*
(Pentecost)

THE HYMN VERSE or this:

[4]*Christ is risen!*
Let the gospel trumpets speak,
and the news as of holy fire,
burning and flaming and inextinguishable,
run to the ends of the earth.

Christ is risen!
Let all creation greet the good tidings
with jubilant shout;
for redemption has come,
the long night is passed, the Saviour lives!
And rides and reigns in triumph
now and unto the age of ages.

Christ is risen!

Silence

A PRAYER OF PENITENCE *may be said,*
of the week, or this:

[5]*O God, give us a well of tears*
to wash away the hurts of our lives.
O God, give us a well of tears
to cleanse the wounds,
to bathe the battered face of our world.
O God, give us a well of tears
or we are left, like arid earth,
unsanctified.

Silence

Heal us and your grieving world
of all that harms us.
By the power of your resurrection
restore us to new life
set us on new paths
bring us from darkness to light
help us to choose hope. Amen

*One of the following **CANTICLES** may be said:*

1. *RESURRECTION*[6]

Rise, beloved Christ,
like a dove rising high in the sky,
its white feathers glistening in the sun.
Let us see the purity of your soul.
Like a sparrow keeping constant watch
over its nest of little ones,
watch over us day and night,
guarding us against all physical and spiritual danger.
Like a turtledove hiding its offspring from all attackers,
hide us from the attacks of the Devil.
Like a swallow, swooping towards the earth,
swoop down upon us
and touch us with your life-giving Spirit.

Rise, beloved Christ.

2. *CHRIST THE LAMB*[7]

Christians, praise the paschal victim!
Offer thankful sacrifice!

Christ the lamb has saved the sheep,
Christ the just one paid the price,
Reconciling sinners to the Father.

Death and life fought bitterly
For this wondrous victory;
The Lord of life who died reigns glorified!

O Mary, come and say
what you saw at break of day.

"The empty tomb of my living Lord!
I saw Christ Jesus risen and adored!

"Bright angels testified,
Shroud and grave clothes side by side!

"Yes, Christ my hope rose gloriously.
He goes before you into Galilee."

Share the good news, sing joyfully:
His death is victory!
Lord Jesus, victor King,
Show us mercy. Amen.

3. THE TABLE[8]

Lord Christ, we pray your mercy on our table spread,
And what your gentle hands have given to us
Let it be by you blessed:
Whatever we have came from your lavish hand,
And all that is good is yours, for you are good.
And you that eat, give thanks for it to Christ,
And let the words you utter be only peace,
For Christ loved peace: he himself said,
Peace I give to you, my peace I leave with you.
Grant that your own may be a generous hand
Breaking the bread for all the poor, sharing the food.
Christ shall receive the bread you gave his poor,
And shall not tarry to give you reward.

I am the bread of life

4. THE WATER OF LIFE[9]

God the Father all-powerful, benign,
Jesu the Son of tears and of sorrow,
With thy co-assistance, O! Holy Spirit.

The Three-one, ever-living, ever-mighty, everlasting,
Who brought the children of Israel through the Red Sea,
And Jonah to land from the belly of the great creature of the ocean,

Who brought Paul and his companions in the ship,
From the torment of the sea, from the colour of the waves,
From the gale that was great, from the storm that was heavy.

When the storm poured on the Sea of Galilee.

Sain us and shield us and sanctify us,
Be thou, King of the elements, seated at our helm,
And lead us in peace to the end of our journey.

With winds mild, kindly, benign, pleasant,
Without swirl, without whirl, without eddy,
That would do no harmful deed to us.
We ask all things of Thee, O God,
According to Thine own will and word.

5. *HOLY FIRE*[10]

I see flames of orange, yellow and red,
shooting upwards to the sky piercing the whole clouds.

I see the clouds themselves chasing the flames upwards,
and I feel the air itself reaching for the heavens.
Down below I see great, grey rocks beating against the earth,
as if they were pushing their way down to hell.
At your resurrection
that which is light and good rises up with you,
and that which is heavy and evil is pushed downwards.
At your resurrection goodness breaks from evil,
life breaks free from death.

Christ is risen!

6. *ASCENSION*[11]

Blessed are you, Sovereign God, reigning in glory.
Cloud and deep darkness proclaim your holiness;
radiant light shows forth your truth.
Jesus has entered the cloud of your presence;
he has taken his seat at the right hand of Majesty.
Perfect sacrifice, he has put away sins.
Merciful high priest, he pleads for our weakness.
Always our brother, he prepares our place in heaven.
Ruler of all, he establishes your reign.

Dawning light for the righteous, hope of sinners,
Blessed are you, Sovereign God, high over all.

7. THE ROYAL ROAD [12]

O my Lord,
how obvious it is that you are almighty!
As we love and obey you,
we can be certain that you will direct us on to the right path.
And as we tread that path,
we will know that it is your power and love that has put us there.
It is said that the path which leads to you is narrow and rough,
with steep cliffs on either side,
plunging down into dark valleys.
Yet the path on which you have put me is a royal road,
broad and smooth.
It is safe for anyone who chooses to take it.
And your Son holds the hand of all who walk on it.
If we become tired or discouraged,
we need only to look up to see your smiling face in the distance,
inviting us to share your joy.

8. SWEET FIRE, SWEET FLAMES [13]

Great God, how I love you; O how I love you!
I feel myself burning; you are the fire that burns me.
O pain, O infinitely happy pain of love!
O sweet fire! O sweet flames!

You, O sweet Lord, have set my heart ablaze,
Your fire destroys my sinful self, reducing it to ashes.
Stop, stop! I cannot pull myself away from such fire.
No, let me stay! Let the fire consume me.

Come, Lord Jesus! My heart is now open to you.
All the sin that encrusted my heart is reduced to ashes.
Let your holy body take the place of my sinful body.
Let your Holy Spirit infuse my spirit.

Silence

THE PROCLAMATION OF THE WORD *for the day*

Silence

*This **RESPONSARY** may be said:*

[14] Be joyful in God, all you lands;
sing the glory of his name.
He gives life to our souls.

Come now and see the word of God
how wonderful he is toward all people.
He gives life to our souls.

He turned the sea into dry land,
so that they went through the water on foot.
He gives life to our souls.

Then we rejoiced in him.
In his might he rules forever.
He gives life to our souls.

THE PSALM *for the day*

THE PRAYERS
for the week, free prayer, or one of the following:

[15] *Let us rejoice during the Great Fifty Days of Easter, for God has raised Jesus up from the dead!*
We pray:

That our hearts may be open to Christ's promised Spirit sent from God:
Risen Christ have mercy.

That God who has forgiven our sins through the life, death and resurrection of the Son may give us strength to forgive those who sin against us: *Risen Christ, have mercy.*

That the sufferings of those who are wounded in body, mind or spirit may be our sufferings: *Risen Christ, have mercy.*

That the churches may ache with the desire to be the one church: *Risen Christ, have mercy.*

That there may soon be peace in one corner of the world that has not known it: *Risen Christ, have mercy.*

That domestic discord, with or without its violence, may yield to a measure of peace: *Risen Christ, have mercy.*

[16]O God, whose blessed Son made himself known to his disciples
in the breaking of bread: Open the eyes of our faith,
that we may behold him in all his redeeming work;
who lives and reigns with you,
in the unity of the Holy Spirit,
one God, now and for ever. Amen.

Or
THANKSGIVING

[17] You love humankind, O Christ, and I glorify you for that.
You are the only Son, the Lord of all things.
You alone are without sin.
You gave yourself up to death for me, an unworthy sinner,
the death of the cross.
Through this suffering,
you have delivered all human beings from the snares of evil.
What shall I render to you, Lord, for such goodness?

Glory to you, friend of us all!
Glory to you, O merciful Lord!
Glory to you, longsuffering God!
Glory to you, who takes away all sins!
Glory to you, who came to save us!
Glory to you, who became flesh in the womb of a virgin!
Glory to you, bound in chords!
Glory to you, whipped and scourged!
Glory to you, mocked and derided!
Glory to you, nailed to the cross!
Glory to you, buried and risen!
Glory to you, proclaimed to all humankind, who believe in you!
Glory to you, ascended to heaven!

THE LORD'S PRAYER

THE PRAYER FOR THE DAY
or this:

[18]Christ, you are risen with the sun;
you are light in our darkness,
warmth in our cold.
You are peace and hope and joy,
for you went willingly to death.

You turned defeat and failure to victory for all.
You live eternally, with you live the millions,
living and dead, who trust in you.

Easter

[19]*May we who in baptism die to sin,*
rise again to new life
and find our true place in your living body.
May the new covenant sealed in your blood
through us bring healing and reconciliation
to this wounded world.
Alleluia! You are risen! We are risen with you!
Praise and glory to the living God!

Ascension

[20]*Give praise to God,*
for the risen Christ is with us now
in power and majesty,
in grace and peace.
May we live in him as he lives in the glory
of the eternal Trinity.

Pentecost

[21]*God of power,*
may the boldness of your Spirit transform us,
may the gentleness of your Spirit lead us,
may the gifts of your Spirit
be our goal and our strength
now and always

EVENING PRAYER
for the season of
EASTER

[22] *He has risen! He is not here. See the place where they laid him.* (Easter)

[23] *Why do you stand there looking into the sky?* (Ascension)

[24] *Receive the Holy Spirit!* (Pentecost)

THE HYMN VERSE
or this:

[25] *You are risen, my Lord and my God!*
Rise up, my heart, give thanks, rejoice!
And do you, O Lord, deign to enter it
despite the shut doors.
Show me your hands and your side,
that I may know it is you.
Send me about your business,
servant of the living King, the King of kings;
and hide my life in yours
for ever and ever.

A PRAYER OF PENITENCE *may be said;*
of the week, or this:

[26] O Jesus Christ, risen master and triumphant Lord,
we come to you in sorrow for our sins,
and confess to you our weakness and unbelief:

We have lived by our own strength,
and not by the power of your resurrection.
In your mercy, forgive us:
Lord, hear us and help us.

We have lived by the light of our own eyes,
as faithless and not believing.
In your mercy, forgive us:
Lord, hear us and help us.

We have lived for this world alone,
and doubted our home in heaven.
In your mercy, forgive us:
Lord, hear us and help us.

Lift our minds above earthly things,
set them on the things above;
show us your glory and your power,
that we may serve you gladly all our days. Amen.

*One of the following **CANTICLES** may be said:*

1. *RESURRECTION!* [27]

I have stretched out my hands and offered myself to the Lord.
The stretching out of my hands is the sign of that offering,
The stretching out on the wood
Where the Just One was hanged, by the roadside

I am risen, I am with them,
I am speaking through their mouth.
I have laid upon them the yoke of my love.

Hell saw me and was vanquished.
Death let me depart, and many with me.
I was gall and vinegar to it.
I descended to the depths of hell.
Death could not bear my face.
I made of the dead an assembly of the living.
I spoke to them with living lips
so that my word should not be in vain.

They ran towards me, the dead.
They cried out, Take pity on us, O Son of God.
Deliver us out of the darkness that fetters us.
Open the gate for us that we may go out with you.
We see that death has no hold on you.
Deliver us also, for you are our Saviour.

And I heard their voices and I traced my name on their heads.
So they are free and they belong to me.
Alleluia!

2. THE PASCH OF THE LORD [28]

This is the paschal feast, the Lord's passing:
so cried the Spirit.
No type or telling, this,
no shadow;
Pasch of the Lord it is, and truly.
The blood that is shed is a sign of the blood to be shed,
the first indication of what the Spirit will be,
a glimpse of the great anointing;
"I, seeing the blood, will protect you."

You have indeed protected us, Jesus,
from endless disaster.
You spread your hands like a Father
and fatherlike gave cover with your wings.
Your blood, a God's blood, you poured out over the earth,
sealing a blood bargain for us
because you loved us.
What anger threatened you turned away from us;
instead you gave us back God's friendship.

The heavens may have your spirit, paradise your soul
but O may the earth have your blood.

The pasch came from God, came from heaven to earth:
from earth it has gone back to heaven.

3. EUCHARIST [29]

And I shall clothe myself in your eternal will,
and by this light I shall come to know
that you, eternal Trinity,
are table and food and waiter
for us.
You, eternal Father, and the table
that offers us as food
the Lamb, your only-begotten Son.
He is the most exquisite of foods for us,
both in his teaching,
which nourishes us in your will,
and in the sacrament
that we receive in holy communion,
which feeds and strengthens us

while we are pilgrim travellers in this life.
And the Holy Spirit
is indeed a waiter for us,
for the Spirit serves us this teaching
by enlightening our mind's eye with it
and inspiring us to follow it.
And the Spirit serves us charity for our neighbours
and hunger to have as our food.

4. THE LIVING FOUNTAIN[30]

How well I know that fountain's rushing flow
Although by night.

Its deathless spring is hidden Even so
Full well I guess from whence its sources flow
Though it be night.

Its origin (since it has none) none knows:
But that all origin from it arose
Although by night.

I know there is no other thing so fair
And earth and heaven drink refreshment there
Although by night.

Full well I know its depth no man can sound
And that no ford to cross it can be found
Though it be night.

Its clarity unclouded still shall be:
Out of it comes the light by which we see
Though it be night.

Flush with its banks and streams so proudly swells;
I know it waters nations, heavens and hells
Though it be night.

The current that is nourished by this source
I know it to be omnipotent in force
Although by night.

From source and current a new current swells
Which neither of the other twain excels.
Though it be night.

The eternal source hides in the Living Bread
That we with life eternal may be fed
Though it be night.

Here to all creatures it is crying, hark!
That they should drink their fill though in the dark,
For it is night.

This living fount which is to me so dear
Within the bread of life I see it clear
Though it be night.

5. *FIRE* [31]

Let the Christbrand burst!
Let the Christbrand blazon!
Dartle whitely under the hearth-fire,
Unwind the wind, turn the thunderer,
And never, never thinning,
Forfend fear.
Flare up smartly, fix, flex, bless, inspire,
Instar the time, sear the sorcerer,
And never, never sparing,
Save all year
Let the Christbrand burst!
Let the Christbrand blazon!

6. *ASCENSION* [32]

Lord Jesus,
I put my faith in you.
I place my hope in you, and I love you
with my whole mind and my whole strength.
When you rise up to heaven,
I long to be carried up to heaven,
that my faith may be vindicated,
my hope fulfilled, and my love rewarded.
Lord Jesus,
as you sit on your throne in heaven,
redeem those who are lost,
sanctify those who are redeemed,
and give joy to those who are sanctified.

7. A STEADY COURSE [33]

Good Lord,
Steer the ship of my life to your quiet harbour,
where I shall be safe from the storms of sin and conflict.
Show me the course I should take.
Renew in me the gift of discernment,
so that I can always see the right direction in which I should go.
And give me the strength and the courage to
choose the right course,
even when the sea is rough and the waves are high,
knowing that through enduring hardship and danger
in your name
we shall find comfort and peace.

8. VENI, SANCTE SPIRITUS [34]

O holy God behind the silent stone
Beneath the under and the elder fire,
Beyond the Milky Way, within the bone,
The grace desired and grace of our desire.

The night is spent; the day is near at hand.
We who have wrestled lonely with the flesh
Listen in solitude for your command,
Our fingers on the curtains, in the mesh.

Of cords and concepts which your glory hide.
Come whom no word of ours can symbolize.
Let wiring of your word in us abide.
Light us in every dark and make us wise,

Wise that through all the night our souls may see
The Father and the Son alive in thee.

Silence

THE PROCLAMATION OF THE WORD *for the day*

Silence

*This **RESPONSARY** may be said:*

[35] Here are the words you may trust
Remember Jesus Christ, risen from the dead:
He is our salvation, our eternal glory.

If we die with him, we shall live with him:
if we endure we shall reign with him.

If we deny him, he will deny us:
if we are faithless, he keeps faith.

For he has broken the power of death:
and brought life and immortality to light through the gospel.

THE PRAYERS
for the week, free prayer or one of the following:

[36]O God our desire,
in the strangeness of searching
at a place beyond hope,
waiting to understand
what we cannot bear to think of,
we put our trust in you:
For death shall have no dominion.

In the strangeness of recognition
of the selves we have become
at the return of the beloved
when the face of love has changed,
we put our trust in you:
For death shall have no dominion.

In the strangeness of separation,
when we refrain from touching;
when we are blessed with freedom,
and invited to let go,
we put our trust in you:
For death shall have no dominion.

In the strangeness of joy,
when we are offered a new name,
a redeemed authority,
and a fresh surrender,
we put our trust in you:
For death shall have no dominion.

Or
THANKSGIVING

[37]O Lord God, our Father.
You are the light that can never be put out;
and now you give us a light that shall drive away all darkness.
You are love without coldness,
and you have given us such warmth in our hearts
that we can love all when we meet.
You are the life that defies death,
and you have opened for us the way that leads to eternal life.
None of us is a great Christian;
we are all humble and ordinary.
But your grace is enough for us.
Arouse in us that small degree of joy and thankfulness
of which we are capable,
to the timid faith which we can muster,
to the cautious obedience which we cannot refuse,
and thus to the wholeness of life
which you have prepared for all of us
through the death and resurrection of your Son.
Do not allow any of us to remain apathetic or indifferent
to the wondrous glory of Easter,
But let the light of our risen Lord
reach every corner of our dull hearts. Amen.

THE LORD'S PRAYER

THE PRAYER FOR THE DAY
or this:

[38]At Eastertime, Lord God,
the vine renews its sap.
Keep the branches united to the stock,
and grant that a love like Christ's
may lead us to live for others,
in him who dies and rose again for us,
Jesus, the Christ, our Lord. Amen.

Easter
[39] Let everyone who loves God rejoice in this festival of light!
With joy we praise the Lord! Alleluia!
Let the faithful servants gladly enter into the joy of their Lord!
Our hearts are filled with thanksgiving! Alleluia!

Let those who have borne the burden of fasting come now to celebrate the feast!
We walk from darkness into light!
Let those who are inwardly dead now rise and dance with Christ, the Lord of Life.
We are renewed in you, O Christ! Alleluia!

Ascension
[40]*Sing to the Lord,*
who ascended above the heaven of heavens,
our Christ,
our Sunrise,
our Joy,
our King,
crowned in glory - Alleluia!

Pentecost
[41]*O Spirit of God, mighty river, flow over me, in me, through me.*
O Spirit of God, cleanse me, purify the channels of my life.
O Spirit of God, bear me along with thy flood of life-giving service.
O Spirit of God, mighty river, bear me down to the ocean,
the ocean of thy love.
O Sprit of God, mighty fire, glow in me, burn in me,
until thy radiance fills my soul.
O Sprit of God, mighty fire, may thy light illumine my mind.
O Spirit of God, mighty fire, may thy heat consume my will
until I burn for thee alone.
May the flames of thy love ever blaze upon the altar of my heart.

---

[1] Luke 24:5.

[2] Psalm 47:8.

[3] Acts 2:2.

[4] Eric Milner-White, *My God, My Glory,* SPCK and The Friends of York Minster, London, 1994, p. 69, adapted.

[5] Kate McIlhagga, *The Pattern of Our Days: Liturgies and Resources for Worship*, ed. Kathy Galloway, The Iona Community, Wild Goose Publications, Glasgow, 1996, pp. 120-121, adapted from a larger prayer.

[6] Bonaventura, *The Fount book of Prayer*, ed. Robert Van de Weyer, HarperCollins, London, 1993, p. 70.

[7] 'Easter Sequence', Roman Rite, 11th Century, attrib. Wipo of Burgundy, trans. Peter Scagnelli, appearing in *A Triduum Sourcebook*, eds. Gabe Huck and Mary Ann

Simcoe, Liturgy Training Publications, copyright the Archdiocese of Chicago, Chicago, 1983, p. 149.

[8] Alcuin, *More Latin Lyrics*, trans., Helen Waddell, Victor Gollancz Ltd., (Cassell Plc), 1976, adapted.

[9] *Carmina Gadelica I 329,* Scottish Academic Press and Trustees of Prof. J.C. Watson.

[10] Adam of St. Victor, *The Fount book of Prayer*, p. 18.

[11] Michael Vasey, *Enriching the Christian Year*, ed., Michael Perham, SPCK, 1993.

[12] Teresa of Avila, *The Fount book of Prayer*, 347-348.

[13] Gemma Galgani, *The Fount book of Prayer*, p. 163.

[14] *The Book of Alternative Services of the Anglican Church of Canada,* copyright the General Synod of the Anglican Church of Canada, 1985, p. 108.

[15] Gerard Sloyan, from a service celebrated at Trinity Episcopal Cathedral, Cleveland, Ohio, USA, appearing in *Liturgy: Easter Day*, Journal of the Liturgical Conference, Winter, 1996, Volume 13, No. 4., pp. 70-71, adapted.

[16] Collect for Wednesday in Easter Week, *Book of Common Prayer*, of the Protestant Episcopal Church in the United States of America, The Church Hymnal Corporation, New York.

[17] Ephraim, fourth century, trans. Agnes Cunningham, *A Triduum Sourcebook*, eds. Gabe Huck and Mary Ann Simcoe, Liturgy Training Publications, copyright the Archdiocese of Chicago, Chicago, 1983, p.21.

[18] *A New Zealand Prayer Book*, copyright The Church of the Province of New Zealand, 1989, p. 537.

[19] Op. cit., p. 537.

[20] Op. cit., p. 540.

[21] Op. cit., p. 541.

[22] Mark 16:6.

[23] Acts 1:10.

[24] John 20:22.

[25] Eric Milner-White, *My God, My Glory,* SPCK and The Friends of York Minster, London, 1994, p. 69, adapted.

[26] *Church Family Worship*, ed., Michael Perry, Hodder & Stoughton, London, copyright Michael Perry, Mrs B. Perry and Jubilate Hymns, 1986, No 244.

[27] Ode 42, adapted, *The Odes of Solomon*, J.R. Harris and A. Mingana, 2 vols. Manchester University Press, Longmans, Green & Co., 1916 and 1920.

[28] Attributed to Hippolytus, third century, *Early Christian Prayers*, ed. A. Hamman, trans W. Mitchell, Longmans, Green & Co., London, 1961.

[29] Catherine of Siena, *The Prayers of Catherine of Siena*, ed. Suzanne Noffke, OP, Paulist Press, New York.

[30] St. John of the Cross, *Poems,* trans. Roy Campbell, Harvill, 1951, Penguin Books, 1960, pp. 61-62.

[31] Francis J. O'Malley, *Scholastic Magazine*, December, 1974, University of Nôtre Dame, Nôtre Dame, Ind. USA.

[32] Bonaventura, *The Fount book of Prayer*, p. 71.

[33] Basil of Caesarea, *The Fount book of Prayer*, p. 57.

[34] George Every, *Anthology of Religious Verse,* ed. Norman Nicholson, 1942, p. 42, appearing in *Seasons of the Spirit*, ed., George Every, Richard Harris, Kallistos Ware, SPCK/Triangle, London, 1984.

[35] 2 Timothy 2:11-13, RSV.

[36] Janet Morley, O God of our desire (Mary Magdalene John 20:1-18), *All Desires Known,* SPCK, London, and Morehouse Publishing, Harrisburg, Penn., 1992, p. 71.

[37] Karl Barth, *The Call of God*, trans. A. Mackay, SCM Press, London, 1967.

[38] *Proclaiming All Your Wonders,* Dominican Publications, Dublin, 1991, Bayard Presse International, Paris, 1983, p. 67.

[39] St. John Chrysostom, *The Book of A Thousand Prayers*, compiled by Angela Ashwin, HarperCollins Religious, London, 1996, p. 327, No. 823.

[40] Source unknown, *The Book of A Thousand Prayers,* compiled by Angela Ashwin, HarperCollins Religious, London, 1996, p. 332, No. 836.

[41] Chandran Devanesan, *The Book of a Thousand Prayers*, compiled by Angela Ashwin, HarperCollins Religious, London, 1996, p. 333-334, No. 840.

LECTIONARY FOR A SECOND READING

The purpose of this lectionary is to provide for those who worship twice daily, and who may wish to use an additional reading and psalm to the ones printed in the main body of the book. The readings are on a semi-continuous basis, but some of them do reflect the seasonal themes.

	YEAR 1	YEAR 2	YEAR 3	PSALM
ASH WEDNESDAY				
W	Ro 1:18-32	Ro 9:1-13	Jas 1:1-11	19
T	Job 1:1-12	Job 22:1-14	Job 32	17:1-11
F	Job 1:13-22	Job 22:15-30	Jas 1:12-18	88:13-18
S	Ro 2:1-16	Job 23:1-7	Job 33:1-11	62:1-8
LENT I:				
TEMPTATION				
S	Job 3:1-17	Ro 9:14-29	Job 33:12-22	88:1-6
M	Job 4:1-17	Job 23:8-17	Jas 1:19-27	88:7-12
T	Ro 3:21-31	Ro 9:30-10:4	Jas 2:1-13	34:1-7
W	Job 5:1-16	Job 24:1-12	Job 33:23-33	27:7-14
T	Job 5:17-27	Job 24: 13-25	Job 34:1-15	4
F	Job 6:1-13	Job 25	Job 34:16-28	13
S	Job 6:14-30	Job 26	Job 34:29-37	15
LENT II:				
THE FALL				
S	Ro 4:1-12	Ro 10:5-13	Job 35:1-8	32:1-7
M	Ro 4:13-25	Ro 10:14-21	Jas 2:14-26	112
T	Ro 5:1-11	Job 27:1-12	Jas 3:1-12	12:1-6
W	Ro 6:15-23	Ro 11:10-12	Jas 3:13-18	!9:7-end
T	Job 7	Job 27:13-23	Job 35:9-16	143:1-6
F	Job 8	Job 28:1-8	Job 36:1-12	143:7-11
S	Job 9	Job 28:9-19	Job 36:13-21	123
LENT III:				
THE RETURN				
S	Job 10	Ro 11:13-24	Job 36:22-36	94:14-19
M	Ro 7:1-6	Ro 11:25-36	Jas 4:1-12	55:1-8
T	Ro 7:7-13	Job 28:20-28	Jas 4:13-5:6	119:33-40
W	Job 11	Job 29:1-10	Job 37:1-13	102:1-8
T	Job 12	Job 29:11-17	Job 37:14-20	102:23-28
F	Job 13	Job 29:18-25	Job 37:21-24	86:1-7
S	Job 14	Ro 12:1-8	Job 38:1-15	77:1-15

	YEAR 1	YEAR 2	YEAR 3	PSALM

LENT IV:
THE COST

	YEAR 1	YEAR 2	YEAR 3	PSALM
S	Ro 7:14-26	Ro 12:9-21	Job 38:15-24	131
M	Ro 8:1-11	Ro 13:1-7	Jas 5:1-12	49:12-20
T	Ro 8:12-17	Ro 13:8-14	Jas 5:13-20	112
W	Job 15	Job 30:1-8	Job 38:25-33	139:6-12
T	Job 16	Job 30:9-19	Job 38:34-41	139:13-18
F	Job 17	Job 30:20-31	Job 39:1-12	73:21-26
S	18	Ro 14:1-12	Job 39:13-30	19:1-6

LENT V:
THE NARROW GATE

	YEAR 1	YEAR 2	YEAR 3	PSALM
S	Ro 8:18-30	Ro 14:13-23	Job 40:1-14	26
M	Job 19:1-12	Job 31:1-8	Job 40:15-24	90:13-17
T	Job 19:13-29	Job 31:9-15	Job 41:1-8	89:46-51
W	Job 20:1-16	Job 31:16-23	Job 41:9-24	70
T	Job 20:17-29	Job 31:24-24	Job 41:25-34	80:3-7
F	Job 21	Job 31:35-40	Job 42:1-6	119:169-176
S	Ro 8:31-39	Ro 15:1-13	Job 42:7-16	116

HOLY WEEK

	YEAR 1	YEAR 2	YEAR 3	PSALM
S	Mark 1:1-11	Mt 21:1-11	Lk 19:28-40	24:7-10
M	Jer 7:1-11	Isa 5:1-13	Jer 20:7-11	Lam 3:4-12
T	Eze 3:4-9	Jer 26:7-11	Jer 15:10-21	Lam 3:13-21
W	Jer 37:6-16	Jer 26:20-24	Jer 17:5-10, 14-17	Lam 3:55-63
T	Jer 12:7-13	Zec 13:7-9	Jer 11:18-20	Lam 2:20-21
F	Zec 12:9-11	Ge 22:1-14	*Wis 1:16-2:1 2:12-24	Lam 1:12-14
S	Micah 7:7-15	*Bar 3:9-15	Zep 3:14-20	Lam 3:22-33

EASTER:
CHRIST IS RISEN!

	YEAR 1	YEAR 2	YEAR 3	PSALM
S	Heb 1:1-5	Heb 4:1-7	Heb 9:15-21	118:1-5
M	Heb 1:6-9	Heb 4:8-13	Heb 9:22-28	148
T	Heb 1:10-14	Heb 4:14-16	Heb 10:1-6	149
W	Heb 2:1-4	Heb 6:1-6	Heb 10:7-14	145:13:21
T	Heb 2:5-9	Heb 6:7-12	Heb 10:15-18	146
F	Ex 2:1-14	Nu 10:1-10	Dt 1:1-8	138
S	Ex 2:15-24	Nu 10:11-13, 29-36	Dt 1:9-18	118:6-14

	YEAR 1	YEAR 2	YEAR 3	PSALM

EASTER I:
THE PASSOVER

	YEAR 1	YEAR 2	YEAR 3	PSALM
S	Heb 2:10-13	Heb 7:1-10	Heb 10:19-25	110:1-4
M	Heb 2:14-18	Heb 7:11-17	Heb 10:16-31	37:3-9
T	Heb 3:1-6	Heb 7:18-22	Heb 10:32-39	95:1-7
W	Heb 3:7-11	Heb 7:23-28	Heb 11:1-10	31:19-24
T	Heb 3:12-19	Heb 8:1-6	Heb 11:17-23	22:27-31
F	Ex 13:1-16	Nu 11:1-9	Dt 4:1-8	78:1-8
S	Ex 13:17-22	Nu 11:10-17	Dt 4:9-14	78:9-16

EASTER II:
THE BREAD OF LIFE

	YEAR 1	YEAR 2	YEAR 3	PSALM
S	Heb 5:1-5	Heb 8:7-13	Dt 4:15-24	85:8-13
M	Heb 5:6-10	Heb 9:1-10	Heb 11:24-39	Lk 1:68-75
T	Ex 14:1-14	Nu 11:18-23	Dt 4:25-35	78:17-30
W	Ex 14:15-22	Nu 11:24-35	Dt 5:1-21	78:32-39
T	Ex 14:23-31	Nu 12:1-9	Dt 5:22-33	78:40-55
F	Ex 15:1-21	Nu 12:10-16	Dt 6:1-12	78:56-64
S	Heb 5:11-14	Nu 13:1-20	Dt 6:13-25	75

EASTER III:
THE WATER OF LIFE

	YEAR 1	YEAR 2	YEAR 3	PSALM
S	Ex 15:22-27	Nu 13:21-31	Dt 7:6-11	78:65-72
M	Rev 1:9-16	Rev 2:1-7	Rev 1:1-8	45:1-4,6-7
T	Rev 1:17-20	Rev 3:1-6	Rev 3:14-22	101
W	Rev 2:8-11	Rev 3:7-13	Rev 14:6-13	18:1-6
T	Rev 2:12-17	Rev 4:1-6	Rev 14:14-20	18:7-12
F	Ex 16:6-20	Nu 14:1-5	Dt 8:1-10	16
S	Ex16:21-36	Nu 14:6-12	Dt 8:11-20	81:1-7

EASTER IV:
FIRE & LIGHT

	YEAR 1	YEAR 2	YEAR 3	PSALM
S	Ex 17:8-15	Nu 14:13-19	Dt 9:1-5	81:8-16
M	Rev 2:18-29	Rev 5:1-5	Rev 19:1-3	100
T	Rev 6:1-6	Rev 5:6-14	Rev 19:4-10	18:13-19
W	Ex 18:1-12	Nu 14:20-25	Dt 10:12-22	106:1-5
T	Ex 18:13-27	Nu 14:26-35	Dt 11:1-12	106:6-12
F	Ex 19:1-8	Nu 14:36-45	Dt 12:1-11	106:13-23
S	Ex 19:9-15	Nu 20:1-13	Dt 13:1-5	106:24-33

	YEAR 1	YEAR 2	YEAR 3	PSALM

EASTER V:
RISEN! ASCENDED! GLORIFIED!

	YEAR 1	YEAR 2	YEAR 3	PSALM
S	Ex 19:16-25	Nu 14:13-19	Dt 9:1-5	106:40-48
M	Rev 6:7-11	Rev 12:1-6	Rev 19:11-16	18:20-24
T	Rev 6:12-17	Rev 12:7-12	Dt 18:15-22	18:25-36
W	Ex 20:1-21	Nu 21:4-8	Dt 26:1-11	89:1-8
T	2 Kings 2:1-15	Eze 1:4-5,26-28	SS 3:29-37	93
F	Ex 24:1-11	Nu 21:4-8	Dt 28:1-6	107:10-22
S	Ex 24:12-18	Nu 21:9-20	Dt 28:7-14	2

EASTER VI:
PILGRIMAGE

	YEAR 1	YEAR 2	YEAR 3	PSALM
S	Ex 32:1-14	Nu 22:2-15	Dt 30:1-10	107:23-32
M	Rev 7:1-8	Rev 12:13-17	Rev 20:1-6	107:33-43
T	Rev 7:9-12	Rev 13:1-4	Rev 20:7-15	144:1-9
W	Rev 7:13-17	Rev 13:5-10	Rev 21:1-8	99
T	Rev 11:1-6	Rev 13:11-18	Rev 21:9-21	98
F	Ex 32:15-26	Nu 22:21-35	Dt 30:11-30	127
S	Ex 32:27-35	Nu 22:36-41	Dt 32:1-12	130

PENTECOST

	YEAR 1	YEAR 2	YEAR 3	PSALM
S	Isa 30:15-25	2 Sa 23:1-5	Micah 3:1-8	134
M	Rev 11:15-19	Rev 14:1-5	Rev 22:1-5	84:1-7
T	Ex 33:1-10	Nu 23:1-12	Dt 32:1-12	101
W	Ex 34:1-10	Nu 23:13-20	Dt 32:48-52	124
T	Ex 40:1-16	Nu 23: 21-30	Dt 33:1-6	122
F	Ex 40:17-33	Nu 24:1-9	Dt 34:1-4	128
S	Ex 40:34-38	Nu 27:12-22	Dt 34:5-12	131

* From the Apocrypha

RESOURCES

ASH WEDNESDAY

WEDNESDAY: **Acclamation:** Stichera of the Triodion, No. 3, *Byzantine Daily Worship,* Alleluia Press, Allendale, N.J., 1969, p. 790, used with permission; **Litany of Penance:** *The Book of Common Prayer* of the Episcopal Church of the United States of America, The Church Hymnal Corporation, New York, 1979, pp. 267-8; **Prayer:** Brian A. Wren, *Bring Many Names,* copyright and © 1989 Hope Publishing Company for the USA, Canada, Australia and New Zealand and Stainer & Bell Ltd., London, England for all other territories. Reproduced from 'Piece Together Praise'. v.1; *THURSDAY:* **Acclamation:** from Matins for the first Monday of Lent, adapted, *The Lenten Triodion,* trans. Mother Mary & Archimandrite Kallistos Ware, Faber & Faber, London, 1978, p.23; **Prayer:** Commission francophone cistercienne, *Proclaiming All Your Wonders,* Dominican Publications, Dublin, 1991, Bayard Presse International S.A., 1983, p.46; *FRIDAY:* **Acclamation:** from Matins for the first Monday in Lent, *The Lenten Triodion,* p. 191; **Prayer:** *A New Zealand Prayer Book,* copyright The Church of the Province of New Zealand, 1989, p. 532; *SATURDAY:* **Acclamation:** from Vespers for the Wednesday in the week before Lent, *The Lenten Triodion,* p. 23, adapted; **Prayer:** *A New Zealand Prayer Book,* p. 573; **Prayer of Penitence:** Chris Bowater, copyright Sovereign Lifestyle Music, Leighton Buzzard, 1990; **The Prayers:** copyright Jan Berry, appearing in *Bread of Tomorrow,* ed., Janet Morley, SPCK/Christian Aid, London, 1992, p. 81.

MEDITATIONS: *WEDNESDAY:* Genesis 3:19; *THURSDAY:* A Monk, *The Hermitage Within,* trans. A. Neame, Darton, Longman & Todd, London, 1977, p. 81; *FRIDAY:* St. Jerome; *The Lion Christian Quotation Collection,* compiled by Hannah Ward and Jennifer Wild, Lion Publishing Plc, Oxford, 1997, p. 38; *SATURDAY:* St. Ambrose, *The Lion Christian Quotation Collection,* p.19; Madeleine L'Engle, *Weather of the Heart,* copyright Crosswicks, Harold Shaw Publishers, Wheaton, Il., USA, 1978.

WEEKEND READINGS: Saturday – Year 1: Mark Searle, *Assembly,* Vol. 8, No. 3, University of Notre Dame Press, Notre Dame, In., USA; **Year 2:** Thomas Merton, *Meditations on Liturgy,* A.R. Mowbray & Co., Ltd., (Cassell Plc), Oxford, 1976, p. 127 (USA title, *Seasons of Celebration,* copyright 1950, 1958, 1962, 1964, 1965, by the Abbey of Gethsemani, pb. Farrar, Straus & Giroux, Inc.); **Year 3:** Maximus the Confessor, Centuries on Charity, *Drinking from the Hidden Fountain: A Patristic Breviary,* Thomas Spidlik, trans. Paul Drake, New City, London, 1992, p. 76.

LENT 1: TEMPTATION

SUNDAY: **Hymn:** G.H. Smyttan & F. Pott, *AMR* 92, v.1; **Prayer:** *Proclaiming All Your Wonders,* p. 39; *MONDAY:* **Hymn:** v.2; **Prayer:** *A New Zealand Prayer Book,* p. 573; *TUESDAY:* **Hymn:** v.4; **Prayer:** John Baillie, *A Diary of Private Prayer,* Oxford University Press, 1936, adapted; *WEDNESDAY:* **Hymn:** v.3; **Prayer:** Collect for the Third Sunday of Lent, *The Book of Alternative Services of the Anglican Church of Canada,* copyright the General Synod of the Anglican Church of Canada, Anglican Book Centre, Toronto, 1983, p. 290; *THURSDAY:* **Hymn:** v.5; **Prayer:**

Proclaiming All Your Wonders, p. 48; *FRIDAY:* **Hymn:** v.6; **Prayer:** *Book of Common Order of the Church of Scotland,* p. 432; *SATURDAY:* **Hymn:** Charles Wesley, *AMR* 90; **Prayer:** Bishop Brooke Foss Wescott, *The Oxford Book of Prayer,* ed., George Appleton, Oxford University Press, 1985, p. 124, adapted; **Prayer of Penitence:** Eric Milner-White, *My God, My Glory,* SPCK and Friends of York Minster, London, 1954, 1994, p. 35 (I), adapted; **The Prayers:** Prayers for Lent 1, *Book of Common Order of the Church of Scotland,* p. 434.

MEDITATIONS: *SUNDAY:* Thomas Merton, *Raids on the Unspeakable,* Burns & Oates/Search Press Ltd, Tunbridge Wells, 1977, p. 16, by kind permission of the publishers; *MONDAY:* John Milton, *Paradise Regained,* The Fourth Book, The Works of John Milton, Wordsworth Editions Ltd., Ware, 1994, lines 606-608; *TUESDAY:* Jerome Emiliani, fifteenth century, *The Lion Christian Quotation Collection,* p. 96; *WEDNESDAY:* Reginald Somerset Ward, *God at Every Gate,* ed., Brendan O'Malley, The Canterbury Press, Norwich, 1997, p. 102; *THURSDAY:* United Society for the Propagation of the Gospel, London; *FRIDAY:* Luke 11:4; *SATURDAY:* Simone Weil, *Waiting on God;* trans. Emma Craufurd, Routledge, 1951, p. 175; A Prayer of the Venerable Bede, *God at Every Gate,* p. 104.

WEEKEND READINGS: Sunday – Year 1: From the discourses of St. Augustine on the Psalms, *The Divine Office,* copyright 1974 the hierarchies of Australia, England and Wales, and Ireland, Collins, London; **Year 2:** Edward Schillebeeckx, *For the Sake of the Gospel,* trans. John Bowden, SCM Press, London, 1989, p. 57; **Year 3:** A Carthusian, *The Wound of Love: A Carthusian Miscellany,* copyright Darton, Longman & Todd Ltd., London, 1994, and Cistercian Publications, Kalamazoo, Mi., 1993, pp. 101-102, adapted. **Saturday – Year 1:** Evelyn Underhill, *The School of Charity,* The Longman Group Ltd., London, 1934; **Year 2:** George Herbert, The Tempter (I), appearing in *The English Poems of George Herbert,* ed. C.A. Patrides, J.M. Dent & Sons Ltd., London, 1974, p. 74, by kind permission of Everyman's Library Ltd; **Year 3:** François de la Mothe Fénelon, *Life and Letters,* A.R Mowbray & Co., Ltd. (Cassell Plc), 1906, pp. 93f.

LENT II: THE FALL
SUNDAY: **Acclamation:** for the week – the "Jesus Prayer"; **Lament:** Sessional Hymns at Mattins, Monday, Tone Two, *The Lenten Triodion,* p. 672, adapted; **Prayer:** Sarapion of Thmuis, *A Lent Sourcebook: Book One,* eds. J. Robert Baker, Evelyn Kaehler, Peter Mazar, Liturgical Training Publications, Chicago, 1990, p. 141; *MONDAY:* **Lament:** The Sunday of Forgiveness, vespers on Saturday Evening, Tone Six, *The Lenten Triodion,* pp. 168-169, adapted; **Prayer:** from Byzantine Vespers, *A Lent Sourcebook: Book One,* p. 30; *TUESDAY:* **Lament:** Sunday of the Prodigal Son, Mattins, Canticle Six, *The Lenten Triodion,* p. 118; **Prayer:** *Celebrating Common Prayer,* (Mowbray) copyright the European Province of the Society of St. Francis, 1992, p. 532, (material from *Celebrating Commn Prayer* is used with permission); *WEDNESDAY:* **Lament:** From the Great Canon of St. Andrew of Crete, Canticle Two, Hugh Wybrew, *Orthodox Lent, Holy Week and Easter: Liturgical Texts with Commentary,* SPCK, 1995, pp. 46-47; *THURSDAY:* **Lament:** (1) Raissa Maritain, *A Lent Sourcebook: Book One,* p. 135, (2) *The Alternative Service Book 1980,* copyright The Central Board of Finance of the Church of England, 1980, p. 143; **Prayer:** (1)

Proclaiming All Your Wonders, p. 40, (2) A Prayer of the Breton Fishermen, Nancy Martin ed., *Prayers Through the Centuries,* Bishopsgate Press, 1990, p. 9; *FRIDAY:* The Song of God's Children, vss. 1-6, *Book of Common Order of the Church of Scotland,* pp. 578-579; **Prayer:** *Book of Common Order of the Church of Scotland,* p. 433; *SATURDAY:* **Lament:** Sessional Hymns at Mattins, Monday, Tone One, *The Lenten Triodion,* p. 668, adapted; **Prayer:** From Vespers of the Sunday of the Prodigal Son, *Orthodox Lent, Holy Week and Easter:Liturgical Texts with Commentary,* pp. 23-24; **Prayer of Penitence:** From the Great Canon of St. Andrew of Crete, Canticle One, *Orthodox Lent, Holy Week and Easter: Liturgical Texts with Commentary,* p. 45; **The Prayers:** David Adam, *The Open Gate: Celtic prayers for growing spirituality,* Triangle/SPCK, 1994, p. 52.

MEDITATIONS: *SUNDAY:* I John 1:8; *MONDAY: The Lenten Triodion,* p. 175, adapted; *TUESDAY:* Italian Sacramentary, *Messale Romano,* Liberia Editrice Vaticana, trans. Peter Scagnelli, copyright 1983; *WEDNESDAY:* Lamentations 3:35-36; *THURSDAY:* Etty Hillesum, *An Interrupted Life: The Diaries of Etty Hillesum, 1941-1943,* trans. Arno Pomerans, Jonathan Cape Ltd., Pantheon Books a division of Random House Inc.; *FRIDAY:* Ruth Burrows, English Carmelite Nun, *The Lion Christian Quotation Collection,* p. 240; *SATURDAY:* Romans 3:23; John Milton, *Paradise Lost,* Book XII, The Works of John Milton, Wordsworth Editions Ltd., Ware, 1994, lines 633-649.

WEEKEND READINGS: Sunday – Year 1: D.M. Baillie, *God Was In Christ,* Faber & Faber, London, 1948, 1961, p. 204; **Year 2:** Karl Barth, *Church Dogmatics: Volume I The Doctrine of the Word of God,* trans. G.W. Bromily, T & T Clarke, Edinburgh, 1975, pp. 407-408; **Year 3:** Reinhold Niebuhr, *The Nature and Destiny of Man, Volume I,* Macmillan College Publishing Company, New York, 1941, pp. 256-259, 266-267; **Saturday – Year 1:** George Herbert, *The English Poems of George Herbert,* pp. 58-59, by kind permission of Everyman's Library Ltd; **Year 2:** Maria Boulding OSB, *The Coming of God,* SPCK, London, 1982, pp. 98-99; **Year 3:** The Exeter Book, c. 950, *The Fount Book of Prayer,* ed. Roger Van de Weyer, HarperCollins, London, 1993, pp. 138-139.

LENT III: THE RETURN

SUNDAY: **Hymn:** Charles Wesley, *Hymns & Psalms,* Methodist Publishing House, Peterborough, 1983, No. 528, v.1; **Lament:** Latin Hymn, 10th Century, *A Lent Sourcebook: Book Two,* eds. J. Robert Baker, Evelyn Kaehler, Peter Mazar, Liturgy Training Publications, Chicago, 1990, p. 33; **Prayer:** Edward Hays, *Prayers for a Planetary Pilgrim,* copyright Forest of Peace Publishing Inc., Levenworth, Kansas, USA; *MONDAY:* **Hymn:** Charlotte Elliott, *AMR* 349, v.1; The Prayer of Manasseh, 1a, 4, 6-7, 9a, 9c, 11-12, 14b, 15b, *RSV;* **Prayer:** *Proclaiming All Your Wonders,* p. 41; *TUESDAY:* **Hymn:** v.2; **Prayer:** Thomas More, *The Book of A Thousand Prayers,* ed. Angela Ashwin, HarperCollins, London, 1996, p. 133; *WEDNESDAY:* **Hymn:** v.4; **Prayer:** *Proclaiming All Your Wonders,* p. 37; *THURSDAY:* **Hymn:** v.3; **Prayer:** St. Augustine, Confessions IV, 6, *God at Every Gate,* p. 143; *FRIDAY:* **Hymn:** v.5; **Prayer:** *Proclaiming All Your Wonders,* p. 47; *SATURDAY:* **Hymn:** Charles Wesley, *Hymns & Psalms* 528, v.4; **Prayer:** George MacDonald, nineteenth century, *A Reconciliation Sourcebook,* eds., Kathleen Hughes and Joseph A. Favazza, Liturgy

Training Publications, copyright the Archdiocese of Chicago, 1997, p. 87; **Prayer of Penitence:** Lent 5, Year B, *A Prayer Book for Australia,* copyright The Anglican Church of Australia Trust Corporation, 1995, pp. 491-492; **The Prayers:** *Gates of Prayer: The New Union Prayer Book,* copyright The Central conference of American Rabbis, New York, and Union of Liberal and Progressive Synagogues, London, 1975, p. 392.

MEDITATIONS: *SUNDAY:* Orthodox (source unknown); *MONDAY:* Psalm 51:10,11; *TUESDAY:* Paul Tillich, *The New Being,* Macmillan Publishing Company and Charles Scribner's Sons, 1955 (copyright 1983, Hannah Tillich); *WEDNESDAY: The Gates of Prayer,* p. 392; *THURSDAY:* Mechtild of Magdeburg, *God at Every Gate,* p. 153; *FRIDAY:* William Temple, *The Lion Christian Quotation Collection,* p. 220; *SATURDAY:* St. John of the Cross, *Complete Works,* trans. E. Alison Peers, Burns & Oates/Search Press Tunbridge Wells & The Newman Press, New York, USA, 1963; John Milton, *Paradise Regained,* The Fourth Book, *The Works of John Milton,* lines 602-639.

WEEKEND READINGS: Sunday – Year 1: Metropolitan Anthony of Sourozh, *The Essence of Prayer,* Darton, Longman and Todd Ltd., London, 1966, pp. 63-64; **Year 2:** A reading from a sermon by John Keble on Ezekiel, *From The Fathers To The Churches: Daily Spiritual Readings,* ed., Brother Kenneth CGA, Collins Liturgical Publications, London, 1983, pp. 182-183; **Year 3:** William Temple, *Personal Religion and the Life of Fellowship,* Longmans Green & Co., London, 1926, p. 46; **Saturday – Year 1:** John Donne, A Hymn to God the Father, *The Lion Christian Poetry Collection,* ed. Mary Batchelor, Lion Publishing Plc., Oxford, 1995, p. 45; **Year 2:** Simone Weil, *Waiting on God,* pp. 174-175; **Year 3:** Madeleine L'Engle, *And It Was Good: Reflections on Beginnings,* Crosswicks, Harold Shaw Publishers, Wheaton, Il., USA, copyright 1983.

LENT IV: THE COST

SUNDAY: **Hymn:** Charles Wesley, *Hymns and Sacred Poems,* John Wesley and Charles Wesley, Williams Strahan, London, 1739, pp. 117-119, v.1; **Prayer:** *A New Zealand Prayer Book,* p. 572; *MONDAY:* **Hymn:** v.2; **Prayer:** Editor, after Isaiah 43; *TUESDAY:* **Hymn:** v.3; **Prayer:** *Proclaiming All Your Wonders,* p. 35; *WEDNESDAY:* **Hymn:** v.4; **Prayer:** written by young people in Kenya, *Pray with Us,* ed. Maureen Edwards, Lion Publishing Plc; *THURSDAY:* **Hymn:** v.5; **Prayer:** (1 & 2) *A New Zealand Prayer Book,* p. 572; *FRIDAY:* **Hymn:** v.6; **Prayer:** Society of St. Francis; *Celebrating Common Prayer,* p. 521; *SATURDAY:* **Hymn:** quoted by D.M. Baillie in *God Was In Christ,* p. 178; **Prayer:** Joseph the Visionary, a Syrian Father of 8th century Iraq, *The Book of a Thousand Prayers,* p. 316; **Prayer of Penitence:** Good Friday liturgy, Western Rite, *The Oxford Book of Prayer,* p. 246; **The Prayers:** Eric Milner-White, *My God, My Glory,* p. 117, adapted.

MEDITATIONS: John Donne, *The Lion Christian Poetry Collection,* p. 306.

WEEKEND READINGS: Sunday – Year 1: George Herbert, *The English Poems of George Herbert,* p. 60, by kind permission of Everyman's Library Ltd; **Year 2:** John Donne, *The Works of John Donne,* Wordsworth Editions Ltd., Ware, 1994, p. 253; **Year 3:** Peter Abelard, *Expositio in Epistolam ad Romanus, 2,* in J.P. Migne, *Patrologia Latina,* 178.832C-D; 836A-B; **Saturday – Year 1:** D.M. Baillie, *God Was*

In Christ, Faber & Faber, London, 1948, 1961, pp. 174-175; **Year 2:** Irenaeus, *Sources Chretiennes*, vol. 153, ed. A. Rousseau, L. Doutreleau, and C. Mercier, Les Editions du Cerf, Paris, 1979; 18.19 -20.20; **Year 3:** *Clement of Alexandria: The Exhortation to the Greeks; The Rich Man's Salvation*, trans. G.W. Butterworth, Loeb Classical Library Edition, Harvard University Press, Cambridge, Mass., 1919, p. 346, reprinted by permission of the publishers and Loeb Classical Library.

LENT V: THE NARROW GATE

SUNDAY: **Hymn:** S. Crossman, *AMR* 102, v.1; **Prayer:** Good Friday Reproaches, Janet Morley, *All Desires Known*, expanded edition, SPCK, London, and Morehouse Publishing, Harrisburg, Penn., 1992, pp. 43-45, v.1; *MONDAY:* **Hymn:** v.2; **Prayer:** Good Friday Reproaches, v.2; *TUESDAY:* **Hymn:** v.3; **Prayer:** Good Friday Reproaches, v.7; *WEDNESDAY:* **Hymn:** v.3; **Prayer:** Good Friday Reproaches, v.6; *THURSDAY:* **Hymn:** v.4; **Prayer:** Good Friday Reproaches, v.4; *FRIDAY:* **Hymn:** v.6; **Prayer:** Good Friday Reproaches, v.8; *SATURDAY:* **Hymn:** v.7; **Prayer:** Prayer for Lent 5, *Book of Common Order of the Church of Scotland*, p. 436; **Prayer of Penitence:** Adapted from *The Book of Common Prayer (1662)*, *A Prayer Book for Australia*, p. 4; **The Prayers:** Adapted by Christopher Duraisingh from 'A Litany of the Disciples of the Servant', used in Andhra Theological College, Hyderabad, India, *Morning, Noon and Night*, ed. John Carden, Church Missionary Society, London, 1976, pp. 67-69, adapted.

MEDITATIONS: *SUNDAY:* Theodora, desert mother, *Sayings of the Desert Fathers*, trans. Benedicta Ward SLG, A.R. Mowbray & Co., Ltd., (Cassell Plc), London, 1975; *MONDAY:* Hosea 6:6; *TUESDAY:* I Kings 18:17; *WEDNESDAY:* Wisdom 6:7; *THURSDAY:* John 16:31; *FRIDAY:* Dorothy L. Sayers, The Greatest Drama Ever Staged in *Creed or Chaos?* Methuen & Co., Ltd., and by kind permission of David Higham Associates Ltd, London, 1947, p. 4; *SATURDAY:* Matthew 7:13; Michel Quoist, *Prayers of Life*, copyright translation Sheed & Ward Inc., 1963, M.H. Gill & Son Ltd., Dublin, 1963, p. 117.

WEEKEND READINGS: Sunday – Year 1: Jacques LeClercq, *A Year with the Liturgy: Meditations and Prayers*, Scepter Ltd., Dublin, copyright 1959; **Year 2:** *A Word in Season: Monastic Lectionary for the Divine Office*, Augustinian Press, Villanova, Pennsylvania; **Year 3:** Leonardo Boff, Way of the Cross, Way of Justice, *A Lent Sourcebook: Book Two*, p. 154; **Saturday – Year 1:** Hans Kung, *On Being A Christian*, English translation copyright William Collins & Sons Ltd., and Doubleday & Co., Inc., 1976, p. 320; **Year 2:** Karl Barth, *Church Dogmatics: Volume I The Doctrine of the Word of God*, p. 387, adapted; **Year 3:** Herbert Butterfield, *History and Human Relations*, William Collins & Sons Ltd., London, 1951, pp. 61-63.

HOLY WEEK

PALM SUNDAY: **Hymn:** H.H. Milman, *AMR* 99, v.1; **Prayer:** Source Unknown, India, *The SPCK Book of Christian Prayer*, London, 1995, p. 388; *MONDAY:* **Hymn:** John Clare, *AMRNS* 335, v.1.; **Lament:** Excerpted from *Ashes to* Fire, Supplemental Worship Resource 8, copyright 1979 by Abingdon; **Prayer:** Janet Morley, *All Desires Known*, p. 12; *TUESDAY:* **Hymn:** v.2; **Lament:** Excerpted from *From Ashes to Fire*; **Prayer:** Kay Bullock, *Read, Mark and Pray*, The Prayer Handbook 1992, copyright

1991, The United Reformed Church in the United Kingdom, used by permission; *WEDNESDAY:* **Hymn:** v.3; **Lament:** Excerpted from *From Ashes to Fire*; **Prayer:** Janet Morley, From 'Beforehand for the Burial', Women in Theology quiet day, Holy Week, 1985, appearing in *Celebrating Women*, eds., Hannah Ward, Jennifer Wild, Janet Morley, SPCK, 1995, p. 46; *THURSDAY:* **Hymn:** *Urbi Charitas*, trans. James Quinn SJ, copyright Geoffrey Chapman a division of Cassell Plc., v. 1; **Lament:** Exerpted from *From Ashes to Fire*; **Prayer:** *A New Zealand Prayer Book*, p. 585; *GOOD FRIDAY:* **Lament:** Exerpted from *From Ashes to Fire;* Joseph of Arimathea, *Byzantine Daily Worship*, p. 833, adapted; **Hymn:** 'And sleeps my Lord in silence yet', copyright Timothy Dudley-Smith, *Lift Every Heart*, Collins/Hope, 1984, p. 51, v.1 and v.2; *SATURDAY – THE VIGIL:* Opening words, Julia Esquivel, *A Sourcebook about Liturgy*, ed., Gabe Huck, Liturgy Training Publications, copyright the Archdiocese of Chicago, 1994, p. 116; From an ancient homily, Office of Readings, Holy Saturday, Roman Rite, *A Triduum Sourcebook*, eds., Gabe Huck and Mary Ann Simcoe, Liturgy Training Publications, copyright the Archdiocese of Chicago, 1983, pp. 64-65; **Prayer of Penitence:** *Book of Common Order of the Church of Scotland*, pp. 438-439, adapted; **The Prayers:** (1)An Obsecration Before The Crucifix, *Cuddesdon Office Book*, Oxford, 1940; (2) *Liturgy: From Ashes to Fire Cycle A, Planning for the Liturgical Season*, Journal of The Liturgical Conference, Volume 10, No. 2, copyright 1992, The Liturgical Conference Inc., p. 56.

MEDITATIONS: *SUNDAY:* William Penn, English Quaker, *The Lion Christian Quotation Collection*, p. 152; *MONDAY:* Dorothy L. Sayers by kind permission of David Higham Associates Ltd; *TUESDAY:* (1) Matthew 20:17-19, (2) Blaise Pascal, *The Lion Christian Quotation Collection*, p. 131; *WEDNESDAY:* (1) Mark 14:9, (2) Teresa of Avila, *The Lion Christian Quotation Collection*, p. 107; *THURSDAY:* (1) John 6:53-54, (2) Choan-Seng Song, a Taiwanese theologian, *The Lion Christian Quotation'Collection*, p. 314; *THE WATCH:* (1) Matthew 26:40; (2) W.H. Vanstone, *The Lion Christian Quotation Collection*, pp. 324-325; *FRIDAY:* (1) George Mcleod, *The Lion Christian Quotation Collection*, p. 281, (2), Leonardo Boff, *The Lion Christian Quotation Collection*, p. 234, (3) Hadewijch of Brabant, *Beguine Spirituality*, trans. O. Davies, ed., F. Bowie, SPCK, London, 1989; *SATURDAY:* Extract from a longer poem by Marion Pitman, appearing in *The Lion Christian Poetry Collection*, p. 311.

MEDITATIONS FOR GOOD FRIDAY: *THE WAY OF THE CROSS:* **The Prayers** (with the exception of those following No. 7 and No. 11) and are extracts from "Prayers on the Way of the Cross" by Michel Quoist, in *Prayers for Life*, pp. 117-135; prayer following No. 7, editor; prayer following No. 11, Eric Milner-White, *A Procession of Passion Prayers*, SPCK, London, 1956, p.100; **Reflection** following No. 4, is an extract from *Stations of the Cross: Mary Meets Jesus*, appearing in *Celebrating Women*, pp. 55-57. *THE SEVEN WORDS FROM THE CROSS:* **The Prayers** following the First Word and the Fourth Word are by Eric Milner-White, *A Procession of Passion Prayers*, p. 99, and p. 106. **The Hymn** ("O Come and stand beneath the cross") following the Second, Third, Fifth, Sixth and Seventh Words From The Cross, is copyright by the editors of *The New English Hymnal*, (No. 98), **Hymn:** p. 163, "When I survey the wondrous Cross", Isaac Watts, *NEH* 95; **Poem:**

Edwin Muir, *Collected Poems 1921-1958*, Faber & Faber Ltd., and Oxford University Press Inc., USA, copyright Willa Muir.
WEEKEND READINGS: Sunday – Year 1: A Reading from the addresses of St. Andrew of Crete, copyright *The Daily Office*, 1974; **Year 2:** Giles Fletcher, *The Lion Christian Poetry Collection*, p. 298; **Year 3:** Dietrich Bonhoeffer, *Letters and Papers from Prison*, SCM Press, London, 1953.

EASTER: CHRIST IS RISEN!
SUNDAY: **Hymn:** Lyra Davidica, *AMR* 134, v.1; **Song of Praise:** Easter Canon of John of Damascus, Third Ode, *Byzantine Daily Worship*, p. 849, adapted; **Prayer:** Gregory of Nazianzus, *The Book of a Thousand Prayers*, p. 327; *MONDAY:* **Hymn:** C.F. Gellers, trans. Frances E. Cox and Others, *AMR* 140, v.1; **Prayer:** *Book of Common Order of the Church of Scotland*, p. 439; *TUESDAY:* **Hymn:** v.2; **Song of Praise:** Easter Canon of John of Damascus, Fifth Ode, *Byzantine Daily Worship*, pp. 850-851, adapted; **Prayer:** *Book of Common Order of the Church of Scotland*, pp. 440-441, adapted; *WEDNESDAY:* **Hymn:** Charles Wesley, AMR 141, v.1; **Prayer:** Brother Roger of Taizé, Ateliers et Presses de Taizé, France; *THURSDAY:* **Hymn:** v.2; **Prayer:** *Proclaiming All Your Wonders*, p. 66; *FRIDAY:* **Hymn:** v.3; **Prayer:** Prayer of the Day for Easter Day, Year B, *A Prayer Book for Australia*, p. 503; *SATURDAY:* **Hymn:** v.4; **Prayer:** *Lent-Holy Week-Easter: Services and Prayers*, copyright The Central Board of Finance of the Church of England, 1984, 1986, p. 229; **Prayer of Penitence:** *Patterns and Prayers for Christian Worship*, copyright The Baptist Union, Oxford University Press, 1991, pp. 53-54; **The Prayers:** From a Resurrection Litany in the Service of the Lord's Supper, The Church of South India, Oxford University Press, Madras, adapted.
MEDITATIONS: (1), John 11:25; (2) Jacques LeClercq, *This Day Is Ours*, trans. Dinah Livingstone, SPCK, London, and Editions du Seuil, Paris, 1980, p. 108, (3) Michael Ramsey, former Archbishop of Canterbury, *The Lion Christian Quotation Collection*, p. 299.
WEEKEND READINGS: Sunday – Year 1: Gerd Theissen, *The Shadow of the Galilean*, trans. John Bowden, SCM, London, 1987, Christian Kaiser Verlag, Munich, 1986, pp. 184-185; **Year 2:** Oscar Cullman, *Immortality and Resurrection*, ed. Krister Stendahl, Macmillan, New York, 1965, p. 19; **Year 3:** Janet Morley, *All Desires Known*, p. 105; **Saturday – Year 1:** Karl Rahner, *Everyday Faith*, trans. W.J. O'Hara, Burns & Oates Ltd/Search Press, Tunbridge Wells, and Crossroad Publishing Co., New York, 1967, pp. 76-77; **Year 2:** Trustees of copyright of Dylan Thomas, J.M. Dent & Sons Ltd., and New Directions, David Higham Associates; **Year 3:** Jacques LeClercq, *This Day Is Ours*, pp. 116-117.

EASTER I: THE PASSOVER
SUNDAY: **Hymn:** T. Olivers, based on the Hebrew Yigdal, *AMR* 631, v.1; **Prayer:** *Byzantine Daily Worship*, p. 856; *MONDAY:* **Hymn:** Isaac Watts, *AMR* 165, v.1; **Prayer:** Janet Morley, Collect for the Sixth Sunday Before Christmas, *All Desires Known*, p. 4; *TUESDAY:* **Hymn:** Dayyenu, *Celebrating an Authentic Passover Seder*, Jospeh M. Stallings, Resource Publications, Inc., San Jose, CA, USA, copyright 1994, pp. 85-88, adapted, reprinted with permission; **Prayer:** Charles MacDonnell,

Celebrating Common Prayer, p. 623; *WEDNESDAY:* **Hymn:** as for Tuesday; **Song:** *The Gates of Prayer: The New Union Prayer Book*, p. 463; **Prayer:** *The Gates of Prayer: The New Union Prayer Book*, p. 463. *THURSDAY:* **Hymn:** as for Tuesday; **Prayer:** Michael Perham, *Celebrating Common Prayer*, p. 663; *FRIDAY:* **Hymn:** as for Sunday, v. 9; **Prayer:** Victimae Paschali, 11th century, *AMR* 138, v.1 and v.2; *SATURDAY:* **Hymn:** as for Sunday, v. 10; **Prayer:** Ad cenam Agni providi, Tr. J.M. Neale and Compilers, *AMR* 129, v.1; **Prayer of Penitence:** Collect for Ash Wednesday, Janet Morley, *All Desires Known*, p. 10; **The Prayers:** Dayyenu, *Celebrating an Authentic Passover Seder*, pp. 85-88, adapted, last verse editor's addition.

MEDITATIONS: (1) Desmond Tutu, *Hope and Suffering*, William B. Eerdmans Publishing Co., Grand Rapids, Mi, USA, 1984; (2) From a Latin Breviary hymn, trans. Robert Campbell, *NEH* 104.

WEEKEND READINGS: Sunday – Year 1: Michele Guinness, *A Little Kosher Seasoning*, Hodder & Stoughton, London, 1994, pp. 246-247, reproduced by permission of the publishers; **Year 2:** Stichera of the Resurrection, *Byzantine Daily Worship*, pp. 858-859, adapted; **Year 3:** Louis Bouyer, *The Paschal Mystery: Meditations on the Last Three Days of Holy Week*, trans. Sister Mary Benoit, George Allen & Unwin Ltd., London, 1951, and Les Editions du Cerf, Paris, 1947; **Saturday – Year 1:** A reading from a paschal homily by and ancient author, *The Divine Office*, 1974; **Year 2:** From a homily on the Pasch, Melito of Sardis, *The Divine Office*, 1974; **Year 3:** Orations 45, 23-4, Gregory of Nazianzen, *The Divine Office*, 1974.

EASTER II: THE BREAD OF LIFE

SUNDAY: **Hymn:** G.H. Bourne, AMR 400, v1; **Prayer:** *Book of Common Order of the Church of Scotland*, p. 193; *MONDAY:* **Hymn:** v.5; **Prayer:** *Proclaiming All Your Wonders*, p. 91; *TUESDAY:* **Hymn:** J. Conder, *AMR* 411, v.1; **Prayer:** *A New Zealand Prayer Book*, p. 619; *WEDNESDAY:* **Hymn:** Luke Connaughton, *Hymns Old & New with supplement*, eds. Kevin Mayhew, Tony Barr, Robert Kelly, copyright Kevin Mayhew Ltd., Bury St. Edmunds, 1989, used by permission, No. 559, v.1; **Prayer:** Edward Schillebeeckx, *For the Sake of the Gospel*, p. 80; *THURSDAY:* **Hymn:** v.2; **Prayer:** David Stancliffe, *Celebrating Common Prayer*, p. 594; *FRIDAY:* W. Bright, *AMR* 397, v.2; **Prayer:** Charles MacDonnell, *Celebrating Common Prayer*, p. 545; *SATURDAY:* **Hymn:** as for Wednesday, v.3; **Prayer:** (1) *A New Zealand Prayer Book*, p. 619, (2) W. Chatterton Dix, *AMR* 399, v.3; **Prayer of Penitence:** David Adam, *The Open Gate*, pp. 54-55; **The Prayers:** Janet Morley, *Bread of Tomorrow*, p. 96.

MEDITATION: Aidan Kavanagh, *Elements of Rite: A Handbook of Liturgical Style*, copyright The Order of St. Benedict, Inc., published by The Liturgical Press, Collegeville, Mn., 1982, p. 75.

WEEKEND READINGS: Sunday – Year 1: Edward Schillebeeckx, *For the Sake of the Gospel*, p. 78; **Year 2:** Alexander Schmemann, *The Eucharist: Sacrament of the Kingdom*, copyright St. Vladimir's Seminary Press, New York, 1987, p. 9; Aidan Kavanagh, *The Shape of Baptism: The Rite of Christian Initiation*, copyright The Order of St. Benedict Inc., published by The Liturgical Press, Collegeville, Mn., 1978; **Saturday – Year 1:** Madeleine L'Engle, *The Risk of Birth*, Harold Shaw Publishers,

Wheaton, Il., USA; **Year 2:** Evelyn Underhill, *Immanence,* copyright Tessa Sayle Literary and Dramatic Agents; **Year 3:** John Masefield, *The Everlasting Mercy,* copyright The Society of Authors as the literary representative of the Estate of John Masefield.

EASTER III: THE WATER OF LIFE

SUNDAY: **Hymn:** Charles Wesley, in *Hymns & Psalms* 318, v.1; **Prayer:** Catherine of Siena, *The Prayers of Catherine of Siena,* ed. Suzanne Noffke OP, Paulist Press, (copyright 1983); *MONDAY:* **Hymn:** v.2; **Prayer:** Gail Ramshaw & Gordon Lathrop, *A Baptism Sourcebook: An Order for Daily Prayer,* eds., Gabe Huck, Gail Ramshaw, Gordon Lathrop, Liturgy Training Publications, copyright the Archdiocese of Chicago, 1993, pp. 163-164 (Days 15-21); *TUESDAY:* **Hymn:** v. 3; **Prayer:** Roger Schultz, "Freed", *Eerdman's Book of Famous Prayers: A Treasury of Christian Prayers through the Centuries,* compiled by Veronica Zundel, copyright A.R. Mowbray & Co., Ltd., (Cassell Plc), & William B. Eerdmans Publishing Co., Grand Rapids, MI., USA; *WEDNESDAY:* **Hymn:** v.4; **Prayer:** Brendan O'Malley, *God at Every Gate,* p. 57; *THURSDAY:* **Hymn:** v.5; **Prayer:** from the Syrian Liturgy of St. Clement of Alexandria, *The Book of a Thousand Prayers,* p. 29; *FRIDAY:* **Hymn:** H. Bonar, *AMR* 351, v.2; **Prayer:** Catherine of Siena, *The Book of a Thousand Prayers,* p. 5; *SATURDAY:* **Hymn:** John of Damascus, *A Treasury of Early Christianity;* **Prayer:** Therese of Lisieux, *The Fount Book of Prayer,* edited by Robert Van der Weyer, HarperCollins, London, 1993, p. 357; **Prayer of Penitence:** Ephraim the Syrian, *Nicene and Post Nicene Fathers,* Volume XIII, William B. Eerdmans, Grand Rapids, MI., USA; **The Prayers:** Eric Milner-White, *My God, My Glory,* p. 52, adapted.

MEDITATIONS: Henry Vaughan, lines from "The Waterfall", *The Lion Christian Poetry Collection,* p. 121; Christina Rossetti, *The Lion Christian Poetry Collection,* p. 177.

WEEKEND READINGS: Sunday – Year 1: Alexander Schmemann, *Of Water and the Spirit,* St. Vladimir's Seminary Press, New York, p. 61; **Year 2:** *St. John Chrysostom: Baptismal Instructions,* trans. Paul W. Harkins, Longmans, Green & Co., London, 1963, and The Newman Press, Westminster, Maryland, USA; **Year 3:** Getrude the Great, from Part II of the Revelations of St. Gertrude, *Medieval Women's Visionary Literature,* ed., Elizabeth Alvilda Petroff, copyright Oxford University Press, Oxford & New York, 1986, pp. 223-224; **Saturday – Year 1:** Hans Urs von Balthasar, *Heart of the World,* trans. Erasmo S. Leiva, Ignatius Press, San Francisco, 1979; **Year 2:** Instruction 13 from the Instructions of St. Columbanus, copyright *The Divine Office,* 1974; **Year 3:** from the instructions of St. Cyril of Jerusalem to catechumens, copyright *The Divine Office,* 1974.

EASTER IV: FIRE & LIGHT

SUNDAY: **Hymn:** Sir R. Grant based on W. Kethe (1561), *ARM* 167, v.1; **Prayer:** St. Augustine, *The Hodder Book of Christian Prayer,* ed. Tony Castle, Hodder & Stoughton, 1986; *MONDAY:* **Hymn:** v.3; **Prayer:** *Celebrating Common Prayer,* p. 26; *TUESDAY:* **Hymn:** v.2; **Prayer:** Michael Vasey, *Celebrating Common Prayer,* p. 564; *WEDNESDAY:* **Hymn:** "From the night of ages waking", copyright Timothy

Dudley-Smith, *Songs of Deliverance*, Hodder & Stoughton, 1988, p. 19, v.1, reproduced by permission of the publishers; **Prayer:** Anonymous, twentieth century; *God at Every Gate*, p.p. 74-75; *THURSDAY:* **Hymn:** v.2; **Prayer:** Catherine of Siena, *The Book of a Thousand Prayers*, p. 46; *FRIDAY:* **Hymn:** v.3; **Prayer:** John Henry Newman, *The Book of a Thousand Prayers*, p. 12; *SATURDAY:* **Hymn:** v. 4; **Prayer:** from *Pentecostarion*, the Sisters of St. Basil the Great, Uniontown, Pennsylvania, USA; **Prayer of Penitence:** Ciaran of Clonmacnois, 'Irish Litany', 6th century, *Celtic Christian Spirituality*, eds., Oliver Davies and Fiona Bowie, SPCK, London, 1995; **The Prayers:** Charles Wesley, *Hymns & Psalms* 745.

MEDITATIONS: Aidan Kavanagh, *The Shape of Baptism: The Rite of Christian Initiation*, copyright The Order of St. Benedict Inc., published by The Liturgical Press, Collegeville, Mn., 1978; Heather Murray Atkins, *Liturgy: Easter Day*, Journal of the Liturgical Conference, Vol. 13, No. 4., Winter, 1996, copyright 1997 The Liturgical Conference Inc., pp. 40-41.

WEEKEND READINGS: Sunday – Year 1: St. John of the Cross, *The Complete Works of St. John of the Cross*, ed., E. Alison Peers, Burns & Oates/Search Press, Tunbridge Wells, & Newman Press, New York, USA, 1963; **Year 2:** Gertrude the Great, *Medieval Women's Visionary Literature*, p. 228; **Year 3:** Catherine of Siena, *The Fount Book of Prayer*, p. 88; **Saturday – Year 1:** extract from Prayer for the New Light, *Byzantine Daily Worship*, pp. 835-836; **Year 2:** Julian of Norwich, *Revelations of Divine Love*, in *From the Fathers to the Churches: Daily Spiritual Readings* , ed. Brother Kenneth CGA, Collins Liturgical Publications, London, 1983, pp. 559-60; **Year 3:** Bishop John of Naples, Sermon 7, *The Divine Office*, 1974.

EASTER V: RISEN! ASCENDED! GLORIFIED!

SUNDAY: **Hymn:** Charles Wesley, *AMR* 216, v.1; **Prayer:** Prayer For Ascension Day, *A Prayer Book for Australia*, pp. 517-518; *MONDAY:* **Hymn:** v.2; **Prayer:** *Proclaiming All Your Wonders*, p. 82; *TUESDAY:* **Hymn:** v. 3; **Prayer:** Janet Morley, Collect for the Sunday After Ascension, *All Desires Known*, p. 17; *WEDNESDAY:* **Hymn:** v.4; **Prayer:** *Proclaiming All Your Wonders*, p. 80; *THURSDAY:* Charles Wesley, T. Cotterill, and Compilers, *AMR* 147, v.1; **Prayer:** Janet Morley, Collect for Ascension Day, *All Desires Known*, p. 17; *FRIDAY:* **Hymn:** Bishop Christopher Wordsworth, *AMR* 148, v.3; **Prayer:** *Book of Common Order of the Church of Scotland*, pp. 441-442; *SATURDAY:* **Hymn:** v.4; **Prayer:** *Proclaiming All Your Wonders*, p.76; **Prayer of Penitence:** *Patterns and Prayers for Christian Worship*, p. 54; **The Prayers:** *Patterns for Worship*, A Report by the Liturgical Commission of the General Synod of the Church of England, GS 898, copyright The Central Board of Finance of the Church of England, 1989, p.203.

MEDITATIONS: (1) Matthew 28:20; (2) Eric Milner-White, *My God, My Glory*, p. 70, adapted.

WEEKEND READINGS: Sunday – Year 1: Karl Rahner, *Everyday Faith*, p. 208; **Year 2:** John Donne, *The Works of John Donne*, p. 247; **Year 3:** John Brooks Wheelright, extract from Forty Days (The Second Ascension of Christ), in *The New Oxford Book of Christian Verse*, ed., Donald Davie, Oxford University Press, 1981, pp. 266-269; **Saturday – Year 1:** St. Augustine, from a Sermon on the Ascension, *The Divine Office*, 1974; **Year 2:** Extract from the Stychera of the Ascension,

Byzantine Daily Worship, p. 882; **Year 3:** Hans Kung, *On Being a Christian*, pp. 358-359.

EASTER VI: PILGRIMAGE

SUNDAY: **Hymn:** W. Williams, trans. P. & W. Williams, *AMR* 296, v.1; **Song:** St. Augustine, *God at Every Gate*, p. 16; **Prayer:** Ruth Burgess, *The Book of a Thousand Prayers*, p. 47; *MONDAY:* **Hymn:** v.2; **Prayer:** from *Daily Prayer*, eds. Eric Milner-White and G.W. Briggs, Oxford University Press, 1941; *TUESDAY:* **Hymn:** v. 3; **Prayer:** Brendan O'Malley, *A Welsh Pilgrim's Manual*, Gomer Press, Llandysul, Dyfed, 1989; *WEDNESDAY:* **Hymn:** B.S. Ingemann, trans. S. Baring-Gould, *AMR* 292, v.1; **Prayer:** Kathy Galloway, *The Pattern of Our Days: Liturgies and Resources for Worship*, ed. Kathy Galloway, Wild Goose Publications, Glasgow, 1996, pp. 40-41, adapted from a longer prayer; *THURSDAY:* **Hymn:** v. 2; **Prayer:** Jim Cotter, *By Stony Paths*, A Version of Psalms 51-100, Cairns Publications, Sheffield, 1991; *FRIDAY:* **Hymn:** v.3; **Prayer:** *Proclaiming All Your Wonders*, p. 79; *SATURDAY:* **Hymn:** v.4; **Prayer:** Boethius, *The Book of A Thousand Prayers*, p. 5; **Prayer of Penitence:** Kathy Galloway, *Pattern of Our Days: Liturgies and Resources for Worship*, ed., Kathy Galloway, Wild Goose Publications, Galsgow, 1996, pp. 36-37; **The Prayers:** Kathy Galloway, Flight into Egypt: a benediction, in *Coracle*, 3/11, copyright The Iona Community, 1992.

MEDITATIONS: (1) Editor; (2) Anonymous, from "The Wanderer", *The Lion Christian Poetry Collection*, p. 184.

WEEKEND READINGS: Sunday – Year 1: *An Interrupted Life: The Diaries of Etty Hillesum, 1941-1943*; **Year 2:** K. George, *The Silent Roots: Orthodox Perspectives on Christian Spirituality*, World Council of Churches, 1994; p. 46; Sir Walter Raleigh, *The Lion Christian Poetry Collection*, p. 188; **Saturday – Year 1:** John Bunyan, *Pilgrim's Progress*; **Year 2:** St. Augustine, *Sermo 306, In Natalie Martyrum Massae Candidate*, Ch. 11; **Year 3:** Basil Hume OSB, *To Be A Pilgrim*, St. Paul (formerly St. Paul Publications), Slough, 1984, p.22, used with permission.

PENTECOST

SUNDAY: **Hymn:** Bianco da Siena, trans. R.F. Littledale, *AMR* 235, v.1; **Prayer:** *A New Zealand Prayer Book*, p. 604; *MONDAY:* **Hymn:** v.2; **Prayer:** Eric Milner-White, *My God, My Glory*, pp. 74-75, III; adapted *TUESDAY:* **Hymn:** v.3; **Prayer:** Anonymous, *Out of Darkness: paths to inclusive worship*, copyright the Australian Council of Churches, Sydney, 1986; *WEDNESDAY:* **Hymn:** v.4; **Song:** Janet Morley, adapted from a eucharistic prayer for Pentecost in *All Desires Known*, pp. 56-57; **Prayer:** *Proclaiming All Your Wonders*, p. 86; *THURSDAY:* **Hymn;** Bishop J. Cosin, based on Veni, creator Spiritus, *AMR* 157, v.1; **Prayer:** Eric Milner-White, *My God, My Glory*, p. 73, adapted; *FRIDAY:* **Hymn:** v.2; **Song:** *RSV,* Romans 8:2, 14, 15b-17, 19; **Prayer:** (1) Synesius of Cyrene, *The Book of a Thousand Prayers*, p. 334, (2) St. John of the Cross, as for (1), p. 31; *SATURDAY:* **Hymn:** v.3; **Song:** An American Indian's Prayer to God, *God at Every Gate*, p. 128; **Prayer:** Janet Morley, Collect for Pentecost, *All Desires known*, p. 17; **Prayer Of Penitence:** *Patterns and Prayers for Christian Worship*, pp. 55-56; **The Prayers:** copyright Jan Berry, appearing in *Bread of Tomorrow*, p. 145.

MEDITATION: Mechtild of Magdeburg, *God at Every Gate*, p. 73.

WEEKEND READINGS: Sunday – Year 1: Richard Challoner, *Meditations for every day in the year*, Vol. 1, 1767, p. 311; **Year 2:** James K. Baxter, *Collected Poems*, Oxford University Press; **Year 3:** Kahlil Gibran, *The Prophet,* Wordsworth Editions Ltd., Ware, 1996, pp. 57-58; **Saturday – Year 1:** Edward Schillebeeckx, *For the Sake of the Gospel*, pp. 72-73; **Year 2:** Hans Kung, *On Being a Christian*, p. 468; **Year 3:** William Temple, *Readings in St. John's Gospel*, Macmillan & Co., Ltd., 1945, pp. 288-289.

Abbreviations

AMR   Hymns Ancient & Modern Revised, Hymns Ancient & Modern Ltd., Norwich, 1950.

AMRNS Hymns Ancient & Modern New Standard Edition, The Canterbury Press, Norwich, 1986.

NEH   New English Hymnal, The Canterbury Press, Norwich, 1986.

Note

Where the same hymn is used each day the author and source are noted on the fist day of use, then only the verse number is given thereafter.

BIBLIOGRAPHY

A Baptism Sourcebook, eds. J. Robert Baker, Larry J. Nyberg, Victoria M. Tufano, Liturgy Training Publications, copyright the Archdiocese of Chicago, 1993.

A Diary of Readings, ed. John Baillie, Oxford University Press, Oxford, 1981.

A Dictionary of Liturgy & Worship, ed. J.G. Davies, SCM, London, 1972.

A Lent Sourcebook: The Forty Days, Book One, eds. J. Robert Baker, Evelyn Kaehler, Peter Mazar, Liturgy Training Publications, copyright the Archdiocese of Chicago, 1990.

A Lent Sourcebook: The Forty Days, Book Two, eds. J. Robert Baker, Evelyn Kaehler, Peter Mazar, Liturgy Training Publications, copyright the Archdiocese of Chicago, 1990.

A New Zealand Prayer Book, The Church of the Province of New Zealand, Collins Liturgical Publications, London, 1989.

Adam, David, *Power Lines: Celtic Prayers About Work,* SPCK, London, 1992.

Adam, David, *The Open Gate: Celtic prayers for growing spirituality,* SPCK/Triangle, 1994.

Adam, David, *The Rhythm of Life: Celtic Daily Prayer,* SPCK, London, 1996.

A Prayer Book for Australia, copyright The Anglican Church of Australia Trust Corporation, Broughton Books, 1995.

A Reconciliation Sourcebook, eds., Kathleen Hughes, Joseph A. Favazza, Liturgy Training Publications, copyright the Archdiocese of Chicago, Chicago, 1997.

A Sourcebook about Liturgy, ed., Gabe Huck, Liturgy Training Publications, copyright the Archdiocese of Chicago, Chicago, 1994.

A Triduum Sourcebook, eds., Gabe Huck, Mary Ann Simcoe, Liturgy Training Publications, copyright the Archdiocese of Chicago, Chicago, 1983.

An Easter Sourcebook, eds., Gabe Huck, Gail Ramshaw, Gordon Lathrop, Liturgy Training Publications, copyright the Archdiocese of Chicago, Chicago, 1988.

An Anglican Prayer Book, The Provincial Trustees of the Church of South Africa, Collins Liturgical Publications, London, copyright 1989.

Baillie, D.M., *God Was In Christ – An Essay on Incarnation and Atonement,* Faber and Faber, London, 1961.

Baptist Praise and Worship, Oxford University Press, Oxford, 1991.

Byzantine Daily Worship, Alleluia Press, Ontario, 1969.

Book of Common Order of the Church of Scotland, the Panel on Worship of the Church of Scotland, Saint Andrew Press, Edinburgh, 1994.

Bloom, Anthony (Metropolitan Anthony of Sourozh), *The Essence of Prayer,* Darton, Longman & Todd, London, 1986.

Bonhoeffer, Dietrich, *Letters and Papers from Prison,* SCM Press, London, 1953.

Boulding, Maria, O.S.B., *The Coming of God,* SPCK, London, 1982.

Boulding, Maria, O.S.B., *Marked for Life: Praying in the Easter Christ,* SPCK, London, 1979.

Bouyer, Louis, *The Paschal Mystery,* trans. Sister Mary Benoit, George Allen & Unwin Ltd., London, 1951, Les Editions du Cerf, Paris, 1947.

Bread of Tomorrow: Praying with the World's Poor, ed., Janet Morley, SPCK, Christian Aid, London, 1992.

Celebrating Common Prayer: A Version of The Daily Office SSF, The Society of St. Francis, Mowbray, London, 1992.

Celebrating Women, eds., Hannah Ward, Jennifer Wild, Janet Morley, SPCK, London, 1995.

Clement, Olivier, *The Roots of Christian Mysticism*, trans. Theodore Berkeley O.C.S.O., revised by Jeremy Hummerstone, New City, London, 1993.

Dudley-Smith, Timothy, *Lift Every Heart: Collected Hymns 1961-1983 and some early poems*, Collins Liturgical Publications/Hope Publishing Company, 1984.

Dudley-Smith, Timothy, *Songs of Deliverance: 36 New Hymns written between 1984 & 1987*, Hodder & Stoughton/Hope Publishing Company, 1988.

Dudley-Smith, Timothy, *A Voice of Singing: 36 New Hymns written between 1988 & 1992*, Hodder & Stoughton/Hope Publishing Company, 1993.

Dudley-Smith, Timothy, *Great is the Glory: 36 New Hymns written between 1993 & 1996*, Hope Publishing Company, 1997.

Egeria: Diary of a Pilgrimage, translated and annotated by George E. Gingras, Newman Press, New York, 1970.

Faith in Her Words: Six Centuries of Women's Poetry, compiled by Veronica Zundel, Lion Publishing, Oxford, 1991.

From the Fathers to the Churches: Daily Spiritual Readings, ed., Brother Kenneth CGA, Collins Liturgical Publications, London, 1983.

Gates of Prayer: The New Union Prayer Book, Central Conference of American Rabbis, New York, and Union of Liberal and Progressive Synagogues, London, 1975.

Gibran, Kahlil, *The Prophet*, Wordsworth Editions Ltd., Ware, 1996.

Guinness, Michele, *A Little Kosher Seasoning*, Hodder & Stoughton, London, 1994.

Guiver C.R., George, *Company of Voices: Daily Prayer and the People of God*, SPCK, London, 1988.

Huck, Gabe, *The Three Days: Parish Prayer in the Paschal Triduum*, revised edition, Liturgy Training Publications, copyright the Archdiocese of Chicago, Chicago 1992.

Harris, Paul, ed., *The Fire of Silence and Stillness*, Darton, Longman & Todd, London, 1995.

Human Ritesa: Worship Resources for an Age of Change, compiled by Hannah Ward and Jennifer Wild, Cassell Plc, London, 1995.

Hymns & Psalms, Methodist Publishing House, Peterborough, 1985.

Hymns Ancient & Modern New Standard, compilation Hymns Ancient & Modern Ltd., The Canterbury Press, Norwich, 1986.

Hymns Ancient & Modern Revised, Hymns Ancient & Modern Revised Ltd., Norwich, 1950.

Hymns Old & New: Anglican Edition, compiled by Patrick Appleford, Kevin Mayhew, Susan Sayers, Kevin Mayhew Ltd, Bury St. Edmunds, 1986.

St. John of the Cross, *Poems*, trans, Roy Campbell, Harvill 1951, Penguin Books, 1960.

Kung, Hans, *On Being a Christian*, trans Edward Quinn, Fount, Glasgow, 1978.

LeClercq, Jacques, *This Day is ours*, trans, Dinah Livingstone, SPCK, London, 1980, Editions du Seuil, Paris, 1976.

Lent-Holy Week-Easter: Services and Prayers, copyright Central Board of Finance of the Church of England, Church House Publishing, Cambridge University Press, SPCK, 1984, 1986.

Liturgy: From Ashes to Fire [A] Planning for the Paschal Season, The Journal of the Liturgical Conference, Vol. 10. No. 2, Summer 1992, Silver Spring, MD, USA.

Liturgy: From Ashes to Fire [B] Planning for the Paschal Season, The Journal of the Liturgical Conference, Vol. 11. No. 2, Fall, 1993, Silver Spring, MD, USA.

Liturgy: From Ashes to Fire [C] Planning for the Paschal Season, The Journal of the Liturgical Conference, Vol. 11. No. 4, Spring, 1994, Silver Spring, MD, USA.

Liturgy: Easter Day, The Journal of the Liturgical Conference, Vol. 13, No. 4, Winter, 1996, Silver Spring, MD, USA.

Milner-White, Eric, *My God, My Glory,* SPCK/Triangle, London, 1954, 1994.

Milner-White, Eric, *A Procession of Passion Prayers,* SPCK, London, 1956.

Morley, Janet, *All Desires Known,* expanded edition, SPCK, London, and Morehouse Publishing, Harrisburg, Penn., 1992.

Morning, Noon And Night: prayers and meditations from the Third World, ed., John Carden, Church Missionary Society, London, 1976

Moses, John, *The Desert: An Anthology for Lent,* Canterbury Press, Norwich, 1997.

O'Malley, *God at Every Gate: Prayers and blessings for pilgrim's,* Canterbury Press, Norwich, 1997.

Patterns & Prayers for Christian Worship, Baptist Union of Great Britain, Oxford University Press, Oxford, 1991.

Patterns for Worship, A Report by the Liturgical Commission of the General Synod of the Church of England, GS 898, Church House Publishing, London, 1989.

Perham, Michael, and Stevenson, Kenneth, *Waiting for the Risen Christ: A Commentary on Lent- Holy Week- Easter: Services and Prayers,* SPCK, London, 1986.

Petroff, Elizabeth Alvilda, ed., *Medieval Women's Visionary Literature,* Oxford University Press, New York and Oxford, 1986.

Prayers Through the Centuries, ed., Nancy Martin, Bishopsgate Press, London, 1990.

Proclaiming All Your Wonders: Prayers for a Pilgrim People, French Language Liturgy Commission of the Cistercians, trans. Vincent Ryan O.S.B., Nivard Kinsella O. Cist., Dominican Publications, Dublin, 1991.

Quoist, Michel, *Prayers of Life,* trans. Anne Marie Commaile and Agnes Mitchell Forsyth, Gill & Son Ltd., Dublin, 1961. Translations copyright, Sheed & Ward Inc., London, 1963.

Rahner, Karl, *Everyday Faith,* Burns & Oates Ltd./Search Press, Tunbridge Wells, and Herder and Herder, New York, 1968.

Robinson, Martin, ed., *Sacred Places, Pilgrim Paths: An Anthology of Pilgrimage,* HarperCollins, London, 1997.

Sayers, Dorothy L., *Creed Or Chaos? and other Essays in popular Theology,* Methuen & Co., Ltd., London, 1947.

Schillebeeckx, Edward, *For the Sake of the Gospel,* trans., John Bowen, SCM Press, London, 1989.

Schmemann, Alexander, *The Eucharist,* trans. Paul Kachur, St. Vladimir's Seminary press, New York, 1988.

Seasons of the Spirit: Readings through the Christian Year, selected by George Every, Richard Harris, Kallistos Ware, SPCK, London, 1990.

Service Book: United Reformed Church in the United Kingdom, Oxford University Press, Oxford, 1989.

Spidlick, Thomas, ed., trans., Paul Drake, *Drinking from the hidden Fountain: A Patristic Breviary*, New City, London, 1992.

Stallings, Joseph M. *Celebrating an Authentic Passover Seder*, Resource Publications, Inc., San Jose, California, 1994.

Stevenson, Kenneth, *Jerusalem Revisited: The Liturgical Meaning of Holy Week*, The Pastoral Press, Washington, 1988.

Synopsis of the Four Gospels: Greek-English Edition of the Synopsis Quattuor Evangeliorum, ed., Kurt Aland, United Bible Societies, 1979.

Taft, Robert, *The Liturgy of the Hours in East and West – The Origins of the Divine Office and its Meaning for Today*, Second Revised Edition, The Liturgical Press, Collegeville, Mn., 1993.

Talley, Thomas J., *The Origins of the Liturgical Year*, second edition, Pueblo, The Liturgical Press, Collegeville, 1991.

The Alternative Service Book 1980, Cambridge University Press, William Clowes, SPCK, and Hodder & Stoughton, 1980.

The Bible: New International Version Inclusive Language Edition, Hodder & Stoughton, London, 1995, 1996.

The Bible: New Revised Standard Version with Apocrypha, Anglicized Edition, Oxford University Press, Oxford, 1995.

The Book of a Thousand Prayers, compiled by Angela Ashwin, Marshall Pickering, London, 1996.

The Book of Alternative Services of the Anglican Church of Canada, The Anglican Book Centre, Toronto, 1985.

The Christian Theology Reader, ed., Alister E. McGrath, Blackwell Publishers Ltd., Oxford, 1995.

The Cloud of Witnesses: A companion to the Lesser Festivals and Holydays of the Alternative Service Book 1980, compiled by Martin Draper with collects written by G.B. Timms, HarperCollins, London, 1982.

The Daily Office, The Joint Liturgical Group, ed. Ronald C.D. Jasper, SPCK and Epworth Press, London, 1968.

The English Poems of George Herbert, ed., C.A. Praides, J.M. Dent & Sons Ltd., London, 1974.

The Festal Menaion, trans. Mother Mary and Archimandrite Kallistos Ware, Faber & Faber, London, 1969.

The Fount Book of Prayer, ed., Robert Van de Weyer, HarperCollins Religious, London, 1993.

The Hidden Tradition – Women's spiritual writings rediscovered, ed., Lavinia Byrne, SPCK, London, 1991.

Theissen, Gerd, *The Shadow of the Galilean*, trans.. John Bowden, SCM Press, 1987, Christian Kaiser Verlag, 1986,

The Lion Christian Poetry Collection, compiled by Mary Batchelor, Lion Publishing Plc, Oxford, 1995.

The Lion Christian Quotation Collection, compiled by Hannah Ward and Jennifer Wild, Lion Publishing Plc., Oxford, 1997

The Lion Prayer Collection, compiled by Mary Batchelor, Lion Publishing Plc, Oxford, 1995.

The New English Hymnal, compilation The English Hymnal Company Ltd., The Canterbury Press, Norwich, 1986.

The New Oxford Book Of Christian Verse, ed., Donald Davie, Oxford University Press, Oxford, 1981.

The Oxford Book of Prayer, general editor George Appleton, Oxford University Press, Oxford, 1985.

The Pattern of Our Days: Liturgies and Resources for Worship, ed., Kathy Galloway, The Iona Community, Wild Goose Publications, Glasgow, 1996.

The Psalms the version as adapted for English usage from the *Standard Book of Common Prayer of the Episcopal Church in the USA*, by the Society of St. Francis in *Celebrating Common Prayer*.

The Revised Common Lectionary, The Consultation on Common Texts, The Canterbury Press, Norwich, 1992.

The Roman Missal for Sundays and Holy Days, C.B.C. Distributors, Newry, 1975.

The Study of Liturgy, eds., Cheslyn Jones, Geoffrey Wainwright, Edward Yarnold S.J., Paul Bradshaw, Revised Edition, SPCK, London, Oxford University Press, Oxford, 1992.

The Way of Silent Love: Carthusian Novice Conferences, A Cathusian, trans., An Anglican Solitary, Darton, Longman & Todd, London, 1993.

The Weekday Missal, Collins Liturgical Publications, London, 1975.

The Works of John Donne, Wordsworth Editions Ltd., Ware, 1994

The Works of John Milton, Wordsworth Editions Ltd., Ware, 1994

Thurian, Max, *Confession*, trans. Edwin Hudson, SCM Press, London, 1958, Delachaux & Nestle S.A. Switzerland, 1953.

Underhill, Evelyn, *An Anthology of The Love of God (from her selected writings)*, eds., Lumsden Barkway and Lucy Menzies, A.R. Mowbray & Co., Ltd., (Cassell Plc), London & Oxford, 1976.

Weil, Simone, *Waiting on God: The Essence of Her Thought*, trans, Emma Craufurd, Routledge, 1951.

Wybrew, Hugh, *Orthodox Lent, Holy Week and Easter: Liturgical Texts with Commentary*, SPCK, London, 1995.